THE DUKE LACROSSE CASE

A Documentary History and Analysis of the Modern Scottsboro

R.B. Parrish

ISBN: 1-4392-3590-2

ISBN-13: 9781439235904

LCCN: 2009903282

Visit www.booksurge.com to order additional copies.

"It is not because the truth is too difficult to see that we make mistakes... we make mistakes because the easiest and most comfortable course for us is to seek insight where it accords with our emotions - especially selfish ones."

--Alexander Solzhenitsyn

Table of Contents

PREFACE

In March 2006 two sophomore members of the Duke University Lacrosse team attended an off-campus party hosted by the team's captains. Spring Break had arrived, but unlike the rest of the student body--many of whom fled to the beaches of nearby South Carolina and Florida--the team had to remain behind for practice; the party was the substitute for missing the week's Break.

Neither sophomore had been eager to attend. But it would have seemed boorish, and not in keeping with team spirit, not to at least put in an appearance. Unlike the popular image of lacrosse players, neither of them came from inherited wealth. The father of one of them, though white, had been raised by a black family. The father of the other had been so poor when he married that he had to borrow money for an engagement ring. After he made his fortune, he spent a portion of it funding medical clinics in Africa, after his family priest--a friend from the age of six--felt called to minister there.

The party–virtually an all-male affair—was sedate, and even dull, producing neither loud noise nor complaints; and could not compete with the fracas of the beachgoers. As an afterthought the team captains decided to hire strippers—a fact many of the team members remained unaware of until they were asked to contribute to the hiring fee. Some twenty other Duke organizations hired strippers that year, including sororities as well as fraternities. Pictures from at least one previous sorority party with (male) strippers had been displayed on the Internet.

For the sophomores' brief interval spent at the lacrosse party, and for their team captains' copying of a frequent Duke practice, they and a team captain were sentenced to endure the next year in hell.

> *...to be honest, we all knew it was so transparently false that [we felt that] no charges would ever be brought but as time went on, I mean, we, we always felt that nothing would ever come of this ... and as time wore on we realized that Mr. Nifong said they were going to do things the old fashioned way and to us, I've never had to deal with courts before...and everyone started to get...this is really going to happen to us, this, something is going to happen and we assumed that, she said it was three people, and three people lived in the house, and they were three seniors, and we thought, OK, it'll probably be the three guys and its a terrible tragedy that it's going to happen to those three but you know this is how they're conducting this ...and to be completely honest with you I never thought in a million years that I would ever be a suspect and I was being told that there's no way ... I wasn't even listed as having been at the party and I ... in my mind it could never be, it could never be me...*
>
> -- testimony of Reade Seligmann before
> the Disciplinary Hearing Commission
> of the North Carolina State Bar,
> June 15, 2007

CASE NARRATIVE : Before the Beginning

Setting the Durham scene

Before the lacrosse case Durham, North Carolina was noteworthy for a number of things, including its status as a former hub of the tobacco industry; its minor league baseball team; being the home of Duke University; as well as the site of the South's "Black Wall Street" during the early decades of the twentieth century.

It was less well known as the hometown of Frank Matthews, the notorious "Black Caesar", who for a time in the late 1960s and early 1970s controlled much of the East Coast heroin trade.

> By the early 1970s, Matthews's organization was handling multi million dollar shipments in at least 21 states. According to the U.S. government, "Matthews controlled the cutting, packaging and sale of heroin in every major East Coast city."
>
> --Black Caesar by Ron Chepesiuk

Matthews had been left motherless as a child, and been raised by an aunt who was married to a Durham police lieutenant. He moved New York where he made his headquarters and kept an apartment filled with bags stuffed with cash, but he never forgot Durham. He trusted Durhamites and hired many of them to be his associates, believing that "local boys" were less corruptible and likely to remain more loyal to him than "city boys". at his peak, it seemed it was impossible for him to be arrested; even when law enforcement officers observed him dealing drugs in plain sight, he was not accosted. Eventually, he was taken into custody; but then his bail was inexplicably lowered and he skipped town, never to be seen again. It was rumored that he had "paid his dues" for many years by doing favors for the government, which later repaid the debt in kind.

The sums for his bail came from Durham, and were presumably repaid anonymously sometime thereafter.

Matthews' successor was Frank Lucas, another Carolinian (portrayed by Denzel Washington in the recent film, *American Gangster).* He, too, was from North Carolina, and also liked to employ locals.

"...a country boy, he ain't hip . . . he's not used to big cars, fancy ladies, and diamond rings. He'll be loyal to you...A city boy will take your last dime, look you in the face, and swear he ain't got it . . ."

"The Return of Superfly" by Mark Jacobson, New York Magazine, August 14, 2000

By rumor, Lucas arranged the shipment of drugs from Southeast Asia by hiding them in the returning coffins of US servicemen; or, as other rumors have it, by hiding the drugs inside the cadavers themselves. *"Who the hell is gonna look in a dead soldier's coffin? Ha ha ha."*

How much money these two may have poured in, and through, the Durham economy is unknown; but the social and political effects on a rural southern community which has millions of dollars of illegal drug profits pumped through it cannot be calculated.

> In recent years, Durham's dope habit has been reckoned as big as $10 million a day. That figure may be 'way off the fact, but, even if marked down, the city's trade in illicit substances has been, and continues to be, considerable.
>
> --Jim Wise, "A Small Name's a Big Legend", The Durham News, January 12, 2008

> District Attorney [later judge in the lacrosse case] Ronald L. Stephens has called the SBI [State Bureau of Investigation] into the investigation involving allegations that a prostitution ring operated out of the police department and the handling of an in-house probe of the charges.
>
> -- News & Observer, February 1, 1992

> In September, police officials conceded that officers had photocopied at least 20 times a blank subpoena that included the signature of a prosecutor [District Attorney Ronald L. Stephens].
>
> -- News & Observer May 19, 1994

FBI crime statistics : estimated arrests for prostitution, Durham county, North Carolina, (population 245,000) :

Year 2000----------------total arrests : 8

Year 2001----------------total arrests : 5

Year 2002----------------total arrests : 4

Year 2003----------------total arrests : 0

Year 2004----------------total arrests : 9

Year 2005----------------total arrests : 0

FBI crime statistics : estimated arrests for prostitution, Wake County, North Carolina, (population 785,000; includes city of Raleigh) :

Year 2000---------total arrests : 107

Year 2001---------total arrests : 196

Year 2002---------total arrests : 171

Year 2003---------total arrests : 204

(no information available for 2004)

Year 2005---------total arrests : 311

FBI crime statistics : estimated arrests for prostitution, Forsyth County, North Carolina (population 332,000; includes city of Winston-Salem) :

Year 2000---------total arrests : 48

Year 2001---------total arrests : 76

Year 2002---------total arrests : 115

Year 2003---------total arrests : 96

(no information available for 2004)

Year 2005---------total arrests : 66

FBI crime statistics : estimated arrests for prostitution, Mecklenburg County, North Carolina (population 825,000; includes city of Charlotte) :

Year 2000--------total arrests : 285

Year 2001--------total arrests : 346

Year 2002--------total arrests : 259

Year 2003--------total arrests : 345

(no information available for 2004)

Year 2005--------total arrests : 318

Prostitution is a money-making business. It is both illegal and profitable. When laws against it are not enforced and it is permitted to operate more or less without receiving any attention from law enforcement, then the presumed quid pro quo is that some of the money from the business flows back to the officials who are allowing it to flourish. Such payments are not included on the tax forms of the recipients; and the money earned by the owners of the businesses often is invested in other illegal activities (drugs, gambling). The officials who turn a blind eye to prostitution therefore often end up turning a blind eye to these other ills, as well.

A city which has a long history of not enforcing laws against particular vices likely has roots of corruption which have grown very deep; they would eventually affect much of the judicial and law enforcement structure--unless, of course, the city's law enforcement and judicial structure are simply monumentally incompetent; in which case their enforcement of any laws needs to be called into question.

> In the past three years, 79 percent of the Durham [police] auction proceeds have gone to expenses, mostly overtime.
>
> ———-
>
> At one Durham police auction, on Oct. 27, 2001, [police property room technician] Brown and her colleagues put in so many hours that the Durham police actually lost money, city records show.
>
> --News and Observer, Dec. 16, 2004

Some random snapshots of Durham justice at work

In 1994 a prison guard named Tim Malloy, who also worked as a convenience store clerk, was accused of rape. An assistant prosecutor, Michael Nifong, pushed to prosecute the case. There was no evidence to support the charges and the accused possessed two tape recordings of phone conversations which would have helped exonerate him.

> The accuser . . . said in a recent interview that until Nifong got involved, she had thought about dropping the case.
>
> "He believed in me, and until that time, I didn't feel anybody else believed in me," she said. "I felt like the system let me down until Mike took the case."
>
> -- News and Observer, October 1, 2006

Nifong disparaged the defense attorneys:

> "Poultry," Nifong said when a defense attorney asked a judge to delay the trial date.
>
> "They're a bunch of chickens," he told the Herald-Sun of Durham to explain his comment. "I have the impression sometimes they are afraid to try cases."
>
> --News and Observer, October 1, 2006

While in the possession of the state, portions of these two tapes were somehow erased. The prosecution fought vigorously against sending the tapes to an out of state expert to be reconstructed; when the tapes were nevertheless repaired and returned, they helped prove the defendant's innocence.

(Records of this case, though reported in the press, appear to be no longer available in the Durham courthouse records.)

In 1992 a man named Leon Brown was tried for rape. This was true even though Brown's DNA wasn't found on the victim but that of another man was. The other man confessed to the rape. The other man was identified by the victim, who was his cousin (i.e., she likely knew him well enough to make an accurate identification). But, the other man was granted immunity from prosecution in exchange for his testimony against Brown, whom the prosecutors alleged was the instigator and had also raped the victim.

The case was prosecuted by Tracey Cline--who would later be slated to try the Duke lacrosse case alongside Michael Nifong. Brown was kept in jail for a year awaiting trial. When the jury retired, they took all of five minutes to find Brown not guilty. The foreman said the trial was "a waste of time... We all wondered what we were doing there. The evidence was nonexistent. We're very comfortable with the decision we made. I can't understand why that man spent a year in jail when there was no evidence whatsoever against him. It made no sense to us. Where's the justice?"

Nevertheless, the one man who was known to be an actual rapist, was therefore permitted to go free, in accordance with his grant of immunity; leading some unkind observers to ponder if a deal of some sort hadn't been worked out.

> [Erick] Daniels was a 14-year-old Chewning Middle School student when two armed men wearing bandanas broke into the home of [Durham police property room employee] Ruth Brown and stole thousands of dollars she said was in her purse. There was no physical evidence linking Daniels (or anyone else) to the crime, and Brown

> identified Daniels as one of her assailants after picking his picture out of a Chewning yearbook. She said she recognized his eyebrows.
>
> That's it. That's all the "evidence" there was connecting Erick Daniels to the robbery. As a result, a 15-year-old boy was sentenced to 10 years in prison
>
> --(Durham) Independent Weekly, May 23, 2007

An appeals' lawyer for Daniels uncovered the fact that Brown was actually hosting an illegal poker game, a fact which was likely known to the robbers. Initially Brown described her robber as light skinned and wearing braided hair; Daniels fit neither description. After Daniels' conviction another man sent word to the prosecutor that he was ready to confess to the crime; but the prosecution didn't follow up on the matter. Hence Daniels was prosecuted and convicted on the strength of a questionable witness ID and nothing else.

Subsequently, a reporter attempted to contract Brown about the case. He phoned her twice, each time leaving a message on her answering machine. "The messages were respectful and were a routine part of the reporting process, and if Brown didn't want to comment, he said, she could have simply told him so." (the reporters committee for freedom of the press, November 16, 2004) For these attempts at making inquires, Brown made out a complaint for harassment and Lee was arrested and jailed. It took the strenuous efforts by local journalists to get him released.

The uneasy symbiosis of Durham and Duke

Duke university is Durham's largest employer. In fact, since the demise of the tobacco industry, it is virtually Durham's only employer of note--the "one industry" in a "one industry town".

The university leases some 30% of the available downtown office space, employs some twenty-thousand locals, and contributes several billion dollars annually to the local economy (in salaries, and monies spent in local businesses, particularly by its students). The university has contributed some seven million dollars to the construction of a local performing arts center (a venture which has nothing to do with the educational mission of the university) and provides some fifty million annually in local philanthropy, including assisting with the construction of homeless housing, better health care, and mentoring local schools.

Nevertheless, as the single biggest industry, Duke is constantly seen by local government as a possible source for even more funds. Whenever Duke requires a building or zoning permit, it must apply to the city; whereupon the city, before its approval, often raises the issue of increased contributions to the city, either through the imposition of some form of property taxes (which Duke, as a tax-exempt charitable foundation, is not required to pay), other taxes, or fees. In recent years, when Duke has been anxious to secure approvals for its anticipated $500 million expansion program, it has been especially vulnerable to pressures from the city. And no amount of spending within the city of Durham seems to have bought the university the sort of good will it has sought: and it is still viewed by at least a substantial and vocal number of Durhamites as an extraneous plantation set on a hill, a place of privilege, to be viewed through the cracked lens of envy.

> The city of Durham wants Duke University to pay $1 million a year in lieu of property taxes for the next 10 years and to pony up at least $10 million to help pay for a proposed downtown performing arts center.
>
> --Herald-Sun, May 13, 2004

A noisy neighborhood

The lacrosse team party was held at 610 N. Buchanan St., a rented house in a neighborhood called Trinity Park, directly across from the University campus. The area had become home to many off-campus students, whose relations with local residents were sometimes stormy. When the legal drinking age was raised to 21, universities around the country found themselves in a quandary whether to permit what had now become illegal drinking on their campuses. Their solution in most instance was to push the drinking off campus, where the universities could disclaim responsibility. It also meant in many cases that the universities would also renounce supervision. Fraternities, sororities, and sports teams located their partying off-campus, along with the resultant noise and confusion. Trinity Park residents had waged a ten-year losing battle with the university to supervise its students' partying, but were not ready to give up the fight in 2006.

In the new school year, in cooperation with the Durham police department, stringent enforcement was to be applied to student violations. No infraction, no matter how small, was to be overlooked; "zero tolerance" was the order of the day--a policy also endorsed by the university. Students who lived in off-campus housing in Trinity Park, having been forewarned of this policy, were alert to the possibility that even a noise violation could bring them a court date, and a resulting criminal record.

Thus, in the fall of 2005, local law enforcement authorities had conducted what they named the "Back-to-School Operation." Just two days after the start of school, dozens of officers surrounded some off-campus housing where they believed alcohol was being consumed. No one present was allowed to leave. Students who could not produce identification showing they were over 21 were made to line up and undergo breath testing, but with equipment that was used over and over, providing many false positives. Any who refused the testing were charged. No Miranda warnings were given, and premises were entered and searched without warrants. More than 200 Duke students were cited and required to appear in court. After a three-day hearing, a judge finally dismissed all 200 cases, saying the police had acted illegally.

To civil libertarians, this resounded of unequal enforcement of the laws, and the targeting of Duke students. (Two years later, statistics showed that Duke students were still more than thirty times as likely to receive citations for alcohol violations as were students at nearby North Carolina State University.)

The response of Duke University was to apologize, not to the students, but to the community. President Richard Brodhead of the university told National Public Radio that "I have great regret for what the neighbors of these party houses have had to experience. They have been the victims of boorish behavior."

That same fall four students were arrested at an apartment complex; one was thrown to the ground by police and had his face bloodied, and was then charged with trespassing--at his own residence. At trial he was acquitted; evidence, including video, showed he did nothing to provoke the attack by the officer.

In October 2005 the Rolling Stones gave a concert on the Duke campus. At an off-campus party, a student threw a bottle which broke on the sidewalk. A nearby neighbor then told the party-goers that she had called the police to complain about the noise. Immediately the party broke up and the students scattered, fearful of being cited. When the police arrived a few minutes later, the house was empty, and quiet.

In the meantime, a Sgt. Mark Gottlieb of the Durham Police Department was preparing for a warrant to raid the house and arrest the student renters. His justification for the warrant asserted the house was the locale of noise and alcohol violations; and that a Duke flag which resembled one that had been stolen from the front of the Duke Administration building ("stolen property") was on display in house. In order to obtain the identities and physical descriptions of the renters, which he needed for his warrant request, he contacted Duke University; and the university provided him with that information (in violation of the Family Educational Rights and Privacy Act--"FERPA").

At 3:00 a.m. the house was surrounded by Durham police and then entered. Everyone inside was handcuffed, some while still in bed, and taken to the police station. One student was dragged by his feet down the steps while handcuffed, his head banging against every step. (This sort of treatment, if meted out to a suspected terror suspect, would be assailed by every civil rights organization in the country.) Because there was no proof that any of the residents had personally violated a noise or alcohol ordinance, the charges against them were amended to 'aiding and abetting'. All were acquitted at trial, except for one student whom the complaining neighbor could identify as one she spoke with the night of the party.

The flag alleged to be stolen property was a cheap copy of the Duke emblem, printed on only one side, such as were purchased by many Duke students for display on their walls. Nevertheless, Sgt. Gottlieb requested and obtained the testimony of Duke Executive Vice President Trask that it at least looked like the same flag. The student owner was acquitted.

The response of the university was to consider possible disciplinary action for the students (despite their acquittal). No one, it seems, complained that the noise from the nearby Rolling Stones concert exceeded anything emanating from the student residences.

In January, 2006, a Trinity Park resident called police to complain of excessive noise by students emptying trash at

610 N. Buchanan St. An officer responded but found no one at the trash cans. Nevertheless he entered the house (without a warrant and without consent) and told the student renters, two captains of the Duke university lacrosse team, that he was going to charge them with noise violations. He told them that he had been given a "directive from [his] supervisor" to do so. According to his recollections, both captains were polite and understanding. One captain was later tried and acquitted. The other, David Evans, was convicted on the same facts and evidence by a different judge (one deliberately chosen by Nifong) and given a probation agreement.

By then, Sgt. Gottlieb had acquired a reputation for animosity toward Duke students. Students recounted his pulling his patrol car across the sidewalk to block their path; being verbally abusive; interrogating them bullishly on the street; threatening one student (whom he wrongly thought was foreign-born) with deportation; and telling others he would put them "in a cell with a couple of crack whores to show them what life was really like".

In a study done later by a local newspaper, the News and Observer, seventy-one percent of Gottlieb's arrests between May of 2005 and February of 2006 were shown to be Duke students (20 of 28), while only three percent of the arrests made by others in the same area were Duke students (2 of 64).

Another examination of Gottlieb's record showed that of 32 people he charged during one period, 19 of them were Duke students. Of the 19, 16 were taken to the police station and jailed (whereas, of the remaining non-Duke students charged, only six were jailed). Fifteen of the Duke students were being charged with noise or alcohol violations; while the non-Duke students, many of whom had potentially more severe offenses (including carrying a concealed handgun) were not jailed. It was alleged by some that Gottlieb would conveniently "create" facts during court testimony in order to bolster the prosecution's case; and sometimes add additional "facts" which were irrelevant to the case itself but which would serve to humiliate the defendants.

Sgt. Gottlieb had his supporters. Ellen Dagenhart, a Trinity Park resident and longtime acquaintance of Gottlieb, defended him: "There were a lot of homeowners and taxpayers who were calling the cops saying, 'Please come and make yourself seen... Anyone who's seen kids passed out in a puddle of vomit is certainly happy to see the police show up. You can't blame Mark Gottlieb for that." (Dagenhart's husband, John, president of the Trinity Park Neighborhood Association. would be interviewed on Larry King Live and elsewhere in the media after the rape charges were made.)

In the ten years or so in which Trinity Park residents had been fighting noise from students, they had never attained their goal. Communities near other universities had tried different measures; police had treated partying students not like adult felons but like immature students; taxis were summoned and they were offered rides home; and stickers were placed in the windows of houses where noise had been found to be excessive; if the police had to return to those houses at any time in the next six months for noise complaints, heavy fines would be imposed on both the renters and the owners. These measures had achieved some degree of success. In Trinity Park, the same battles were fought year after year, as the student population changed every year.

In late February, 2006, Gottlieb was transferred from the precinct which included Trinity Park, possibly as a result of complaints against him, and given a desk job. It is possible that Duke university, which was informed about the complaints, was instrumental in his transfer.

CASE NARRATIVE :
The Party

On March 13, 2006, the Duke lacrosse team held a party at 610 N. Buchanan St., in Trinity Park. The team captains, who as seniors were permitted to live off campus, were renters of the house. Team members came and went throughout the day and as a late addition it was decided to hire strippers to perform. In previous years the team had celebrated once a year by attending en masse a strip club performance; but the lowering of the drinking age had made this impossible, and hiring the strippers was considered to be a substitute for the annual party, as well as compensation for the team's having to miss Spring Break. Many of the partygoers were unaware that strippers had been hired and found out only when they were asked to contribute their share to the hiring fees.

By midnight the dancers had arrived and began their performance. They were Kim (Pittman) Roberts and Crystal Mangum. Mangum sometimes worked as a dancer at the Platinum club. She had made a claim some years previously that she had been gang-raped, seized by three men and taken inside a bathroom and held against her will. She had also claimed that her former husband had once dragged her into the woods and tried to kill her. Neither claim was ever prosecuted.

It was evident from the outset that she would be unable to perform this night. Some of the partygoers thought she might have been either drunk or under the influence of drugs. When the dance began she started leaning heavily on Roberts, and then fell to the floor. She alternately crawled and mumbled unintelligibly. Roberts attempted to keep up the performance, asking if any members of the audience wanted to join her, or if any had brought any sex toys which she might use in the act. Pictures show the players, who were seated in rows against the wall, and who said afterwards that they felt uncomfortable or even disgusted by the act, idle and looking bored or pained.

One player, in an attempt at humor, held up a broomstick and jokingly suggested she might use that. Roberts then claimed that she was insulted and took Mangum with her off into the bathroom and shut the door. It is not unknown in stripper circles for dancers who have been paid in advance, and feel that there is no more money to be made at a location, to abruptly end their performance on some pretext and depart, a scenario called "cash and dash". Whatever the cause, the performance that night, for which $800 had been paid, and which had been expected to last for two hours, had lasted all of four minutes.

Inside the bathroom, Mangum attempted to apply some false fingernails, and some phone calls were made, possibly to the booking agency about other gigs or to drivers. These cell phone records were sealed by a judge later in the interests of protecting the privacy of other parties whose numbers might appear on the phones.

The partygoers, angry at what they considered being cheated, wanted for the dancers to return their money and leave. One player threatened to call the police; another offered to shove additional money under the bathroom door ($100 extra) if only they would leave; and an argument developed over returning their fee. Angry words were exchanged at curbside as the dancers were getting into their car, with Roberts calling the players "little ___ white boys" and one player responding to Roberts with "Thank your grandpa for my nice cotton shirt!", a line which some claimed was taken from a show by a nationally-known African-American comedian.

Roberts responded with, "That's a hate crime! I'm calling the police!".

During all this time the other dancer, Mangum, had been incoherent, sometimes attempting to return to the house and resume her performance, saying to Roberts, "There's more money to be made"; and sometimes meandering about the back yard. The players locked the back door when she attempted to enter, before she stumbled once again on the stairs. Pictures taken at this time show her smiling.

After the dancers had departed, the team captains advised everyone to leave, saying they feared that if the dancers did complain to the police, Durham officers, in keeping with their known policy, would automatically cite everyone at the house for alcohol and noise violations.

By then several of the players had already left. Shortly after the brief performance--which ended at 12:04, according to data from photographs-- two sophomores had left the party with friends. Beginning at 12:05, Reade Seligmann made the first of eight separate attempts to reach numbers on his cell phone; after which he called for a taxi about 12:14. At 12:19 he and a friend were picked up by a cab at a corner. They were taken first to an ATM where pictures showed Seligmann made a withdrawal; then to a fast food place; and then back to the campus, where Seligmann entered his dorm at 12:46, according to his key card information.

Collin Finnerty also began using his cell phone. After leaving the party, at 12:22 he called a member of the team to see if he wanted to join him for something to eat. He walked a short distance to another student rental house, in order to retrieve a Playstation. While there he was himself called by another member of the team at 12:27. At 12:30 he called to order a pizza. At 12:33 he called to cancel the pizza, and he and three friends left the second rental house and went to an eatery, where at 12:56 they paid for their meal with a credit card. Finnerty re-entered his dormitory at 1:04, and made another call beginning at 1:16.

David Evans, the third of the players who would later be indicted, began a phone call to his girlfriend at 12:34, which would last for the next sixteen minutes.

Photographs show Magnum being helped into a car at the Buchanan house at 12:41 (the car departed a few moments later). If she was raped by Reade Seligmann alone it must have taken place between 12:04 and the first of Seligmann's calls at 12:05. If she was raped by Collin Finnerty alone it must have been sometime after approximately 12:15 to 12:20, when she was seen by a neighbor in the back yard arguing about money, and before 12:22, when Finnerty was making a call. She made her own call to her escort service at 12:26. Time-stamped photos show her standing outside the house at 12:30 and 12:37. If she was raped by Seligmann, Finnerty, and David Evans together, all three of them must have all been gathered in the bathroom for one minute between 12:04 and 12:05. Fingerprinting of the entire bathroom proved that Finnerty had never been in the bathroom. None of them individually was ever out of sight of other partygoers. Neither were they ever as a group out of sight of others. Neither of the sophomores was present when the dancers left, both having departed twenty to twenty-five minutes earlier. And a large number of time-stamped photographs, plus two phone videos of the night's events, further confirm that there was no seizure of the dancers, nor any struggle; nor anything but a group of bored and naive college students who were eager for their over-expensive entertainment to leave.

> The photos show some guys looking away [from the dance]. One looked at his feet. One was sending a text message on his phone. Another had his thumb pointed down.
>
> ——
>
> Reade Seligmman was shrinking back in one photo with a look of distaste. "I didn't like the tone of the party... And I just--it made me uncomfortable"
>
> ——
>
> Collin Finnerty didn't like it either. "It wasn't fun to watch. People were talking over them [the dance and the dancers]... it wasn't appealing at all."
>
> ——
>
> "It was boring. I was itching to get out of there, because it was. I'd rather be going to sleep personally, to tell you the truth." (Devon Sherwood)
>
> --Until Proven Innocent, Stuart Taylor and K.C. Johnson, pp. 24-25)

But the facts have never been known to get in the way of a good story--especially one that involves accepted stereotypes. In the Alabama of the 1930s it was immediately understood that if nine black men had hidden in a railroad gondola car with two white women, then the nine black men must have been consumed with thoughts of rape.

> A Negro will always, in their opinion, rape a white woman if he gets the chance. These nine Negroes were riding alone with two white girls on a freight car. Therefore, there was no question that they raped them, or wanted to rape them, or were present while the other Negroes raped them -- all of which amounts to very much the same thing in Southern eyes -- and calls for the immediate death of the Negroes regardless of these shades of difference.
>
> --Observations of Hollace Ransdell at the first Scottsboro Trials, April, 1931

Times change, but human nature remains constant. In the 21st century, it is immediately understood that if a white college fraternity or sports team hires strippers, and particularly strippers of another race, then their thoughts must focus on rape.

> Black women; white men. A stripper; and a team blowout. The wealthy white athletes – many from prep schools – of Duke; and the working class woman from historically black North Carolina Central. Race and class and sex. . .
>
> The history of white men and black women – the special fantasies and realities of exploitation – goes back to the nation's beginning and the arrival of slaves from Africa. The patterns associated with this history arouse fears and evoke too many bad memories.
>
> --"Duke: Horror and Truth", Jesse Jackson, April 24, 2006

Yet in such cases there is always the danger that if these general assumptions turn out not to be true, then accepted stereotypes might crack; and an entire world view might be threatened.

Though full of glaring inconsistencies, the [Duke accuser] was nonetheless. . . a victim and entitled to her pound of flesh. Why? Because she is not to be seen simply as an individual but, more as a member of a "weak" group, namely, women -- and a black woman to boot. . . Right over wrong did not matter; only class/group struggle did.

--Rabbi Aryeh Spero, February 15, 2007

For many the lacrosse case was never to be about the three charged players--David Evans, Collin Finnerty, and Reade Seligmann, each a unique human being with a unique makeup of his own. It was to be about "three rich white males". Almost as soon as the news hit the stands, the case became "us vs. them": "black vs. white"; "rich vs. poor"; "male vs. feminist"; "town vs. gown"; "athlete vs. scholar". Sweeping assertions were made about the presumed lifestyles of "athletes", "lacrosse players", "college males", and "children of the rich".

The players had ceased to be treated as individual persons once they were accused. But Reade Seligmann's father was raised by a black family. His putative grandparents were therefore black. Collin Finnerty's family funded medical facilities in Africa. Humans are much too complex to be able to make sweeping generalizations about them just from their ethnicity or their zip code. No two snowflakes are alike. No two humans--infinitely more complex than snowflakes--can be alike, either.

But when the accused were proven to be innocent--then for many with agendas the story became another example of a case that was "too important for innocence to be allowed as a defense".

Western democracy exists because traditional Christian culture taught it that men were loved individually and separately and not as part of a herd. The state had to be restrained because it only had temporary charge of these beings. When a state expresses its willingness to treat individuals as expendable generic and redundant copies of one another, it demonstrates that has lost its understanding of both its function and of the nature of those it governs.

--adapted from Malcolm Muggeridge

The lives of everyone involved were shortly to be changed because of a false charge of rape.

Handwritten Statement of Jarriel Lanier Johnson, Raleigh, NC. The driver for Crystal Gail Mangum

made - 6:37 - 7:50 p.m. April 6, 2006

[statement starts on Friday, March 10, 2006]

STATEMENT:

I was called by Crystal on March 10, 2006 to drive her to Holiday Inn Express in Wakefield.

I picked her up at her parents house around 1:50 p.m. She said her appointment was a 2 p.m. We arrived at the hotel around 2:20 p.m. After I dropped her off I returned home.

———

We got to Platinum [Club] around 11 or 12 [P.M.] where she went in and I remained in the car.

Around 2 a.m. I go inside to find her, she asks if we can stay for about another hour. She then asks me if we can stay just one more hour. We leave at 4:30 when the club closes. She then tells me that she has a job at the Millennium Hotel.

We get there at 5:15 a.m., where she goes in and I remain in the car. At about 6:15 a.m. she returns and I driver her back to her parent's home. We say good bye and I head back to Raleigh. I arrive at my parents home at 7 a.m. and go to bed.

Around 2 p.m. that afternoon Crystal calls me asking if I could drive her that night. I agree and ask what time, she says around 4 p.m. As I get close to her parents house she calls me and says that Matt [Matthew Murchison, her boyfriend] is coming over to bring her something.

I told her that I would wait until she called me at the the car wash on Fayetteville St. Around 5-5:30 p.m. she calls me and tells me that he's gone. About 5-10 minutes later I arrive at her parent's house.

Her daughter lets me in. I sit there and play with her kids while Crystal is getting ready. Once she is ready we leave and ride around for about half an hour. We then go over to Forest Hills Park and sit and talk.

Around 8 or 9 she asks if we could go to Raleigh to find this guy she met. I say okay. We drive around downtown Raleigh trying to find this guy. We have no luck so we decide to get a hotel room and wait to see if he calls. This is about 9 p.m. or so. We go to get something to at a Chinese place over on Wake Forest Rd. Once we get our food we take it back to the hotel and eat. After eating we get into bed and watch TC. While watching TV we engage in sexual intercourse.

Around 12 a.m. I leave. I tell her to call me in the morning so I could pick her up. At around 11 a.m. Crystal calls me asking me to pick her up.

I arrive at the hotel around 11:30 am. I call Crystal to see where she is and she tells me that she went for a walk. I drive up and down Lane St. trying to find her. She calls me back asking me to meet her at the hotel. When I arrive she is with an older gentleman that she says wants to see her perform.

I go back down and wait in my car until I see the man come out. After I see him leave I go to the room and help Crystal gather her things.

We then head over to my parents house and hang out for about 20 min. I told Crystal that I was going to wash my car and she suggest we go to one of the pay car washes. While there I began to wash my car while she talked on the phone. I then told her that I was taking her home.

On the way to I-540 she told me she needed to use the bathroom and wanted me to pull over. Once I did she got out of the car and started walking down Creedmoor Rd. I pulled my car over and got out to chase her down. She told me to leave her alone. I went back to my car and pulled up in front of her. Once again I pulled over and asked her to get in. She again told me to leave her alone. I went up several yards and waited until she came towards me; again I asked her to get in the car. She then got in.

We went back to my parents house where we talked it out. We sat on the couch for a little while and then went to my bedroom. While there we talked and she knocked over her drink which spilled on my phone. After that it was around 4-4:30 p.m. and I took Crystal back to her parent's house.

Later on that night I noticed that my phone wasn't working properly. I called Crystal and told her that it was mess up. At that time she told me that she had a bachelor party to work that night, and asked if I could drive. I agreed. Later on that night I couldn't get my phone to work and called her to let her know that it's not working and wouldn't be able to take her.

She said that was okay and that Brian would take her. I told her to call me when she got home and she said okay. About 1 a.m. or 1:30 a.m. I received a call from Tammy asking if I was Crystal's driver that night. I told her no and she hung up. I tried calling Crystal for the next couple of days and didn't hear from her until Thursday.

———

[Added later, to reconcile the statement with Crystal Mangum's claim that she had not had sex for a week preceeding the party] Looking at my datebook on my cell phone I realized that the dates that I engaged in sexual intercourse with Crystal was off by a week. our last encounter together was the Sunday prior.

Perhaps neither Johnson, nor Kim Roberts who was then driving Crystal away from the house on Buchanan street, was aware that Mangum had previously claimed to have been gang-raped.

Police Report August 18, 1996

Crime/Incidents : Statutory Rape

Crime Incident : Assault on Female

How Attacked or Committed :

Suspects did for a continual time, rape and beat the victim about her person.

Narrative :

On 08/18/96, at about 1815 hours, the reporting officer responded to the police Dept. in reference to taking a report. Upon arrival the R/O spoke with [Crystal Mangum]... stated that three years ago [1993], at an unspecified location on Hillsboro St., three suspects raped and beat her when she was fourteen years old. [Crystal Mangum] stated the three suspects were (1) [name omitted] b/m [black male], unknown address (2) [name omitted] b/m [address omitted], and (3) [name and address omitted], Creedmoor. The R/O advised [Crystal Mangum] to write a chronological ordered statement of the incidents and occurrences that had taken place and return the statement for investigative purposes. No further information.

4/28/06 - 0918

Called victim [Crystal Mangum] in reference to an earlier sexual assault that she reported at Creedmor police department. She stated that she was dating F_____ at the time. She stated that she had ran away from home on previous times and that she had been found hiding at F____'s house after the police came with a search warrant. She stated that she was used by F____ to sell drugs and take the money to him. She stated that when F____ was not there some men would come over, L____, A_____ and S_____. She stated that she would have sex with them when Floyd was not around. She stated later that the men paid F____ to come over and have sex with her. She stated that one day F_____ confronted the victim about the men that were coming over and having sex with her. She stated that she denied it to him and then he brought the three men to the house. She stated in front of her she asked them and they all said that they had been having sex with her. She stated that F____ grabbed her and they went into the bedroom where she stated three men Mr. F____, A____ and L____ "ran the train on her" she stated she was very scared . In her voice I could sense that she was becoming very emotional, she stated that she did tell some of her family members about it and that she went to Duke Hospital about a week after the incident. She stated that Mr. F____ stated to her that no one would believe her and she stated that she didn't think anyone would believe her since she had already had sex with them before. She stated that F_____ was very abusive and stated that if she ever told he would find her and that she was very afraid of him at the time. She stated years later she met her husband Mr. McNiel who she confided with about the incident. She stated he urged her to go report the incident so that she could have some closure and that she wont keep it a secret. She stated she reported it to the Creedmor police who did an investigation. She stated that she was told by the investigators that it would be a long process and that at her young age it would be mentally and physically tough and very hard on her. They told her that all three of the men were currently in jail and that were going to be in jail for a significant time. The victim stated that Mr. F_____ had been in jail for pushing his grandmother down the stairs which killed her. [no evidence has been found of this supposed murder] She stated that when she found out they were currently in jail, she thought she had closure due to the fact that she had let some one know what happened and that they were going to be in jail for a long time she felt satisfied and she did not pursue it further.

--Notes of Investigator Ben Himan on statement of Ms. Mangum about her earlier accusation of gang rape

CASE NARRATIVE :
The Road to the Hospital

At 12:53 Kim Roberts made an anonymous call to 911. But it wasn't to report a rape.

CALLER: *"Hi, I don't know if this is an emergency or not, necessarily, but I'm in Durham, and I was driving down near Duke's campus, and it's me and my black girlfriend, and the guy--there's like a white guy by the Duke wall -- and he just hollered out 'n_____' to me. And I'm just so angry I didn't know who to call."* [Crying or pretending to cry]

Then Roberts changed her story a bit, to say she and her friend were walking by the house instead of driving :

CALLER: *"It's right outside of 610 Buchanan. And I saw them all come out of, like, a big frat house, and me and my black girlfriend are walking by, and they called us 'n______.'"* [Sobbing or pretending to sob]

"...And they didn't harm me in any way, but I just feel so completely offended, I can't even believe it. I thought, you know what I'm saying, times have changed, and I don't even know what's going on."

The Buchanan St. house has no numbers visible from the street, where passersby unfamiliar with the house could have noticed its address. For some reason, the 911 operator did not take the caller's name or contact information. Police responded to the call, even though had they found someone there, they could not have legally have charged anyone since they had no complaining witness nor did they witness the supposed name-calling themselves.

Durham is a city in which residents in some areas complain that police do not respond quickly to calls for help; and that in some instances, even when it has been reported that shots have been fired, they do not respond at all.

In answering this anonymous complaint about name-calling in Trinity Park, not one but two police cars responded within two minutes (120 seconds). Officers inspected the premises, remained some eleven minutes searching the front and back yard for evidence (of a name-calling incident or possibly other violation) before leaving.

Kim Roberts later told the press that the *"trip in that car from the house went from happy to crazy. I tried all different ways to get through to her [Mangum]. I tried to be funny and nice. Then I tried to, you know, be stern with her."* Finally, trying to get Mangum out of the car, Roberts tried to push her out, shouting, *"Get out of my car! Get out of my car!"* Mangum then replied, *"Go ahead, put marks on me. That's what I want. Go ahead!"*

Roberts then drove to the parking lot of a Kroger store looking for an off-duty police officer who would help her get Mangum out of her car. She was unable to locate the officer but asked the security guard in the store, Angel Altmon, for help. Altmon phoned 911 after she too was unable to convince Mangum to leave the car. The 911 operator cited the case to the police as a *"10-56 female refusing to get out of dark colored*

Honda Accord in the Kroger parking lot", "10-56" being code for "drunk and disorderly pedestrian."

When police arrived, their report stated:

"A female walked across the parking lot to my [Sgt. Shelton's] *location and said that it was her car. She told me that she had made the call at 610 N. Buchanan. She stated that she was driving up the street and that the female she had in the car was walking up the sidewalk along the Duke Wall in the 600 block of N. Buchanan. She said that a group of white males was at 610 and they were yelling racial slurs across the street at the female. She said that she did not know if the female was drunk or high, but that in any case, she did not appear that she could take care of herself and she was afraid of what the white males might do to the woman. She said that she offered the woman a ride to a safe location; but that the woman would not get out of her car. She further stated that she did not know the woman. I cautioned her about picking up strangers."*

This was a third version of events, in which Roberts said she did not know Mangum and was not with her but picked her up off the street. Up to this point no one had mentioned rape. In a phone conversation with Investigator Benjamin Himan of the Durham police almost a week later (March 20, 2006), Roberts said (according to Himan's notes) :

"She stated that she heard that Ms. Mangum was sexually assaulted, which she said was a 'crock', and she stated that she was with her the whole time until she left. And the only time she was alone was when she [Mangum] would not leave [the house] and that time period was less than five minutes."

Sergeant John Shelton and another officer tried to get Mangum out of Kim Roberts' car. Mangum was pretending to be unconscious so Shelton broke an ammonia capsule under her nose and Mangum began breathing through her mouth. Shelton therefore concluded she was only feigning unconsciousness.

When Shelton tried to pull Mangum out of the car, she grabbed the parking break and locked her fingers around it. When Shelton with the help of another officer finally managed to get her out of the car, she pretended she was unconscious again.

Mangum had a previous record of altercations with law enforcement.

> Police report of Crystal Mangum 2002 arrest by Deputy John Carroll
>
> The suspect was driving a blue taxi cab [which she had stolen at a topless club]. She was completely left of center within my sight without any lights on the vehicle. She then crossed back right and off the road into the shoulder and turning up dirt. [After traveling 70mph in a 55mph zone,] the suspect was then traveling south in the northbound lane . . . She traveled east until it came to a dead end. She then attempted to turn left and run through a fence but was unable to and it appeared that she was not going to go any further. I put my vehicle in park and exited it, and approached the suspect—telling her to turn the car off and get out.
>
> When she saw me approach, she was laughing and put the vehicle in reverse and backed across the road and into the woods. It appeared that she was stuck. I had to run around my vehicle to get back to the driver's side door, and as I began to approach the vehicle she put it in drive and drove towards me. I jumped out of the way to the right and she missed me. The suspect then struck the right rear quarter of my patrol vehicle . . . and then proceeded west on Briar Creek Parkway, almost striking Deputy Goss in his patrol vehicle.
>
> [Police pursed Mangum and eventually boxed in her vehicle]

> ... was boxed in. Deputy Goss and I approached the vehicle with our guns drawn, pointing at the suspect, giving verbal commands to exit the car. She refused until we were directly next to the car.
>
> She then opened the door and would not get out, with her hand on the steering wheel and leaning out to the rear of the car. She finally got out of the car and laid down on the ground. She was taken into custody at that time. I put her in the back seat of my vehicle. She kept attempting to lay down but was advised to sit up. She was given an alcosensor and submitted, giving a 0.19 reading, and at the same time, while getting all the information together, the suspect passed out and was unresponsive.

Because of her condition, Shelton did not feel he could simply take her home; nor could he take her to jail. Instead, he arranged for other officers to take her to Durham ACCESS, a mental health care clinic, for observation. If admitted at the clinic, Mangum would have been detained for at least twenty-four hours. While still at the Kroger, an officer radioed to report that Mangum (with whose circumstances the police were apparently acquainted) had two young children at home and that someone should alert the Department of Social Services to be prepared to look after them should they be found alone. It is not unreasonable to consider if Mangum might have feared at some point that her children could be taken away from her.

At Durham ACCESS, Mangum was examined by a number of persons. The first supervisor she saw detected alcohol on her breath. Mangum said her name was "Honey" and stated she did not want to go to jail. When Mangum was then taken to see a nurse for evaluation, she at first refused to say anything. She then wrote the names of her children on a piece of paper. When the nurse asked if something had happened to her children, she said no. When the nurse asked if something had happened to her, she nodded. When the nurse asked her if she had been raped, she nodded once again.

The nurse did not believe that she was drunk or high on drugs, but was suffering from disoriented thinking or a break with reality, possibly a form of psychosis. But because she had claimed to be raped, she had to be taken immediately to Duke Hospital for a formal Sexual Assault Examination, instead of being committed at Durham Access.

(Some observers believe that Mangum may have agreed with the rape claim in order to avoid being held for observation.)

On the way to the hospital Mangum did not further describe the rape, nor her attackers; but complained that Roberts had stolen $2000 from her, as well as her purse, bag, cell phone and ID. Once at the hospital she took back her rape claim. Sgt. Shelton, who had arrived at the hospital to question her, then went to phone headquarters and inform them she had changed her mind. Mangum meanwhile still asserted that Roberts had stolen her money, which she wanted returned. At another point she complained that she had left her money behind in a police car. While Shelton was on the phone he was told that Mangum had changed her mind again and was once more saying she had been raped. (Officer Shelton later faced criticism from the police hierarchy and an internal investigation because he expressed honest skepticism about Mangum's rape claim. Curiously, he was the only officer whose conduct the department would examine during the course of the case.)

Throughout the following hours Mangum would variously assert that she had been raped by 2, 3, 5, or 20 white men; that Kim Roberts had (or had not) assisted them; that Roberts had stolen her money; that some of the men had been named Adam, Brett, and Matt; that these were (or were not) aliases;

that some of the attackers may have used more than one alias (with one using as many as three); and that the lacrosse players had (or had not) referred to each other using only their player's numbers. She also claimed that she had been dancing with three other performers, named Nikki, Angel, and Tammy; and that the performance had taken place in the master bedroom of the house (and not the living room, the actual location). It might or might not be relevant that "Nikki" was another stage name of Kim Roberts; "Angel" was the name of Angel Altmon, who phoned in the 911 call; and "Tammy" was the name of an employee of a booking agency from which Mangum sometimes received assignments.

From Scottsboro:

My name is Victoria Price. I live at Huntsville, Alabama. I am twenty-one years old... I was on a freight train--through Jackson County. I got on that train at Chattanooga. Ruby Bates was with me on that train. . . I was riding on a gondola car. That is a car with no top on it. It has sides on it. I was inside of that car. That car was loaded with chert or gravel. It was not full to the top with chert or gravel. It lacked two or three feet on each side being full.

When I first saw the defendants they were coming over the top of the train; they were coming over the top of the box car next to the gondola, into the gondola which I was in. There were some other Negroes with these defendants. Twelve of them, all Negroes, came over the top of that car.

I know which was the first one that got down into the car in which I was riding; it was one of these defendants...When they came into the car I was in, Clarence Norris asked me if I was going to put out. The one that had the gun picked me up in his arms and said he was going to throw me out of the gondola. He got me by the leg and by the ankle and slung me back in the gondola and picked me up like he was going to throw me out of it. Then Clarence Norris grabbed me and had sexual intercourse with me...At the time Norris was having intercourse with me the defendant Weems had a knife at my throat. He had one of his hands on my face and the other hand with his knife, so I could not holler. He would not let me raise up. I struggled, hollered, and screamed. Some of the other defendants were standing around at that time. The little one, the smallest, was holding my legs...

One of these defendants, Clarence Norris, pulled my overalls off me, and had intercourse with me. The other one helped him; he held me while the other one pulled my clothes off.

I did not afterwards put my clothes on before I got to Paint Rock. . . and I didn't remember anything for about an hour after I got off the car...

--Victoria Price, direct testimony in the first Scottsboro trial

From Scottsboro:

My name is Ruby Bates. I live at Huntsville. . . I was in company with Victoria Price on a freight train traveling towards Chattanooga to Point Rock, Alabama...

--Ruby Bates, direct testimony in the first Scottsboro trial

From Scottsboro:

Q You testified at Scottsboro that six Negroes raped you and six Negroes raped her, and one had a knife on your throat; what happened to her was exactly the same thing that happened to you. Who coached you to say that?

A She [Victoria Price] did.

Q Did she tell you what would happen to you if you didn't follow her story?

A She said we might have to lay out a sentence in jail.

--Ruby Bates, direct examination by defense counsel Samuel Liebowitz, Scottsboro trials

From Scottsboro:

If in your mind the conviction of this defendant depends on the testimony of Victoria Price and you are convinced she has not sworn truly about any material point, you could not convict this defendant.

--Judge Horton in his charge to the Scottsboro jury

Press Release
April 28, 2006

As you know, the Associated Press broke a story yesterday alleging that the victim in what has come to be known as the "Duke Lacrosse Rape Case" had reported approximately ten years ago that she had been sexually assaulted approximately thirteen years ago...

Much has been said about the presumption of innocence in conjunction with this case. It is important to keep in mind that it is the finder of fact in any criminal case--the jury--who must presume innocence. Not only is the prosecutor not required to presume a defendant innocent, but it would be a violation of his ethical duties to prosecute any person in whose guilt he did not personally believe. And, if the prosecutor personally believes in a defendant's guilt, it would be a violation of his moral responsibility to the victim and to his community not to prosecute a case because doing so was not popular, or because he was worried that he might not win at trial.

The investigation of this case is not yet complete. All of the facts are not yet known...For the sake of the victim, for the sake of the accused, for the sake of our system of justice, I encourage everyone to step back from this situation and allow that system to do its job.

Mike Nifong
District Attorney
Durham, North Carolina

CASE NARRATIVE: How the Medical Community Responded

MOTION TO SUPPRESS ID

I. Factual Background

The Duke University Medical Center Emergency Room

7. At the Emergency Room, the accuser was met and interviewed by Officer G.D. Sutton. She told Officer Sutton that she was sore and bleeding from her vagina, that there were "20 guys" at a bachelor party at 610 N. Buchanan, and that she performed with three other girls, "Nikki, Angel, and Tammy." (Discovery at 1304) She further told Officer Sutton that "Nikki" [Kim Roberts] wanted "to have sex with one of the guys and tried to talk her into it." When she refused, "she ended up in the bathroom with five guys who forced her to ...perform sexual acts." The accuser further "stated that one of the guys, Brett, penetrated her ...She later stated that she was penetrated by all five of the guys." (Discovery at 1304) She gave no description of her attackers.

8. Shortly thereafter, Sgt. Shelton arrived at the Emergency Room. The accuser told him that she was a stripper who had been hired to dance with one other female at 610 N. Buchanan through an escort service. The accuser said that she and "Nikki" [Kim Roberts] "put on a show" for the men at the party and that "they left and got into 'Nikki's' car." The accuser then said that one of the men asked them to come back inside, that Nikki wanted to return, but that the accuser did not want to and she and Nikki "got into an argument." The accuser then said that "at that point some of the guys from the party pulled her from the vehicle and groped her. She said that no one forced her to have sex. She then mentioned that someone had taken her money." (Discovery at 445-47:1322-23) She gave no description of her attackers.

9. Sgt. Shelton contacted the Watch Commander to report that the accuser had recanted her claim of rape; however, he was told a few minutes later that the accuser had told the SANE doctor that she had been raped. Sgt. Shelton "called the Watch commander back and told him that she had changed her story back to being raped." He then "returned to the room where she was and asked her if she had or had not been raped. She told me that she did not want to talk to me anymore and then started crying and saying something about them dragging her into the bathroom." (Discovery at 1323)

A Duke Police Officer also noted that the accuser had not only changed her story several times, but that at one point was claiming that she had been raped by 20 white males. (Discovery at 1) She gave no description of her attackers.

10. While at the Emergency Room, the accuser was examined by a number of nurses and physicians. She reported that she was suffering from pain of "10/10"--however, the ESI Pain Documentation portion of the medical records indicates

that she had no facial distress indicating pain, that she was not sweating (a common response to intense pain), that she did not change her body position in any way to indicate that she was uncomfortable, and that she had no changes in her vital signs (pulse, breathing, blood pressure) that would have corroborated her complaints of pain. Indeed, she was noted to be in "No Obvious Discomfort." (Discovery at 526)

11. Examination of the accuser's skin, arms and legs revealed no swelling, no abnormalities, and three small cuts on her right knee and right heel. (Discovery at 524,526) When asked, the accuser specifically and repeatedly denied receiving any physical blows by hands. (Discovery at 523, 550) Further examinations showed no tenderness in the back, chest and neck, and her neck was found to be supple. (Discovery at 523) ...

---

13. The accuser told the physicians at the Emergency Room that she had been raped by the "bachelor" and "other guys" ... (Discovery at 523) She related to the forensic nurse that she was performing at a bachelor party where "Matt was getting married." She said that "Brett asked Nikki for a threesome" but that she said that she wanted to "go home and see my kids". The accuser said that she then "stormed out of the house" and got into a fight with Nikki in the car. Brett and Nikki then carried her back into the house while she "kept telling them No." (Discovery at 537-38) Once in the house, "Adam" closed the door to the bathroom [a near-physical impossibility, with four or more persons inside the tiny bathroom] and told her that she could not leave. She further stated that "Dan Flanigan" was the person who arranged everything, but that this was a "fake name" and that his real name was "Matt." The accuser said that "Matt said I'm getting married tomorrow, I can't do this" but that "Adam" told him "yes you can." At that

point, Matt ...[penetrated] her "and did not use a condom." Adam then... [penetrated her] . (Discovery at 538-39) When asked directly whether she had been hit by the men, the accuser said "they kept grabbing me and threatened to kill" her. The accuser claimed that her attackers also used racial slurs during the attack. . .According to the accuser in this statement, "Brett" did not engage in any sexual assault. She then said that after the rape, the men put her clothes on and took her to the car; once there, Nikki drove her to the Kroger, pushed her out of the car and took her money and her belongings. (Discovery at 540) She gave no description of her attackers.

The University of North Carolina Medical Center

14. The accuser was discharged from the Emergency Room on the afternoon of March 14, 2006. The next day, March 15, she went to the Clinic at the University of North Carolina Medical Center. There she reported that she had been raped the day before while she had been working with other girls, that she had been knocked to the floor on multiple occasions during the rape, and that she had hit her head on the sink. (Discovery at 500-01) The accuser told the physician that she was "drunk," and that she had consumed "a lot of alcohol." She reported that her neck was now painful, but that she had told the physicians at Duke that she was not in pain "because she was drunk and did not feel pain." It was only after she sobered up that she discovered that her neck was painful. (Discovery at 501)

15. The Clinic records at UNC further noted that the accuser had a past medical history of bipolar mental illness. (Discovery at 501.) The physician noted that "due to the patient's long psychological history, she is at very high risk of narcotic abuse, and at clinic, we have recommended not to prescribe the patient any narcotics." (Discovery at 502.1)

S. Summary of Investigation: March 14 and March 15

16. Within the first 36 hours of the events in this case, the accuser denied being raped, claimed she was raped by 20 men, then 5 men, then 2 men and then 3 men, claimed that she was carried against her will from a car by Nikki and "Brett," claimed that she was dancing with three other women, multiple other women and then only one other woman, denied ever being struck with fists, claimed that Matt was getting married, told the forensic nurse that Matt raped... that Adam raped her... and did not mention Brett raping her, while telling other personnel that Brett raped her...without mentioning either Matt or Adam.

17. At no time during this first 36 hours did the accuser ever describe the person(s) who she claimed raped her other than to say that he or they were "white."

From Scottsboro:

She states that on March 25, 1931, she [Victoria Price] was on a freight train traveling through Jackson County from Stevenson to Paint Rock; that Ruby Bates was with her on the train...that one of the negroes [sic] picked her up by the legs and held her over the gondola, and she he was going to throw her off; that she was pulled back into the car and one of the negroes hit her on the side of the head with a pistol causing her head to bleed; that the negroes then pulled off the overalls she was wearing...that they then threw her down on the chert and with some of the negroes holding her legs and with a knife at her throat, six negroes raped her...that she lay there for almost an hour on that jagged rock, with the negroes lying on top of her, some of whom were pretty heavy...

That she got up and climbed over the side of the gondola and as she alighted she became unconscious for a while, and that she didn't remember anything until she came to herself in a grocery store and she was then taken to Scottsboro...

The Court will now present the evidence which will show... that neither Dr. Bridges nor Dr. Lynch saw the wound inflicted on the head by the pistol, the lacerated or bleeding back which lay on jagged rocks...or the blood...on the clothes; any torn garments or clothes; that these doctors testified that when brought to the office that day neither woman was hysterical or nervous about it at all, and that their respiration and pulse were normal...

Returning to the pistol lick on the head. The doctor testifies: "I did not sew up any wound on this girl's head; I did not see any blood on her scalp. I don't remember any attention being called to any blood or blow on the scalp." And this was the blow that the woman claimed helped force her into submission...

Dr. Bridges says that when these two women were brought to his office neither was hysterical, or nervous about it at all. He noticed nothing unusual about their resignation and their pulse was normal.

Such a normal physical condition is not the natural accompaniment or result of so horrible an experience, especially when the women testified she fainted from the injuries she had received. . . If the faint was feigned then her credibility must suffer from such feigned actions. And this witness's anger and protest when the doctors insisted on an examination of her person was not compatible with the depression of spirit likely to be caused by the treatment she said she had received.

--Judge Horton's Opinion overturning the Scottsboro verdict

False accusations of rape frequently bear some characteristics in common. The National Center for Women and Policing, an organization which provides materials and training to law enforcement agencies, while bearing in mind that each case is unique, lists several indicators which might point to a rape accusation being false.

For example, persons making a false accusation often claim to have fought furiously in their own defense; they invent elaborate stories of how they struggled until finally they were overpowered. Frequently they will claim to have been gang-raped (an extension of the above); and often by members of another group or race. They may claim injuries, but on examination these will prove not to be serious or to have been self-inflicted. When it comes time to provide exact details of the rape itself, they may become vague, claiming to have been unconscious or unable to remember. Alternately:

"The accuser may also provide an emotionless, but exquisitely detailed, description of the event. . . Unable to recount objectively something that was done to her, she tends either to become vague and evasive or to cross the cultural barrier and become overly descriptive."

--"Cases and False Accusations", National Center for Women and Policing, a division of the Feminist Majority

Such a person may have a prior history of making false claims; and they may have experienced previous mental difficulties. When investigated, the crime scene and the underlying lab work will not support a rape allegation.

The victim stated she was hit, kicked, and strangled during the assault and she attempted to defend herself, but was overpowered. The victim reported she was sexually assaulted for an approximate 30 minute time period by three males.

--Application for search warrant for 610 N. Buchanan St., April 16, 2006

From Scottsboro:

Q. They didn't spare you in any way, didn't try to make it comfortable for you in any way?

A No sir.

Q Just like brutes?

A Yes sir.

Q You lay on your back there for close to an hour on that jagged rock screaming?

A Yes sir.

Q Was your back bleeding when you got to the doctor?

A I couldn't say.

Q When you got to the jail did you find any blood on your back?

A A little bit.

Q Are you sure about that?

A I ain't sure, that has been two years ago.

--Victoria Price being cross-examined by defense counsel Samuel Liebowitz during the Scottsboro trials

From Scottsboro:

...and supposing further that she states that she was seized very violently, and states further that she was struck several blows in and about different parts of the body, including the face, and supposing that she was picked up and held over the sides of a gondola car by her legs, and then pulled back around, and thrown down on some rough material known as chert, and suppose then and there one of the assailants pushed her head, that is her face roughly, and supposing further that this man that threw her down had intercourse with her... and suppose that six men in succession had intercourse with this woman, against her will, while she was struggling and squirming, and resisting, on this rock, or chert, and suppose, doctor, that she lay on this rock or chert on her back and on her side for over an hour, screaming and struggling with these heavy men on top of her, and suppose after that, she was taken off, and suppose that she claimed that she was in a faint, for a few moments...

--Samuel Liebowitz, Scottsboro defense counsel, summarizing the story told by accuser Victoria Price, during the Scottsboro trials of Haywood Patterson and Clarence Norris, Nov.-Dec., 1933

From Scottsboro:

"I can't be positive."
Victoria Price testifying during the Scottsboro trials

"I couldn't say."
Victoria Price testifying during the Scottsboro trials

"I never did pay any attention to that."
Victoria Price testifying during the Scottsboro trials

"I don't remember."
Victoria Price testifying during the Scottsboro trials.

From Scottsboro:

Mrs. Price said she did not remember anything of the kind at Scottsboro and when Mr. Leibowitz insisted that she tell which version of her story she wanted the jury to believe, Mr. Lawson arose to demand that the court instruct counsel to show some respect for the complaining witness.

--New York Times, July 22, 1937

From Scottsboro:

"One thing I will never forget is that one setting there raped me."

--Victoria Price testifying during the Scottsboro trials.

From Scottsboro:

Trial of Clarence Norris, Scottsboro defendant, December 2, 1933 before Judge William Washington Callahan:

DR. BRIDGES: ...I examined Mrs. Victoria Price [Scottsboro accuser] on the 25th of March, 1931, on the day some trouble is said to have happened on a freight train. I saw her first at the jail house in Scottsboro. It was something around 4 o'clock in the afternoon, probably a little after. I saw her in the company with some other girl, Ruby Bates. . . I don't remember seeing any cut on the top of her head from which any blood came. I did not find any bruises on the face. I don't remember finding any puffed up lips, or swollen lips. If I had seen that, I would have noticed it. We were looking for those things.

Q. Were you instructed by the authorities of Jackson County to make the examination?

MR. KNIGHT [Prosecutor] : That is objected to.

COURT: Sustain the objection.

DR. BRIDGES: I made an examination of the face. I didn't see anything. I didn't see any blood. I was examining her for the purpose of finding marks, if possible, and I made note of everything I saw. I don't remember finding any scratch on her face. I did not examine the chest of this woman on that day; I did the next day. I did examine her abdomen. There were no cuts on the chest nor any cuts on the abdomen. I examined her back. There were no cuts on the back from which blood would come; no cuts on her legs; no abrasions or skin rubbed off on the legs. . . I found a couple of scratches on the wrist of one arm, and on the forearm of the other. I knew these women were taken off a freight train. I heard that; I didn't know it. I did not find any lacerations of any kind outside the scratches on the wrist and forearm. When I examined this woman, her pulse was not fast; it was in the bounds of normal. The respiration was about normal, too. A person under excitement, as a rule, especially a woman, would show rapid pulse and rapid breathing. If a woman come into court and made believe she was fainting, threw herself over in this fashion, if she was just faking or shamming a faint, a doctor could, as a rule, find that out by felling her pulse, but not always. Then can fake it sometimes mighty well.

A NEW YORK SIDEBAR: THE TAWANA BRAWLEY CASE

As a result of the information given to the Poughkeepsie police officer, a rape kit examination was performed by the emergency room physician. As part of that examination, the physician began by asking Ms. Brawley several questions which were answered solely with nods and shrugs. She nodded affirmatively to the questions: "I understand you said you were assaulted?"; "Was this by three men?"; and "Were they white men?"; But when Ms. Brawley was asked,

"Were there more?", she shrugged her shoulders. In response to the question, "Did they hit you?", Ms. Brawley pointed to an area of her scalp behind her left ear. When asked, "Does anything hurt?", Ms. Brawley again pointed to the same area of her scalp, where the physician found a round, flat, discolored bruise approximately the size of a quarter. The bruise did not appear tender or fresh, and when it was pressed, Ms. Brawley did not wince or pull away in pain. The physician asked Ms. Brawley if she was grabbed, pushed, twisted or hurt anywhere else, and Ms. Brawley shrugged her shoulders, indicating a negative answer.

On Monday, November 30, at approximately 1:05 p.m., a detective from the Sheriff's office; two Senior Assistant District Attorneys, one of whom specialized in the prosecution of child sex abuse cases; and a Special Agent for FBI civil rights investigations arrived at the Carmine Drive apartment. Present in the apartment and also present during the interview were Tawana Brawley, her cousin, her mother and aunt, Ralph King, and an attorney with the Public Defender's Office who was also president of the Newburgh Chapter of the NAACP.

Tawana Brawley was lying on a fold-out couch in the living room and appeared somewhat dazed and disheveled, apparently lapsing in and out of consciousness. She did not appear to be fully aware of what was going on around her. She answered most of the detective's questions with a monosyllabic whisper or nod of her head such that he was usually unable to either hear or understand the response. Because of this, her aunt or her cousin related most of Ms. Brawley's answers. In order to obtain a response, the questions generally had to be asked in a leading or suggestive manner.

The interview lasted approximately 45 minutes. It was the last time Ms. Brawley communicated in any manner whatsoever with anyone from a law enforcement agency.

Additional Statements of Ms. Brawley

The limited information that Ms. Brawley provided at St. Francis Hospital on Saturday, November 28, and at her home on Monday, November 30, was the only information that Ms. Brawley ever gave to law enforcement. Neither meeting can truly be called an interview as that term would be commonly understood At the hospital she spoke but one word to law enforcement and often communicated by accepting the options offered to her by the questioner. The height of an assailant was, for example, the same as that of the officer interviewing her and the assailant's hair color was the same as that of the nurse in the room.

The interview in the home on Monday, November 30, was similar. Ms. Brawley's answers were often suggested or filtered through members of her family. One person present at this meeting told us that Ms. Brawley responded only to leading questions.

The information derived from this interview differed in some significant respects from the information the family had provided to the police on the day before. The account her family provided was more specific and graphic than the information Ms. Brawley related. Moreover, the time she got off the bus varied by approximately three hours, and the location where she got off the bus was on a different road about a mile away. There was, however, no opportunity to reconcile these discrepancies.

A witness told us that Ms. Brawley "was definite that there were at least three" assailants. That same witness also testified that she believed the claim of six assailants came from a relative of Ms. Brawley's because that number may have sounded more "effective."

Summary

The allegations as to what may have happened to Tawana Brawley were never made in detail. Her own statements were sketchy and at times contradictory. For example, although she indicated to the black police officer at the hospital that she had been raped, she appeared to indicate to the emergency room physician that she had not.

No Evidence of Sexual Assault

There was no medical or forensic evidence that a sexual assault was committed on Tawana Brawley...

There were no bruises, lacerations, tenderness or blood...

There were no cuts, dried blood, bruising, swelling, deep redness or other injury...

There was no plant material found on Ms. Brawley or her clothing. If an individual was sexually assaulted in a wooded area or spent significant time in a wooded area, there is a high probability that there would have been plant materials on the individual's body and clothing...

--Report of the Grand Jury concerning the Tawana Brawley Investigation

"I could stand on a soap box in downtown Poughkeepsie and read the grand jury report in its entirety and it wouldn't make a difference. People believed what they wanted to believe. Hearts and minds were long past changing over something as evasive as "the facts."

--"Letters from Camp Tawana", by Brian Mahoney

Mangum was discharged from the emergency room that afternoon. The next day she went to the University of North Carolina medical clinic, stating that she had been raped and beaten and asking for some pain killers. Clinic records showed that she had a prior bi-polar condition. The physician there wrote that "due to the patient's long psychological history she is at very high risk of narcotic abuse, and at [the] clinic, we have recommended not to prescribe the patient any narcotics."

That same day Duke and Durham police had decided to close the case, after having found Mangum's rape accusations not believable. However, in some manner Sgt. Gottlieb, who may have been working off duty that day at City Hall, learned of the case; and either volunteered, was maneuvered, or else was directed to take charge of it. The case was turned over to him even though he was no longer technically involved in patrolling the Trinity Park area, and he aggressively re-opened the investigation.

From Scottsboro:

[The state's case] depended on two alleged victims, neither with any character, of lax morals...bumming freight trains with a group of male hobos when the attack occurred, if it occurred at all. [Ruby] Bates repudiated her original testimony. [Judge] Horton said both had perjured themselves. So we ask: what constitutes reasonable doubt in the eyes of an Alabama jury?

--Greensboro Daily News, 1933

DURHAM -- "She [Mangum] basically said, 'I'm going to get paid by the white boys,'" H.P. Thomas, the former security manager at the Platinum Club, said in an interview Friday. "I said, 'Whatever,' because no one takes her seriously."

--News and Observer, November 4, 2006

From Scottsboro:

"Just three blocks from here is the 14th Precinct Police Station. The sergeant behind the desk there probably gets a dozen complaints a day... Now the sergeant is no genius, but years of listening to such complaints has given him some ability to tell whether or not a complainant is lying. Had Victoria Price and Ruby Bates walked into that station house to complain to the sergeant on duty that nine Negro boys had raped them, that sergeant, after questioning them for five minutes, would have known them to be liars. He would have tossed them out of the precinct and that would have been the end of the whole affair."

--Scottsboro defense counsel Samuel Liebowitz to Alabama Lt. Governor Knight

From Scottsboro:

History, sacred and profane, and the common experience of mankind teach us that women of the character shown in this case are prone for selfish reasons to make false accusations both of rape and of insult upon the slightest provocation for ulterior purposes.

These women are shown, by the great weight of the evidence, on this very day before leaving Chattanooga, to have falsely accused two Negroes of insulting them, and of almost precipitating a fight between one of the white boys they were in company with and these two Negroes. This tendency on the part of the women shows that they are predisposed to make false accusations upon any occasion whereby their selfish ends may be gained.

The Court will not pursue the evidence any further. As heretofore stated, the law declares that a defendant should not be convicted without corroboration where the testimony of the prosecutrix [accuser] bears on its face indications of improbability or unreliability and particularly when it is contradicted by other evidence.

The testimony of the prosecutrix in this case is not only uncorroborated, but it also bears on its face indications of improbability and is contradicted by other evidence, and in addition thereto the evidence greatly preponderates in favor of the defendant.

--Judge Horton's Opinion overturning the verdict against the Scottsboro boys

"Give it up, game over, this case is toast, the only reason the D.A. is still trying to hold on to this thing he has 50 hours worth of interviews he's done nationally he's been out there condemning these guys, investing in something and stirring it up.

"It's a joke. He should walk away from this before it becomes a bigger spectacle."

--Mark Geragos, noted defense attorney discussing the Duke lacrosse charges on Larry King Live, April 10, 2006, one week before the first defendants were indicted

CASE NARRATIVE : How Law Enforcement Responded

Officers did not search the Buchanan St. house until March 16, two days after the party. Until then it had not been regarded as a serious case. The three residents, who were all co-captains of the lacrosse team, cooperated fully, even assisting the officers in gathering items for evidence. They then voluntarily accompanied the officers back to the police station, where they were separated and individually questioned for hours through the night. None of them requested counsel. At 2:00 AM they were taken to Duke Medical Center to provide DNA samples. They offered to take lie detector tests, but Gottlieb and his co-investigator, officer Himan, declined their offer. No evidence to support Mangum's claims was found.

That same day officer Himan administered the first photo ID session with Mangum. Mangum had by then described her assailants as shorty and chubby, and weighing more than 250 pounds. (No one on the lacrosse team fit this description.) Mangum was shown 24 pictures of lacrosse team members. There were no pictures of non-lacrosse team members used as "fillers" or for a control group. Pictures of Seligmann and Evans were included, but Finnerty's was excluded because he could not remotely be described as short and chubby. Mangum was only able to recognize five of the twenty-four as having been present at the party, could not recognize the other nineteen, and could not identify her supposed attackers. She was 70% certain that she had seen Seligmann somewhere, but did not say he had raped her. She identified another player with 100% certainty as having been at the party, when in fact he had been in Raleigh that night.

Five days later she was shown another photo ID collection, this time of twelve more players. Again there were no non-lacrosse team members' photos included. Again she was unable to identify anyone; she remarked to an officer that "they all looked the same". However David Evans' photo was shown again, thus making this the second time she had seen his photo without recognizing him.

By March 21 the investigation was stalled and going nowhere.

On March 22 Kim (Pittman) Roberts, the second dancer, was called to the police station to give her written statement. (Crystal Mangum was not asked to provide a written statement until April 6, three weeks after her accusations--a deviation from normal investigative procedures, which encourage a victim or witness to recount the details of any event as soon as possible.) Once at the station Roberts was served with a warrant for her arrest; she was in violation of parole for a previous incident. She wrote out her statement, and then some time later appended an additional note : *"I forgot to mention that the first time Precious [a professional name used by Mangum] came to the car, she left because she felt there was more money to be made. It was after then, that the boys helped her to the car."* This remark provided a brief interval when, separated from Roberts, Mangum could have been raped, and undid the effect of her statement that the rape allegations were a "crock". Roberts was not arrested and what some termed a "sweetheart deal" was arranged to cover her parole violation.

On the same day, Gottlieb secured a judicial order requiring all 46 white members of the Duke lacrosse team to provide DNA samples (the lone black member of the team was excluded since Mangum had said her attackers where white). The Durham police knew by then that several members of the team had not been at the party, and that some had not even been in Durham. Furthermore, it already had DNA samples from the three team captains. Such a broad judicial order, covering all members of a specific group, even some who could not possibly be considered as suspects, is generally considered to be unconstitutional; and was unique in the history of Durham.

Despite this, the District Attorney of Durham County, Michael Nifong, claimed to not been consulted about this order; and to have learned about it by only afterward when he accidently noticed a copy of it which had been left at a copy machine. (Such a lack of knowledge would permit him to avoid being called as a witness to explain how the decision to request such a judicial order was arrived at.)

Had the team members fought the order in court, and demanded that the Durham police provide probable cause to seek their DNA, what became known as the Duke lacrosse case might have ended before it began; because Durham prosecutors could not have offered any material evidence to support Mangum's allegations. But the players, when informed of the order, considered it the fastest way to clear up any doubts. At a meeting where their attorneys were explaining the requirements of the order to them, players were already getting up out of their seats and heading for the doors to go to the courthouse before the attorneys had finished speaking ; in the players' view, going for the tests just made for a day off from regular rigorous team practice.

At the courthouse the players found the doors locked, and they were forced to wait outside in full view of the press, which had been alerted to their arrival--contrary to promises that the team would not be subjected to a press frenzy. Attorneys told the players to cover their faces (as there had been threats) which resulted in providing the media with pictures of apparently ashamed and guilty team members.

> 8-2.1
>
> (b) Law enforcement officers and agencies should not exercise their custodial authority over an accused individual in a manner that is likely to result in ... :
>
> (1) the deliberate exposure of a person in custody for the purpose of photographing or televising by representatives of the news media...
>
> --American Bar Association Standards for Criminal Justice

On March 24 District Attorney Michael Nifong, in an unusual procedure, assumed personal control of the Durham police investigation. (The Durham police are normally subject to the City Manager, not the District Attorney; and both offices operate independently of each other.) It is not known why the police department relinquished supervision of the case to the prosecutor, and instructed its officers who were working on the case to be responsible to him; but effectively, this eliminated oversight of the investigation by senior police officers.

The next day the Durham police department began asserting (incorrectly) that the players had been uncooperative during the search of their house; and that team members had continued to refuse to cooperate with the investigation; and that it was this non-cooperation, and not the need for the prosecution to go on a fishing expedition, which made such things as the judicial order for DNA testing necessary.

The public, confronted with images of a guilty and uncooperative team, which was now portrayed as banding together to hide the crimes of a few, reacted with outrage. A candlelight vigil was held for the victim in front of 610 N. Buchanan St. that night. Marchers commented among other things that they were there to "protest the 'wall of silence'"; and that "if there were 40 of them, somebody must know something". (Herald-Sun, March 26, 2006)

Crystal Mangum, the supposedly injured victim, was described by a relative as being afraid to leave her house even to get milk for her children, and fearful of seeing a white man on the street. In fact she was performing as usual at a strip club, and was pole dancing before an audience at the Platinum club the same night as the candlelight vigil. The media, which had abundant resources and contacts, and spared no effort to cover the candlelight vigil, was strangely not able to find the accuser, who was openly performing in a public place (a place said to be a favorite with many of Durham's police and city officials).

> "We were provided with "sign-in" logs from the "Champagne Room" of the Platinum Club. A "dancer" and her customer are required to sign the sheet pledging that they will not engage in any sex or touching in the room. (I swear that I am not making this up). We have sheets from the latter part of March (and just 2 or 3 days after the "attack") showing that someone named "Precious" [Crystal Mangum] signed in.
>
> This is consistent with what Yolanda Hayes [another dancer at the club] said about Precious [Mangum] in her affidavits (and appears to corroborate the approximate time of the videotape showing her dancing until Yolanda throws her off the stage).

Significantly, we were able to trace Precious' footsteps the weekend before the party. Recall that she told Durham PD that after dancing at the Platinum Club on Friday night, she did her nails, went to a movie, and did her nails some more.

Hardly. We found that after dancing at the Platinum Club she had at least 4 private hotel room engagements with various escort customers. She made approximately 20 to 25 calls to at least 8 escort services that weekend for jobs. We were able to track down at least one of those customers. We were comfortable with what his testimony would have been."

--Defense Attorney James Cooney, after the case was over

AN OFFICER WHO WAS INVESTIGATED

Only one officer's conduct was investigated as a result of the lacrosse case. Officer John Shelton observed the accuser's conduct and demeanor on the night of her arrest. He heard her change her stories, first asserting she was raped, then changing her mind and denying it, then changing her mind once again. On the basis of his experience, he believed she was making a false charge; and he maintained that opinion in the weeks and months that followed. His honesty was a challenge to the entire prosecution's case. For not being a "team player", he immediately came under fire. He was later disparaged by Officers Himan and Gottlieb, by District Attorney Nifong, and was made the subject of an internal police investigation. (In an unusual move, the investigation was handled by an investigator working for the District Attorney, and not by anyone inside the police department.) The City Attorney, Patrick Baker, to whom the Chief of Police reports, asserted vigorously *"I've had a lot of conversations with the investigators in this case and with officials at Duke, and at no time did anyone indicate the accuser changed*

> *her story.*" Yet Shelton still refused to change his report or make it comply with what his superiors likely wanted. Instead he reported honestly as any officer should and maintained his commitment to the truth as he saw it, despite the cost to himself personally and professionally.

Applications for search warrants in the case were submitted, but they were carefully crafted to avoid "cumbersome" details.

> On 3/14/06 at 1:22 am, Durham City Police Officers were called to the Kroger on Hillsborough Road. The victim, a 27 year-old black female reported to the officers that she had been raped and sexually assaulted at 610 North Buchanan Blvd. . . Medical records and interviews that were obtained by a subpoena revealed the victim had signs, symptoms, and injuries consistent with being raped and sexually assaulted...
>
> --Application for Search Warrant
> for Duke dormitory, 3/27/06

Without the mention of "signs, symptoms, and injuries consistent with being raped and sexually assaulted" there would have been no probable cause for warrants to be issued; only Mangum's accusation. In fact, the actual written medical statements--which had not as yet been finished nor delivered to the police (meaning, that the application falsely referred to reports which police did not have and which did not yet exist) reported no signs, symptoms, or injuries consistent with rape, or the struggle as described by Mangum. Ergo, the assertion that Mangum had injuries which supported her story was not only premature, it was ficticious. Yet it was to be repeated endlessly in the weeks to come by journalists as a justification for continuing the prosecution.

In addition, Mangum made no mention of rape until she was asked about rape at the hospital; in the applications, that issue is clouded, and it is made to seem that a phone call asking for police assistance to remove a stranger from a car, was a call asking for help for a rape victim. Though Mangum also complained that $2000 of her money was taken from her (either by her co-dancer, or left behind in a police car), this amount was reduced to only $400 in the warrants, the amount she was paid for the evening, with the Duke students made the possible suspects, not Kim Roberts. (This also avoided the problem of explaining how a poor working mother acquired $2000 cash to carry on her person.) Nor do the applications contain physical descriptions of possible perpetrators, though these were available.

> ...she gave vague descriptions of the three men who allegedly assaulted her... "white male, short, red cheeks fluffy hair chubby face, brn"; "Heavy set short haircut 260-270 [pounds]," and "Chubby." . . . None of Himan's notes came close to matching Collin Finnerty, who is tall, baby-faced and lanky.
>
> --News and Observer, March 5, 2008

These descriptions bore no similitude to any Duke lacrosse player. On this basis alone--and that the applications for search warrants contained false information about what the medical reports stated--the warrants should have been quashed, and the case stopped.

> U.S. Supreme Court
> Malley v. Briggs, 475 U.S. 335 (1986)
>
> Argued November 13, 1985
> Decided March 5, 1986

The question is whether a reasonably well-trained officer in petitioner's position would have known that his affidavit failed to establish probable cause, and that he should not have applied for the warrant. If such was the case, the application for the warrant was not objectively reasonable, because it created the unnecessary danger of an unlawful arrest.

The right of the people to be secure in their persons, houses, papers, and effects, against unreasonable searches and seizures, shall not be violated, and no Warrants shall issue, but upon probable cause, supported by Oath or affirmation, and particularly describing the place to be searched, and the persons or things to be seized.

--Fourth Amendment to the Constitution

NORTH CAROLINA DECLARATION OF RIGHTS AND CONSTITUTION (December 1776)

VII. That, in all criminal prosecutions, every man has a right to be informed of the accusation against him, and to confront the accusers and witnesses with other testimony, and shall not be compelled to give evidence against himself.

X. That excessive bail should not be required, nor excessive fines imposed, nor cruel or unusual punishments inflicted.

XI. That general warrants -- whereby an officer or messenger may he commanded to search suspected places, without evidence of the fact committed, or to seize any person or persons, not named, whose offenses are not particularly described, and supported by evidence -- are dangerous to liberty, and ought not to be granted.

XIII. That every freeman, restrained of his liberty is entitled to a remedy, to inquire into the lawfulness thereof, and to remove the same, if unlawful; and that such remedy ought not to be denied or delayed.

The poorest man may in his cottage bid defiance to all the forces of the Crown; it may be frail, its roof may shake, the wind may blow through it; the storm my enter, the rain may enter; but the King of England cannot enter; all his forces dare not cross the threshold of that ruined tenement.

--Lord Chatham

NO. COA97-1122
NORTH CAROLINA COURT OF APPEALS
Filed: 21 July 1998

STATE OF NORTH CAROLINA v. MICHAEL C. SEVERN,

The defendant made a motion to suppress the evidence seized from his residence on the grounds that there was false information submitted in the affidavit.

Detective McLeod admitted that although he stated in the affidavit that he had obtained drugs from "inside the residence," he had not "personally [gone] inside the residence to get anything." He testified he had deduced that the controlled substances had been used inside the residence. Detective McLeod explained that he "just used common sense in saying that it is in a trash bag along with his mail and other articles that [were] normally used inside of the . . . house" and therefore "it probably came from inside." Detective McLeod stated that he had no intention of misleading the magistrate.

He further testified that he used the terms "investigative means" because he did not want the defendant to know that a trash pick-up was the actual method used in order to obtain a search warrant to search the residence. According to Detective McLeod, "most of the magistrates know that when . . . officers present something in this fashion [that drugs have been recovered from inside of a residence] that it is a trash pickup but is worded in such a way as not to draw attention from the suspect in question."

North Carolina General Statutes section 15A-978 provides that a defendant can challenge the "validity of a search warrant and the admissibility of evidence obtained thereunder by contesting the truthfulness of the testimony" which showed probable cause for the issuance of the warrant. N.C.G.S. section 15A-978(a) (1997). The section defines truthful testimony as "testimony which reports in good faith the circumstances relied on to establish probable cause."

If a defendant establishes by a preponderance of the evidence that a "false statement knowingly and intentionally, or with reckless disregard for the truth" was made by an affiant [officer] in an affidavit in order to obtain a search warrant, that false information must be then set aside.

If the "affidavit's remaining content is insufficient to establish probable cause, the search warrant must be voided and the fruits of the search excluded to the same extent as if probable cause was lacking on the face of the affidavit."

It is true that every false statement in an affidavit is not necessarily made in bad faith. An affiant may be unaware that a statement is false and therefore include the statement in the affidavit based on a good faith belief of its veracity. In this case, however, Detective McLeod admitted that he did not go inside of the residence; therefore, by stating in the affidavit that he had recovered evidence from within the residence, he knowingly made a false statement. A person may not knowingly make a false statement in good faith for the purposes of an affidavit in support of a search warrant.

In so holding we are not persuaded by the State's argument that the addition of the words "using investigative means" transforms the context of the affidavit and reveals that the statement taken as a whole is truthful. It remains undisputed that no one entered the defendant's residence; the statement to the contrary was false and the affiant knew that it was false. Indeed, Detective McLeod's use of the words "investigative means" further supports our holding that the affidavit was entered in bad faith. . .

Because the statements made by Detective McLoed were false and made in bad faith, they must be stricken from the affidavit. Moreover, the State does not contend, nor do we believe, the remaining contents of the affidavit are sufficient to establish probable cause. As a result, the trial court erred in not granting the motion to suppress.

Revised and remanded.

Judges MARTIN, Mark D., and TIMMONS-GOODSON concur.

SILVERTHORNE LUMBER CO., Inc., et al. v. UNITED STATES.
No. 358.
Argued Dec. 12, 1919.
Decided Jan. 26, 1920.

Mr. Justice HOLMES delivered the opinion of the Court:

The proposition could not be presented more nakedly. . . It reduces the Fourth Amendment to a form of words. The essence of a provision forbidding the acquisition of evidence in a certain way is that not merely evidence so acquired shall not be used before the Court but that it shall not be used at all.

MOTION TO SUPPRESS PHOTOGRAPHS, 7 June 2006

3. These discovery materials reveal that the lead investigator possessed relevant impeaching information regarding the veracity of Crystal Mangum's story that she was sexually assaulted and this information was intentionally, deliberately and/or recklessly omitted from the investigator's probable cause affidavit. This affidavit provided the legal basis for Judge Ronald L. Stephens to make his decision to issue Non-Testimonial [DNA] Identification Orders for forty-six Duke Lacrosse Players.

4. By intentionally, deliberately and/or recklessly omitting this relevant and impeaching information from the Application for the Non-Testimonial Identification Order, the State violated the Fourth, Fifth, Sixth and Fourteenth Amendments to the United States Constitution, Article I, Sections 19 & 23 of the North Carolina Constitution. Had the omitted information been furnished to Judge Stephens, he would not have had probable cause to believe that a felony had been committed or reasonable suspicion to believe that the Defendant committed any criminal act.

Kohler v. Englade , Fifth US Circuit Court of Appeals 470 F.3d 1104
November 21, 2006

To determine whether facts omitted from a warrant affidavit are material to the determination of probable cause, courts ordinarily insert the omitted facts into the affidavit and ask whether the reconstructed affidavit would still support a finding of probable cause. This materiality analysis presumes that the warrant affidavit, on its face, supports a finding of probable cause.

In cases such as this one, however, where the warrant affidavit is already lacking in probable cause, any reconstructed affidavit that includes the omitted exculpatory information [tending to show innocence] would necessarily lack probable cause as well, regardless of the materiality of the omitted information.

05/28/2005 - HIGH POINT, NC — Charges of cocaine trafficking against three area people were dropped Wednesday because of an "invalid search warrant," according to court records.

The reason: the search warrant was invalid [amid allegations that a High Point Police Officer provided false information] and there was no other evidence to support a conviction, according to the release order.

DURHAM -- A rare decision was handed down in Durham County Superior Court last week, with Judge Ron Stephens ruling that police unconstitutionally searched a house before arresting a narcotics suspect.

Stephens then threw out evidence seized in the case, depriving authorities of the ability to prosecute Anthony Maxwell on charges of possessing cocaine . . .

---The Herald Sun, Dec. 10, 2007

A ROOKIE NURSE AND A POLICEMAN

Most hospitals (as does Duke Medical Center) keep a SANE (Sexual Assault Nurse Examiner) on duty 24 hours a day. When Crystal Mangum arrived at Duke Medical Center, however, she was not examined for evidence of sexual assault until the following morning. In the intervening hours Mangum was seen by at least seven medical personnel at Duke, and had given varying accounts of what had happened to her; but apparently none had felt the need to call for a SANE. It is possible they did not believe Mangum's differing accounts.

The following morning, however, Dr. Julie Manly, a resident, performed a sexual assault examination of Mangum. She was assisted by Tara Levicy, a SANE-in-training, whose certificate of completed class work would arrive only that afternoon.

Because the evidence collected by a SANE about a possible sexual assault may be used later in court, it must be scrupulously documented and preserved. A number of tests may be done, samples may be taken, and even the presence of all persons at the medical facility who saw the victim must be noted (as these may be witnesses later on).

Frequently a "rape kit" is employed. The term "rape kit" is actually a misnomer; the kit would more correctly be called an "evidence collection" kit (since "rape" is a legal conclusion which can only be made by a jury). The kit, which includes a checklist, helps insure that evidence which might prove a rape is not missed or lost.

All evidence is to be collected at the time of the exam. No changes are permitted to be made to notes afterwards (there must be no suspicion that notes were altered later to suit prosecution or defense requirements) . An alleged rape victim is free to refuse use of the kit, and to refuse the services of a SANE. She may refuse any portion of an examination, such as a test for drugs.

It was Levicy who filled out the examination report. Later, when Officer Himan phoned for information, he contacted Levicy directly and not Manly or other hospital personnel. Levicy was willing to assert for Himan that Mangum's medical exam revealed injuries that were "consistent with" her story of rape. But "consistent with" is a very broad phrase--according to some wags "breathing" may be considered "consistent with" a condition--and in the event the written record, when it was finally produced, did not note any injuries as claimed by Mangum. The subpoena for Mangum's medical records was later brought by Gottlieb not to the hospital administration, as would have been routine; and not to Manly or to Levicy's supervisor; but directly to Levicy, a low-level nurse.

As events would show, Levicy's full notes on the examination were not turned over to the police until April 5th. They bear indications of subsequent strike outs and corrections and emendations, each dovetailing with developments in the case as the police worked out a theory of the rape.

For example, after police discovered a towel in the Buchanan St. house, Levicy added a handwritten note to her report, in which she states that Mangum told her that her attackers had wiped her off afterwards with a rag. (The towel later turned out not to have Mangum's DNA on it and therefore failed to provide evidence of a possible rape.) On Levicy's SANE report, the "No" blank was originally checked after a question about whether any effort had been made to conceal evidence; after the towel was discovered, the "No" was crossed out and the "Yes" blank was checked.

In her early notes, Levicy recorded three times that Mangum had said her attackers did not use condoms. She even stated, in the space for giving a brief account of the attack in the victim's own words, that "no condoms used". Some ten months later, however, Levicy contradicted herself and now said that Mangum hadn't been sure if condoms had been used or not. She also stated that she wasn't surprised when she learned that no DNA from the accused had been found, because "rape is not about passion or ejaculation but about power"--a remark which displayed a profound lack of understanding about DNA testing and its ability to detect even a single human cell from any type of contact.

Without Levicy's willingness to orally state early on that Mangum had injuries "consistent with" her story of rape, there would have been no probable cause sufficient for the issuance of search warrants and judicial orders, and the prosecution could not have continued.

It is also instructive to examine other ways in which the police conducted their investigation of the lacrosse case.

The police refused an offer from the residents of the Buchanan Street house to take lie-detector tests (and to do so without attorneys present). (While evidence from lie-detector tests may not be admissible in court, they still provide investigators with clues and leads.)

Later, attorneys for the indicted defendants offered to turn over evidence to the District Attorney proving their clients were innocent. The District Attorney, contrary to ordinary practice, refused to accept or even look at it. (Prosecutors are normally eager to see what the defense has; and what holes may appear in their case.) By refusing to examine it, the District Attorney could later claim to have been unaware of any evidence which proved the defendants innocent.

(Perhaps for the same reason, some have speculated that President Brodhead of Duke, who was offered the same opportunity to examine all the evidence the defense had, refused to even look at it; this would permit him later to say that he was unware of any evidence of innocence.)

In what must surely be nearly a unique example in an investigation, two suspects, Seligmann and Finnerty, were never questioned at all either the police or the District Attorney during the entire course of the investigation. No one took any statements from them. Evans was questioned only after the initial search of the Buchanan St. house, before he was indicted, when he and two other residents of the house were interviewed for hours without an attorney present, and cooperated fully. (Again, perhaps this was to avoid hearing directly from the defendants testimony which would have proved their innocence.)

And Nifong himself would claim he had never spoken with the accuser about the case, nor to have had anyone from his office speak with her about it, until late December 2006--some ten months after the case began.

> *"To this day [January 2007, nine months after arrests were made] nobody has asked Collin [Finnerty] where he was, who he was with, what kind of exonerating evidence he has...no one has questioned Collin. No one has asked Wade Smith [his attorney]. No one has asked us. How do you get indicted and you're never questioned?"*
>
> --mother of one of the indicted

A next-door neighbor of the Buchanan St. house had witnessed the arrival and departure of the dancers. He gave several interviews to the media (including television) but was never interviewed by the police; and had to volunteer to give the police a statement, which they retrieved from him without asking any further questions. He was never spoken to by law enforcement thereafter.

The accuser's fellow dancer was not asked to make a photo ID of the suspects until after they had been indicted and their names and photographs had already appeared widely in the press.

The co-workers of the accuser were not interviewed for months, if at all.

A wanted poster was issued by the Crimestoppers organization, with photos of most of the lacrosse team. Yet the whereabouts of the team and the wherewithal to contact them through their attorneys was always known (wanted posters are usually issued to seek the public's help in locating suspects). Some believe the poster was pointless unless it was issued only to stir animosity against the players.

Having asserted that there were allegedly dangerous rape suspects on the streets, the District Attorney put off arresting them for two weeks. (Had they been arrested immediately, however, they would have had the right to a Probable Cause hearing, at which they could have presented evidence of their innocence.)

Instead, the District Attorney waited until after the Grand Jury met, which permitted him to obtain indictments against them before arrest. (In North Carolina, persons indicted by a Grand Jury have no right to a Probable Cause hearing.) Because no transcripts are kept of North Carolina Grand Jury proceedings (contrary to the practice in almost all other states), there is no record of what "evidence" might have been offered the jurors. The Jury which indicted the lacrosse players heard over 80 cases during its sitting; which suggests that the amount of time it had to devote to whether or not to charge some Duke students with the serious crime of gang-rape was only a few minutes, at best.

Various prosecutors, police officers, and others involved in the case--which was to become the biggest case in Durham's history and one which received international news coverage--somehow managed to conduct most of their investigation without preserving any notes or records; or putting their names on any relevant documents.

While at the beginning there were some calls from observers for the FBI to investigate the possibility of bringing hate crime charges, these calls abruptly ceased and the District Attorney--even though he insisted there had been a racial component to the crime--studiously avoided the prospect. It has been speculated that the District Attorney wanted to preclude an investigation from any outside agency and what it might uncover. (It should be noted that the defendants were consistent in requesting FBI intervention throughout the case and even afterwards continued to call for a full federal investigation.)

The police chief disappeared from public view during the case yet remained on full salary, though absent for months. Allegedly he was spending the time caring for his sick mother.

In an unusual coincidence Nifong had arrested his daughter on an old warrant shortly after the lacrosse case began.

In all, it was a most peculiar way to run an investigation into a major crime.

On March 27, a couple of days after he had assumed control of the police investigation, officers Gottlieb and Himan briefed Nifong on their progress so far.

> Q. Did you, either through this report or through other sources, become aware that Ms. Mangum had had psychological problems or issues prior to this event?
>
> A. We had discovered at some point in the investigation that she had psychological issues, yes.
>
> ——
>
> Q. Was her history or alleged history of psychological problems discussed with Mr. Nifong during these briefings?
>
> A. The information was provided to Mr. Nifong as far as reports; and as we had found out information on her, that was brought to his attention.
>
> --Deposition of Sgt. Mark Gottlieb for the Disciplinary Hearing Commission of the North Carolina State Bar April 19, 2007

Shortly thereafter--either that day or in the next few days--after learning that there was no DNA evidence linking any lacrosse player to Mangum--Nifong admitted that the prosecution would be hard put to win its case in court, and bluntly admitted, "You know, we're f----d".

Q. Okay. Do you recall, if not the specifics, if you would have talked with him [Nifong] in general that there was inconsistency about what Ms. Pittman [Kim Pittman/Roberts, the second dancer] was saying, what Ms. Mangum was saying?

A. Yes, I know we went over that. But Kim was saying one thing about the money and that --regarding--let's see, I've lost my train of thought.

Q. I had just asked you about whether you discussed generally the inconsistencies between what Ms. Pittman [Roberts] was alleging, stating, and what Ms. Mangum was alleging.

A. We would have talked about it, but I just don't know in what detail we would have gone into. I'm trying to think.

Q. Okay. At the time of the initial meeting with Mr. Nifong where you briefed him up to date--

A. Uh-huh (yes).

Q. --in terms of the statements of people who were actually present at the party that you had done to that point, you had Ms. Mangum's allegations that she had been sexually assaulted?

A. Uh-huh (yes).

Q. And the other statements that you had about the people who were actually at the party were the three captains who had come in to give voluntary statements?

A. Yes.

Q. And Ms. Pittman? [Kim Roberts]

A. Yes.

Q. And all of the other people, besides Ms. Mangum, had stated at one point or another that no sexual assault had occurred at that residence?

A. Correct. But Kim--Kim couldn't verify or deny what Crystal was saying. She said she didn't know if there was a rape occurred or didn't occur. And in the beginning that's what she said, she said it was a crock. And then Kim said that she doesn't know if it happened or not. She didn't witness a rape, but she wasn't for sure that a rape didn't occur.

Q. But she did make a statement that the last time she came in the car Ms. Mangum still wanted to go back into the house?

A. Yes.

Q. And that--wouldn't that seem inconsistent to you with somebody who had been gang-raped by three individuals in the house?

A. Yes. Yes, it would.

----Deposition of Investigator Himan for the Disciplinary Hearing Commission of the North Carolina State Bar May 8, 2007

Yet instead of dropping the charges, Nifong then began a public relations offensive. He was in a close race for election to the office of District Attorney; and, as he said to his campaign manager, the lacrosse case was worth a million dollars' worth of free publicity.

STATE BAR FINDINGS OF FACT IN THE ORDER OF DISBARMENT FOR MICHAEL NIFONG

---

19. Between March 27 and March 31, 2006, Nifong stated to a reporter for the New York Times, "There are three people who went into the bathroom with the young lady, and whether the other people there knew what was going on at the time, they do now and have not come forward. I'm disappointed that no one has been enough of a man to come forward. And if they would have spoken up at the time, this may never have happened."

22. Between March 27 and March 31, 2006, Nifong made the following statements to Rene Syler of CBS News: "There's no doubt a sexual assault took place."

23. Between March 27 and March 31, 2006, Nifong made the following statements to a reporter for NBC 17 TV News: "The information that I have does lead me to conclude that a rape did occur"; "I'm making a statement to the Durham community and, as a citizen of Durham, I am making a statement for the Durham community. This is not the kind of activity we condone, and it must be dealt with quickly and harshly"; "The circumstances of the rape indicated a deep racial motivation for some of the things that were done. It makes a crime that is by its nature one of the most offensive and invasive even more so..."

24. Between March 27 and March 31, 2006, Nifong stated to a reporter for ESPN, "And one would wonder why one needs an attorney if one was not charged and had not done anything wrong."

28. Between March 27 and March 31, 2006, Nifong stated to a reporter for the USA Today newspaper, "Somebody's wrong about that sexual assault. Either I'm wrong, or they're not telling the truth about it."

30. Between March 27 and March 31, 2006, Nifong stated to a reporter for ABC News, "It is a case that talks about what this community stands for."

37. On March 31, 2006, Nifong stated to a reporter for MSNBC, "Somebody had an arm around her like this [demonstrating] which she then had to struggle with in order to be able to breathe . . . She was struggling just to be able to breathe"

40. In April 2006, Nifong stated to a reporter for the Raleigh. News and Observer newspaper, "I would like to think that somebody [not involved in the attack] has the human decency to call up and say, 'What am I doing covering up for a bunch of hooligans?'

41. In April 2006, Nifong stated to a reporter, "They don't want to admit to the enormity of what they have done."

42. In an April 2006 conversation with a representative of the Raleigh News and Observer newspaper, Nifong compared the alleged rape to the quadruple homicide at Alpine Road Townhouse and multiple cross burnings that outraged the city of Durham in 2005 and stated "I'm not going to let Durham's view in the minds of the world to be a bunch of lacrosse players from Duke raping a black girl in Durham."

AVERY FRIEDMAN: . . . The reality is that when this case -- before we even saw the first arrest, Michael Nifong had about 70 interviews with the media. . . But at this point, this makes the Sam Sheppard case which dealt with pretrial publicity, look like nothing. This is going to wind up in the Ringling Brothers hall of fame. This is terrible.

--CNN LIVE SATURDAY April 22, 2006 (five days after indictments of the first two lacrosse players)

Nifong, backed by the aura of his authority as District Attorney, succeeded in establishing in the public mind the image of a team which was not cooperating and which had something to hide; and of the certainty that a terrible crime had been committed on Buchanan St.

A GEORGIA SIDENOTE

Your honor, an astounding and outrageous state of affairs obtained previous to and during my trial. On the streets rumor and gossip carried vile, vicious and damning stories concerning me and my life. These stories were absolutely false, and did me great harm, as they beclouded and obsessed the public mind and outraged it against me. From a public in this state of mind the jury that tried me was chosen. Not alone were these stories circulated on the street, but to the shame of our community, be it said, these vile insinuations crept into my very trial in the courtroom, creeping in insidiously, like a thief in the night. The virus of these damning insinuations entered the minds of the twelve men and stole away their judicial frame of mind and their moral courage. The issues at bar were lost. The poison of unspeakable things took their place.

--Leo Frank speaking to the court before his sentence, 1913 (lynched in 1915)

In May Nifong came from behind to win the primary election, which was tantamount to victory in the fall as he would then be running unopposed. His prominence in the lacrosse case is credited with giving him the victory.

Well before then, however, DNA evidence had been received which proved with certainty the innocence of the lacrosse players.

From the start, the players had asserted their innocence. And they insisted on this even before the DNA test results were returned. Each and every player maintained that there had been no contact with Mangum, by himself or by anyone else. It would be the more common and safer course for players in such a situation to hedge their bets, and say that if there had been any sexual contact, it was consensual. And this is especially so where players are not certain what other players may have done during the course of an evening. But the lacrosse players never varied their stories and maintained an absolute denial that any of them had contact with the accuser. (In other words, this strongly indicates that they were positive beyond all doubt of the complete innocence of themselves and their teammates.)

On March 31, Nifong instructed Gottlieb and Himan to run yet another photo ID session. On April 4, Mangum was presented with photos of 36 members of the lacrosse team, but this time she was only asked to say whether or not she could remember if they had been at the party. In theory, this was to be only a test of her memory of events that night, and not a formal identification session. This justification permitted the inclusion of photos of Reade Seligmann and David Evans, whom she had already seen twice and not identified as her attackers, or not recognized; and Collin Finnerty, who did not remotely fit the description she gave of her attackers. As well, it permitted the police to maintain that since this was not a formal photo ID session, the standard police procedural requirements, designed to guard against false identifications, would not apply.

Nevertheless, this explanation seems spurious. Had police only wanted to jog Mangum's memory, they could have shown her photos of the party itself, instead of mug shots. Officers also claimed that they did not expect Mangum to identify her attackers during the session; yet this was the only ID session which they videotaped.

"Detectives conducted the key photo session with the accuser in the Duke lacrosse case with an eye firmly on how it would play in court, according to one description, despite recent assertions by city officials that they weren't expecting her to identify suspects." (Herald-Sun, May 2007)

Whereas during previous sessions Mangum had been hesitant and unable to differentiate between the players, on this occasion she identified four players as having been her assailants. The session was run by case investigator Sgt. Gottlieb instead of a neutral figure; and because all of the photos were of lacrosse team members, there were no "fillers", and hence there could be no wrong answers. In a statistical curiosity, her picks--other than a fourth player, who was never charged by Nifong--all came from families who lived in areas (as determined by zip codes) with the highest average incomes of any members of the team (leading one wag to suggest that she hadn't so much studied the players' photographs as their tax returns.)

Q. As I understand it, there were four different photo arrays shown on the 16th [of March]?

A. Correct.

———

Q. And do you know whether or not the six individuals in there were members of the lacrosse team?

A. Yes, they were.

Q. Okay. And do you know whether or not she was able to identify anybody as one of the alleged attackers in those arrays on the 16th?

A. No, she didn't identify anyone.

--Deposition of Investigator Benjamin Himan for the Disciplinary Hearing Commission of the North Carolina State Bar May 8, 2007

A. All I can say is he [Nifong] didn't ask for a photographic array [lineup]. He was dealing with, my understanding, he was asking for this to see what she recalled and what she didn't recall.

Q. Okay. Just to make sure I'm clear, it was Mr. Nifong's decision to conduct this photographic presentation as opposed to having her provided photographic arrays as had been done before?

A. Yes. But then again—yes.

Q. Did you discuss during that meeting whether nor not there needed to be photographs from anybody besides lacrosse team members in that presentation?

A. No.

Q. Did you discuss with Mr. Nifong or did he give you any indication about what Ms. Mangum should or should not be told about the identity of the people in the photographs she was shown in the presentation?

A. Just that these were people we had reason to believe had attended the party and tell us if you recognize them and tell us if you don't recognize them and be truthful. That's all. And as to what they were or were not doing.

--Deposition of Sgt. Mark Gottlieb for the Disciplinary Hearing Commission of the North Carolina State Bar April 19, 2007

IMAGE 1 (M______; a resident of the house who had been present the night of the party)

Accuser: I don't recognize him.

Gottlieb: OK.

IMAGE 4 (MW_____)

Gottlieb: Do you recognize the person?

Accuser: He looked like Bret but I'm not sure.

Gottlieb: Who is Bret?

Accuser: One of the guys that assaulted me.

Gottlieb: One of the guys that assaulted you. OK.

Accuser: Mm-hmm.

[There is no follow-up question from Gottlieb. He does not ask how certain she is--percentage-wise--that she can identify him, as he does with the other suspects. This individual was one of four whom the accuser identified as having attacker her; although by this point she was only claiming to have been attacked by three people. This person was never charged by Nifong.]

IMAGE 5 (David Evans)

Accuser [after a lengthy delay]: He looks like one of the guys who assaulted me sort...

Gottlieb: OK. How sure of it are you on this image?

Accuser: He looks just like him without the mustache?

Gottlieb: OK, so the person had a mustache?

Accuser: Yes.

Gottlieb: Percentage-wise, what is the likelihood this is one of the gentlemen who assaulted you?

Accuser: About 90 percent.

[Evans never had a mustache; neither had the accuser ever before mentioned one of the attackers having a mustache.]

IMAGE 7 (Reade Seligmann)

Accuser: He looks like one of the guys who assaulted me.

Gottlieb: How sure are you?

Accuser: 100 percent.

Gottlieb: You're 100 percent sure, OK.

Accuser: Yes.

Gottlieb [FOLLOW UP QUESTION] : How did he assault you? Which one was he?

Accuser: He was the one that was standing in front of me . . .

Gottlieb [FOLLOW UP QUESTION] : What else did he do?

Accuser: That was it.

[Though she had recognized Seligmann in an earlier lineup, saying she was 70% sure he had been at the party, she had not distinguished him in any other way, nor suggested that he had been one of those who assaulted her. She identified him with "Adam", who she said after the rape had helped her to get dressed and then helped her to the car. By that time, however, Seligmann had long since been back in his dorm.]

IMAGE 9 (B______; a person who was never at the party and was in another county that night.)

Accuser: He was there.

Gottlieb: In the bathroom, or at the party?

Accuser: At the party.

Gottlieb: OK, so he was not the person who assaulted you. Do you remember what he was doing at the party?

Accuser: He was standing outside talking to the other dancer.

[This was the second ID session in which the accuser stated she was certain this person had been at the party.]

IMAGE 26 (C______; a person who had been back in his dorm room since 11:00 PM, well before the dancers arrived at the party. The accuser had never seen him.)

Accuser: He was in the living room.

Gottlieb: He was in the living room? What was he doing there?

Accuser: Sitting down.

IMAGE 27 (N______; a person whom the accuser had identified with 100% certainty of having been at the party during an earlier ID session)

Gottlieb: Do you recognize him?

Accuser: No.

IMAGE 30 (F________; another person whom the accuser had identified with 100% certainty of having been at the party during an earlier ID session)

Gottlieb: Do you recognize him?

Accuser: No.

IMAGE 40 (Collin Finnerty)

Accuser: He is the guy who assaulted me.

Gottlieb: What did he do?

Accuser: He [assaulted me]

Gottlieb: Was he the first or second one to do that?

Accuser: The second one.

Gottlieb [SUGGESTIVE FOLLOW UP QUESTION] : Is he the one that strangled you or not?

Accuser: No.

IMAGE 41 (K________; another person whom the accuser had identified with 100% certainty of having been at the party during an earlier ID session)

Gottlieb: Do you recognize him?

Accuser: No.

Gottlieb: Do you need some tissues?

--Transcript of April 4, 2006, photo ID session

Oddly, the accuser did not once refer to her alleged assailants as "Matt", "Brett", or "Adam". *("He looks like Matt...that's Brett...").* Had she forgotten those names? Or had it been suggested that using those names would not look good in a video record to be shown to a jury?

MOTION TO SUPPRESS ID

D. The PowerPoint Identification and the Accuser's Final Version of Events (March 31 through April 6)

63. On March 31, 2006, Sgt. Gottlieb and Inv. Himan met with the District Attorney to discuss doing further photographic identifications using what Sgt. Gottlieb called "the mug shot type photographs" of the Lacrosse team obtained on March 23, 2006. (Discovery at 1825.)

64. As of March 31, 2006, the State was aware that the accuser, according to inv. Clayton's report, had failed to identify a single person as an attacker after reviewing photographs of approximately 36 lacrosse players...

The PowerPoint Identification

65. During the course of the meeting among Inv. Himan, Sgt. Gottlieb and the District Attorney, the District Attorney "suggested we put together the mug shot type photographs into a group since we are under the impression the players at the party were members of the Duke Lacrosse Team, and instead of doing a line up or photographic array, we would merely ask the victim to look at each picture and see if she recalled seeing the individuals at the party." (Discovery at 1825.)

---

67. Following the meeting of March 31 in which the District Attorney directed that only photographs of the Lacrosse team be shown to the accuser, Sgt. Gottlieb assisted Inv. Himan and another investigator in placing all of the pictures of the Lacrosse team into a "PowerPoint" format so that they could be displayed to the accuser. (Discovery at 1825; 14-107.)

———

69. Thereafter, on April 4, 2006, the accuser was brought to the Durham Police Department to view the PowerPoint photographs. Before viewing the photographs, however, the accuser was told by Sgt. Gottlieb that "we were going to sit in the far side of the room at the desk and look at people we had reason to believe attended the party" (Discovery at 1826) Sgt. Gottlieb, who was supervising the investigation for the Durham Police Department and who had put together the PowerPoint photographs, presided over the process; Inv. Himan who was the lead Durham Police Department investigator in charge of the case, also sat in on the identification process.

Sgt. Gottlieb --contrary to both the practice employed at the earlier photo arrays and the procedures of the Durham Police Department --then told the accuser that it was "important" for her to say whether she recalled "seeing any of the persons to be shown and to describe what they were doing." (Discovery at 109.)

70. According to an in-court representation made by the District Attorney on October 27, 2006, during the course of meeting with the accuser on April 11, the District Attorney concluded that she was "too traumatized" to speak of the events of March 13 and 14. The PowerPoint identification procedure that the District Attorney directed police to employ took place one week earlier.

71. At the time that this PowerPoint identification was conducted, and at the time that the District Attorney directed that the accused be shown pictures of only members of the Duke Lacrosse team, the Durham Police Department had in place "General Order 4077" relating to Eyewitness Identification and, specifically, Photographic arrays.

72. General Order 4077 provided, in relevant part, that "photographic arrays should adhere to the following set of guidelines":

(a) "Use an independent administrator. It is preferable that the individual conducting the photographic array should be someone who does not know which member of the photographic array is the suspect. There should not be anyone present during the array procedure who knows the suspect's identity. Only when resources make this practice prohibitive should an Independent administrator not be utilized."

(b) "Include a minimum of five fillers (non-suspects)."

(c) "If there is more than one suspect that fits the description of the perpetrator, there can be more than one suspect in the photographic array; however, the number of fillers should be increased to a minimum of five per suspect."

73. The PowerPoint procedure suggested by the District Attorney and conducted by the Durham Police Department on April 4, 2006, violated General Order 4077 and the policy and procedures of the Durham Police Department.

74. By its terms, General Order 4077 was "based upon recommendations published by the North Carolina Actual Innocence Commission which are endorsed by the Education and Training Committee of the North Carolina Criminal Justice Education and Training Standards Commission."

75. The recommendations of the Actual Innocence Commission, in turn, provide, in relevant part, that:

(a) "Use an independent administrator. The individual conducting the photo or live lineup should be someone who does not know which member of the lineup is the suspect.... Technological tools, such as computer programs that can run photo lineups and record witness identifications without the presence of an investigator, may assist agencies with resource constraints."

(b) "Include a minimum of seven fillers (non-suspects) per photo identification procedure and five for live lineups."

(c) "If there is more than one suspect that fits the description of the perpetrator, there can be more than one suspect in the lineup; however, the number of fillers should be increased to a minimum of seven.... By keeping the proportion of fillers to suspects constant, the reliability of the identification remains constant."

General Order 4077 is similar to the procedures employed by many metropolitan police departments throughout this State. For example, the Hickory Police Department utilizes the guidelines recommended by the Actual Innocence Commission including the administration of the identification by someone who is not familiar with the case and the use of 7 "fillers" for each suspect. The Asheville Police Department similarly uses the Actual Innocence Commission Guidelines including the use of an "independent" administrator and 5 "fillers" per suspect. Indeed, the Guidelines of the Actual Innocence Commission appear to be the policy in whole or in part in Burlington, Chapel Hill, Spencer, Tarboro, Cary, Gastonia, Jacksonville, Rocky Mount, Fayettevilie and Raleigh.

(d) "An independent administrator is the preferred administrator for both sequential and simultaneous presentations. Because there is a greater risk that an administrator may convey unintentional cues during sequential presentations, sequential presentation should only be used if the identification procedure is being conducted by an independent administrator. if an independent administrator is not available, simultaneous presentation of individuals/photos is necessary."

(e) "Administrators should avoid making any comments during the selection procedure and should be aware that witnesses can perceive such things as unintentional voice inflection or prolonged eye contact as messages regarding their selection."

(f) "Witnesses should be instructed as follows prior to the lineup: For sequential presentation:

In a moment, I am going to show you a series of photos. The person who committed the crime may or may not be included. I do not know whether the person being investigated is included....

You should not feel like you have to make an identification. This procedure is important to the investigation whether or not you identify someone.

76. The PowerPoint procedure utilized on April 4, 2006, did not follow or conform to the recommendations of the Actual Innocence Commission.

77. The PowerPoint procedure was videotaped and a transcript of that videotape was prepared. Discovery at 1827-39.

78. During the course of the PowerPoint procedure, the accuser was shown 46 photos in a sequential manner. The accuser:

(a) Identified four of the players as looking like her three attackers:

(e) Claimed to recognize twelve persons who she failed to recognize when shown pictures on the photo arrays on March 16 and 21...

E. Summary of Accuser's Statements

March 16 through April 6

88. Including the statements made to medical personnel, the accuser in this case has made approximately 16 statements concerning the events of March 13 and March 14. Some of the issues raised by these statements include:

Who Did What?

89. In her statement of March 14 to Officer GD Sutton, the accuser claimed that she had been in the bathroom with five men and that Brett had penetrated her ...she would later add that she was penetrated by all five men. (Discovery at 1304.)

In the sexual exam assault report of March 14, the accuser said that Brett and Nikki [the second dancer] carried her back into the house, where Adam closed the door and told her she could not leave. At that point Matt claimed that he was getting married but then raped her [and then Adam raped her]. . . Brett apparently committed no sexual acts. (Discovery at 538-40.)

On March 16, the accuser told Inv. Himan that Adam came to the car and took her back into the house, that Brett first raped...her, followed by Matt, and that Adam forced her...She then said that Adam dragged her back to the car and wiped her off. (Discovery at 1207-08.)

In her handwritten statement of April 6, Dan and Adam came to the car to apologize and bring her back inside, Adam was the attacker who claimed he was getting married, Matt first raped...her, followed by Brett, Dan participated in beating her, and then Nikki [the second dancer] and Adam took her back to the car. (Discovery at 809-11)

How Long Did the Attack Last?

90. In the affidavits used to establish probable cause and secure warrants in this case, the State represented that the accuser was sexually assaulted over a 30 minute time period. See, e.q., Discovery at 460 (Probable Cause Affidavit for March 23, 2006). In her handwritten statement, the accuser wrote that Matt assaulted her for 5 minutes, that Brett assaulted her for 7 minutes, did not put a time on the length of Adam's ... assault, and then describes being beaten before and after the assaults for some length of time. (Discovery at 810.)

However, on September 22, 2006, the District Attorney represented to the court that he did not believe that the entire assault took more than 10 minutes (Transcript at 87) despite the fact that the District Attorney later admitted on October 27, 2006, that he had never spoken with the accuser about the facts of this case.

The second dancer has told investigators that the accuser was never alone in the house for more than 5 minutes. (Discovery at 1213.)

Was She Beaten?

92. While at the Duke University Medical Center Emergency Room the accuser specifically denied that she was hit by fists or hands (Discovery at 550), and told the physician examining her that she had not been hit. (Discovery at 523) The physical exam showed no tenderness in the accuser's neck, no back tenderness, and no swelling, tenderness or edema in her arms or legs. (Discovery at 523-24)

On March 15, when she went to the University of North Carolina Medical Center, the accuser claimed that she had been knocked to the floor and that she had hit her head on a sink, making her neck sore. Her back was noted to be normal and the only pain that she complained of was neck pain. (Discovery at 501, 508)

On March 16, the accuser described being choked or strangled to Inv. Himan and Sgt. Gottlieb; there is no mention in either of their reports of being beaten or kicked or of a fall in which she struck her head on a sink. (Discovery at 1817)

On March 28 she told physicians at the University of North Carolina that when she had been assaulted "she fell and slipped" and hit her knee. (Discovery at 498)

On April 3, she told physicians that the assaulter had squeezed her neck and then kicked her in the back of the neck. (Discovery at 495)

In her handwritten statement of April 6, the accuser describes being kicked in he "behind" as well as her back before the assault, and after the assault being hit in the face and kicked by Dan and Brett; she says nothing about being choked or strangled. (Discovery at 810)

What Did "Nikki" Do?

93. In her statements to the ACCESS nurse, Officer GD Sutton, Officer BS Jones, Sgt. JC Shelton, and on the Sexual Exam Assault Report, the accuser claimed that Nikki [the second dancer] stole her money and carried her back into the house along with the attackers. (Discovery at 1981,1304,1308,1310, 538)

The accuser's statement of April 6 mentions none of these things and portrays the second dancer as a fellow victim of the assault who rescued her, rather than helping the men carry out the assault and then stealing her money.

F. Summary of The Physical Evidence

94. No ...blood, bodily fluid, skin, saliva, hairs, fibers or DNA from Reade Seligmann has been found in the accuser, on the accuser, or on the accuser's clothing.

95. No ... blood, bodily fluid, skin, saliva, hairs, fibers or DNA from Collin Finnerty has been found in the accuser, on the accuser, or on the accuser's clothing.

96. No ... blood, bodily fluid, skin, saliva, hairs, fibers or DNA from Dave Evans has been found in the accuser, on the accuser, or on the accuser's clothing.

97. No ... blood, bodily fluid, skin, saliva, hairs, fibers or DNA from Reade Seligmann has been found in the bathroom at 610 N. Buchanan, where the accuser claims that he assaulted her.

98. No ... blood, bodily fluid, skin, saliva, hairs, fibers or DNA from Collin Finnerty has been found in the bathroom at 610 N. Buchanan, where the accuser claims that he assaulted her.

99. ...testing by another lab using the Y-STR method reportedly found evidence of male DNA in the accuser; the

profile matched the accuser's boyfriend and excluded Reade Seligmann, Collin Finnerty and Dave Evans. The accuser [incorrectly] informed investigators that she had not had sexual intercourse with her boyfriend for a week prior to the alleged assault.

———

102. As of the date of this Motion:

(a) There is no physical evidence of assault or sexual assault linking the accuser to Reade Seligmann;

(b) There is no physical evidence of assault or sexual assault linking the accuser to Collin Finnerty;

(c) There is no physical evidence of assault or sexual assault linking the accuser to Dave Evans;

(d) There is no physical evidence that links Reade Seligmann to the bathroom at 610 N. Buchanan where the accuser claims she was raped;

(e) There is no physical evidence that links Collin Finnerty to the bathroom at 610 N. Buchanan where the accuser claims that she was raped.

The Identification of the Defendants

Reade Seligmann

109. Before the events of March 13 and 14, 2006, the accuser did not know and had never seen Reade Seligmann.

———

111. According to Inv. Himan's notes, the description given by the accuser of "Adam" on March 16 was that he was a "white male, short, red cheeks, fluffy hair, brown, chubby face."

(Discovery at 1290) Reade Seligmann is 6'1" and weighed 215 pounds. His hair is black, not brown.

112. On March 16, 2006, less than 72 hours after the claimed assault, the accuser reportedly indicated during the course of a photo array that she was "70%" sure she recognized Reade Seligmann as having been at the party; however, "she could not remember where exactly she saw [him] at the party." (Discovery at 1667)

---

114. Further, according to the accuser in both her handwritten statement and in Inv. Himan's typewritten report, "Adam" carried her from the bathroom to the car when the rape was finished. (Discovery at 1208) ("Adam dragged her to the car and wiped her off with Nicki [sic] and then they left and she was driven to Kroger on Hillsborough.") ; (Discovery at 810) (Adam opened the door and Nikki [the second dancer] "rushed in and helped Adam to get me dressed." Nikki and Adam then "dragged me out to the car because my legs would not move.").

115. Based on the accuser's handwritten statement, "Adam" (Reade Seligmann), stayed in the house for the entire attack and then carried or dragged the accuser to the car after the attack.

---

117. Photographs that were taken show the accuser and the second dancer performing just after midnight. The last photograph shows the two women leaving the room in which they were dancing... The time recorded by the digital camera's software is 12:03:58.

118. Reade Seligmann's telephone records, as maintained by Verizon Wireless, reveal that he received a telephone call on

his mobile phone at 11:50:31 p.m. (23:50:28) which lasted for 86 seconds (or until 11:51:57 p.m.). They further reveal that the next activity on his telephone was when he made a call at 12:05:49 a.m. (0:05:49) which had a duration of 32 seconds. He then called the same number at 12:06:24 a.m., and 12:07:03 a.m. He then called another number at 12:09:14 a.m. and 12:09:57 a.m. He then attempted to call the first number again at 12:10:14 a.m., 12:12:16 a.m. and 12:13:33 a.m. Finally, at 12:14:46 a.m., Reade Seligmann called the number of a taxi service to pick him up at an the intersection of Watts and Urban, near the house on Buchanan.

119. Moezeldin Elmostafa operates the taxi service that Reade Seligmann contacted; he told Inv. Himan that he received a call at 12:14 a.m. requesting that a cab come to Watts and Urban, and that he arrived at Watts and Urban by 12:19 a.m. (Discovery at 1242-43) Once there, he picked up Reade Seligmann and another man. Mr. Elmostafa's billing records for his telephone indicate that he received the call from Reade Seligmann at 12:14 a.m.

120. After picking up Reade Seligmann and the other person, Mr. Elmostafa drove them to a Wachovia ATM so that Reade could withdraw money and then to Cookout's for food. The Wachovia ATM camera shows that Reade withdrew money from the machine at 12:24 a.m. After buying food, Mr. Elmostafa took the young men to the Duke Campus, where Reade Seligmann entered his dorm using a secure dorm card at 12:46 a.m.

121. Meanwhile, and during the time that Reade Seligmann was in the cab, at 610 N. Buchanan the accuser was photographed standing on the back porch. The time recorded by the digital software of the camera is 12:30:24 a.m.

122. Later, and while Reade Seligmann was still in the taxicab, the accuser was photographed being helped into a car. The time recorded by the camera software for this picture is 12:41:32 a.m. Neither person in the picture is wearing clothing similar to Reade Seligmann.

123. In short, if Reade Seligmann was accurately identified by the accuser as "Adam," then he should still have been at 610 N. Buchanan at the time of this photograph at 12:41 a.m., as the accuser has stated that he carried or dragged her to the car. Instead, he had been in the back of a taxicab since 12:19 a.m.

124. Moreover, the accuser mentions nothing in any of her more than one dozen statements about any of her attackers, let alone "Adam," using a cell phone during the course of the attack. Reade Seligmann began making calls on his cell phone within 2 minutes of the accuser stopping her dance.

Collin Finnerty

125. Before the events of March 13 and 14, 2006, the accuser did not know and had never seen Collin Finnerty.

126. At 6′ 5″ tall, Collin Finnerty towers over most people. He has a very noticeable freckled face, and reddish-brown hair. He weighs 215 lbs., and while he could fairly be described as "lanky," no one would describe him as "chubby" or "heavy set."

127. The accuser described her assailants to Inv. Himan as:

Adam: white male, short, red cheeks, fluffy hair, brown, chubby face

Matt: heavy set, short hair cut, 260 lbs. to 270 lbs.

Brett: Chubby.

128. Collin Finnerty does not match any of the three assailants the accuser described to Inv. Himan on March 16, 2006. In fact, his physical appearance is essentially the opposite of the assailants she described.

129. More importantly, Collin Finnerty has a very noticeably freckled face. As Kim (Pittman) Roberts ["Nikki"], the second dancer told the police on May 11, 2006 when they showed her a picture of Collin:

"Yeah. I remember him. I remember him... One of the reasons I remember him is because of the freckles on his face."

130. Roberts told the police that Collin had been sitting on the floor near the door in the room where the two girls had been performing. She said that once the two girls left the room, she never saw Collin again.

131. The fact that none of the alleged attackers has ever been described as having a freckled face or as being abnormally tall would eliminate Collin Finnerty as one of the assailants.

132. Moreover, during the April 4, 2006 PowerPoint Identification procedure, the accuser identifies Collin Finnerty as "the guy who assaulted me..." The accuser specifically says that Collin was the "second one".

133. In the accuser's handwritten statement given to the police two days after her identification of Collin, she says that the second assailant to penetrate her was the one who went by the name of "Brett." (Discovery at 810)

134. As noted above, on March 16, 2006, two days after the alleged assault, the accuser described "Brett" to Inv. Himan as "chubby." Collin Finnerty, at 6'5" and 215 pounds, would never be described as "chubby."

Dave Evans

135. Before the events of March 13 and 14, 2006, the accuser did not know and had never seen Dave Evans.

136. The accuser was shown a "head-shot" photograph of Dave Evans during the course of the photo array performed on March 21, 2006, eight days after her claimed assault. Despite looking at that picture in the array twice, the accuser did not recognize Dave Evans.

137. The accuser was shown another "head-shot" photograph of Dave Evans during the course of the PowerPoint Identification on April 4, 2006, more than three weeks after the claimed assault.

As shown in this excerpt from this "identification," the accuser looked at this photograph for approximately 45 seconds before saying "he looks like one of the guys who assaulted me sort [of]." She went on to say that she would be 90% certain that Dave Evans was one of her attackers, if he had a mustache: "He looks just like him without the mustache." (Discovery at 1829.6)

138. Dave Evans did not have a mustache on March 13, 2006, as shown by ...photographs taken on March 12 and March 14, 2006.

The PowerPoint Identification Process was Unduly Suggestive, Fundamentally Flawed and Violated the Defendants' Constitutional Rights

140. The first photo array was shown to the accuser on March 16. It had been constructed in such a way so as to include someone from the Duke Lacrosse team named

"Matt," "Adam," or "Brett." Only pictures of members from the Duke Lacrosse team were used. Despite the requirements of General Order 4077, no "fillers" were used for these arrays.

———

143. ...despite the fact that only Lacrosse players were shown to the accuser, according to Inv. Clayton's report the accuser did not identify a single person from the 24 photographs shown to her as one of her attackers.

144. Significantly, according to this report, she did identify Reade Seligmann as having been present at the party, but not as one of her attackers. . .

145. Five days later, and under the same warnings and administered by the same Investigator, the accuser did not identify any of the 12 additional players whose pictures she was shown. One of those players was Dave Evans, whose picture (along with the other 11 in the arrays) she was shown twice. She did not identify him at that time and said nothing about him resembling one of her attackers if he had a mustache, despite being explicitly told to consider whether one of her assailants could have changed his appearance, including a mustache.

146. By April 4, the time of the PowerPoint Identification, the circumstances of the case -- and the procedures that were now being used --had changed dramatically. The accuser had reportedly not identified any of the 36 players shown to her as her attackers; the State was aware that there would be no DNA from, on, or in, the accuser to identify any of the white Duke Lacrosse players as her alleged attackers. Also by April 4, the District Attorney had repeatedly informed the public that it was his opinion that a rape had occurred and that members of the Duke Lacrosse team had committed it. The

PowerPoint Identification directed to be used by the District Attorney simply represented the last chance to identify someone from the Duke Lacrosse team as an attacker.

Consequently, and despite the requirements of General Order 4077, the PowerPoint Identification was conducted in violation of the Durham Police Department's own procedures and in a very different manner than the photo arrays of March 16 and March 21.

147. Rather than being conducted by an investigator with no knowledge of the case or the suspects, the PowerPoint Identification was conducted by Sgt. Gottlieb. (Discovery at 109) Sgt. Gottlieb had supervised the investigation over the preceding weeks and had personally interviewed the accuser and recorded observations in his notes about her actions and demeanor that indicate that he believed that a rape had occurred and that the attackers were lacrosse players from Duke University.

148. Rather than being told that the attackers may not even be in the photographs shown to her, the accuser was told just the opposite: "I... explained to her we were gong to sit in the far side of the room at the desk and look at people we had reason to believe attended the party." (Discovery at 109) In short, the accuser was told that every person she was going to see was a potential attacker or suspect.

149. Rather than being told that "you should not feel like you have to make an identification," the accuser was effectively told the opposite: "I also told her it was important to tell us if she recalled seeing a particular individual at the party and to let us know how she recalled seeing them from that night, what they were doing, and any type of interactions she may have had or observed with a particular individual." (Discovery at 109)

150. As with the earlier photo arrays, no 'fillers" were used. Compounding this is the fact that, by this time, investigators were aware that two white males not on the Lacrosse team had attended the party; neither was included in the PowerPoint presentation, thereby either eliminating two potential suspects, or two further opportunities for the accuser to make an error.

151. Contrary to the procedure used with the photo arrays, the accuser was not shown these images in her home. Rather, the images were shown to her in the police department where she was surrounded by investigators including Sgt. Gottlieb, Inv. Clayton, CSI Ashby and CSI Maddry. (Discovery at 109) Moreover, the accuser was being videotaped and audiotaped in plain view, rather than through one-way glass or other methods. This effectively communicated to the accuser that an identification was expected of her and that the investigators believed that she would identify her attackers in the PowerPoint photographs.

152. Significantly, and as to Reade Seligmann, the accuser was shown photographs of individuals whom she had reportedly identified before as being present at the party -- even though she had indicated that they had not attacked her. Having seen a photograph of a person previously, showing a different photograph of the same person would effectively trigger a recognition of that person based not on the commission of a crime, but simply on the earlier photo array. This significantly increased the risk of misidentification. Moreover, the inclusion of Reade Seligmann in the PowerPoint photographs makes no sense from an investigative standpoint, as the accuser had indicated that he was present at the party but that she could not remember where she saw him -- effectively indicating that he had not attacked her. . .

153. As to Dave Evans, the accuser had previously stated that she did not recognize him --despite being shown his picture twice. Having indicated twice that she did not recognize him, his inclusion in the PowerPoint photographs also makes no sense --other than to increase the risk that the accuser might wrongly identify him because she had seen another picture of him twice approximately two weeks earlier.

154. In sum, the accuser was effectively told that she was going to make an identification, that the identification was important for the case, that she was only going to be shown individuals who the investigators thought could be her attackers, and even if she had previously indicated that someone had not attacked her, she was still going to be shown a different picture of that person. In short, this procedure was designed [would] permit her to pick any person she desired and identify him as an attacker; that person would then be charged with rape.

---

159. During the course of a hearing before this Court on October 27, 2006, the District Attorney represented to the Court that while he had met with the accuser on April 11 -- one week after the PowerPoint Identification -- he could not speak with her about the facts of the alleged attack because she was "too traumatized" to discuss it meaningfully. (Transcript at 6.) If the District Attorney's assessment that the accuser was too traumatized to even discuss the attack in a meaningful fashion is to be credited, that assessment necessarily casts doubt upon the reliability of any identification or description made by her prior to that time.

160. There are significant discrepancies concerning the length of the attack, and thus the length of time that the accuser would have had to observe her attackers. In their

initial affidavits to this Court, investigators claimed that the attack lasted for a period of 30 minutes. (Discovery at 460) In her handwritten statement to investigators on April 6, the accuser specifically assigned time frames to each element of the attack, describing a series of events that would have taken at least 10 minutes before the assault began, a series of sexual assaults that lasted at least 12 minutes, and then a period of time in which she claimed she was dressed, beaten, and dragged back to her car. (Discovery at 810) However, after receiving a Notice of Alibi and other evidence from Reade Seligmann detailing his cell phone calls, cab ride and ATM withdrawal, indicating that he left the party within minutes of the dancers ending their "performance," and after being told by the second dancer that the accuser was never alone for more than 5 or 10 minutes, the District Attorney "speculated" to the Court that he did not believe the entire assault took more than 'five minutes, 10 minutes at the outside." (Transcript at 87: Discovery at 1213) If the attack lasted between 5 and 10 minutes, as the State apparently now contends, there was not sufficient time for a person, allegedly fighting for her life during the course of a brutal rape, to adequately observe each of three attackers, then be unable to identify two of them within a few days of the attack, and yet be able to retain sufficient memory of their appearances to identify them reliably three weeks later. The accuser has made significant errors in identification that demonstrate beyond dispute that there is a "substantial likelihood of misidentification"

161. During the course of the PowerPoint Identification, the accuser actually identified four individuals whom she claimed looked like her three attackers. (Discovery at 1828-29,1829,1829-30, and 1838)

162. The only person that the accuser identified with 100% certainty as being at the party in both the photo array and

the PowerPoint Identification was B______. (Discovery at 385-90,1667,1830) It is undisputed that B______ never attended the party and was in Raleigh during the party. (Discovery at 747-51)

163. During the course of the PowerPoint Identification, the accuser identified C______ as being present at the party. (Discovery at 1834-35) It is undisputed that C______ left the party before the accuser arrived and was in his dorm room at the time of the claimed attack. (Discovery at 859)

———

165. The accuser failed to recognize or identify the person who was photographing her throughout the evening. (Discovery at 1832)

166. On March 16th, the accuser described "Adam" as being a "white male, short, red cheeks, fluffy hair, brown, chubby face." (Discovery at 1290)... In short, the accuser's description of "Adam" to Inv. Himan is substantially different from Reade Seligrnann's actual appearance. This substantial discrepancy makes her description unreliable.

167. During the course of the PowerPoint Identification, the accuser also identified M______ as resembling "Bret." Discovery at 1828-29. Her description of "Brett" to Inv. Himan as being "chubby," also does not resemble M______, who is 6' and weighed 185 pounds. (Discovery at 665)

168. Based upon the accuser's handwritten statement to police on April 6, 2006, Dave Evans would have to be "Matt." The accuser's description of "Matt" to Inv. Himan was that he was "heavy set," had a "short hair cut," and weighed "260lbs to 270 lbs." (Discovery at 1290) Dave Evans is 5'9" and weighed 185 lbs, or 75lbs to 85lbs less than the accuser's description.

(Discovery at 634) In short, the accuser's description of "Matt" to Inv. Himan does not resemble Dave Evans.

169. Moreover, during the course of the PowerPoint Identification, the accuser claimed that Dave Evans had a mustache during her attack; Dave Evans never had a mustache during any time surrounding the party.

170. Putting to one side the substantial evidence that no sexual assault ever occurred at 610 N. Buchanan, there is quite simply no evidence that any of the accuser's identifications or descriptions of her alleged attackers are in any way reliable. Rather, the State is left with an incoherent mass of contradiction and error, one which not only raises the issue of a "substantial likelihood of misidentification," but which establishes that the accuser has in fact misidentified the Defendants.

Supplementation with Further Evidence

This leads to the conclusion that either Sgt Gottlieb -- who took no notes of this meeting and did not record his recollections until later-- was either wrong, or that the accuser gave two very different descriptions of her attackers to Inv. Himan and Sgt. Gottlieb on the same day during the course of the same interview. Sgt. Gottlieb's descriptions, moreover, do not identify which suspect is "Brett," "Adam," or "Matt," again either indicating that Sgt. Gottlieb could not recall which suspect was which person or that the accuser, after giving descriptions by name to Inv. Himan, was unable to do so with Sgt. Gottlieb.

Deposition of Sgt. Mark Gottlieb for the Disciplinary Hearing Commission of the North Carolina State Bar April 17, 2007

Q. Did you raise any concerns with Mr. Nifong about whether what he had proposed would comply with this General Order 4077?

A. No, because what he was asking was not applicable to [General Order] 4077.

Q. Why is that?

A. First of all, it was not a photo array. In order to be a photo array, the very first thing you have to do is have a suspect, and we had no suspect whatsoever.

Q. Are you saying that you did not consider the lacrosse players to be suspects or potential suspects in the crime?

A. I'm not saying that they were not considered to be potential suspects. What I am saying is that we did not have an individual identified as a suspect.

And in cases like this, there are other things we use also, such as yearbook theory. If we know there's a suspect, say, who robs a bank and he is wearing a Riverside High School jacket, we know the suspect is possibly from Riverside High School. We put a Riverside High School yearbook in front of the victim and say, "Go through it and tell me what you see."

In this case, like I said, there was no suspect that was presented. And, on top of that, Mr. Nifong didn't want a lineup, he wanted what I have described earlier.

Q. Okay. Now, I don't mean to quibble with you about words because, as I told you, we're not here to investigate you.

A. No problem.

Q. But in the notes, Exhibit 204 Page 11, your description of the meeting with Mr. Nifong you do actually use the phrase in reference to doing a photographic lineup of "new mug shots".

A. Yes.

Q. Okay.

A. And that was ruled out. We didn't have a suspect.

Q. Is it your understanding that this General Order 4077 does not apply to any photographic identification procedures that the Department conducts?

A. Does it apply to photographic lineups or arrays? Yes, it does.

Q. But you're saying that your understanding is that it does not apply to all photographic potential identification procedures conducted by the Department?

A. No, because it doesn't address, like I said, the yearbook identifications, things of that nature.

Q. Okay. And consistent with the conversation that you had with Mr. Nifong on March 31st, you informed Ms. Mangum that you had reason to believe that the people in the photographs she was going to be shown had attended the party on March 13th?

A. Yes.

Q. Did you use the verbal instruction and certification sheets that we have seen for the photographic arrays that had been used for her?

A. No.

Q. And during the course of--without going through each one, during the course of that procedure she identified four (4) people in that presentation who were potentially attackers?

A. No, sir.

Q. Okay. How many did she identify?

A. She identified three (3) people, and she said one person looks like him, if not him.

Q. Okay. Are you referring to MW--------?

A. I guess that's his name, I had to actually go back and look up who the people were according to item number.

Q. If you will to go page 14 of your typed notes...

A. Yeah, I've got it. "Do you recognize that person? He looked like Bret, but I'm not sure. Who was Bret? One of the guys who assaulted me."

Yeah, she's saying that he looked like him, but she wasn't sure.

Q. Okay. And then right below that, David Evans, her response is, "He looks like one of the guys who assaulted me sort." I don't know if that's supposed to me "sort of".

A. No, actually it was "sort".

Q. All right. But you're saying that she identified Mr. Evans as an attacker?

A. Yes.

Q. Explain to me how her identification of Mr. Evans is different than her identification of Mr. M-------.

A. On the one she said she wasn't sure, and then on the other one she said she is 90% sure.

Q. After the identification procedure--after the photographic presentation as you have described it, did you meet with Mr. Nifong about the results?

A. Yes.

Q. What did you tell him?

A. Told him what had happened.

Q. And what was that?

A. That she had identified the people and gone through it with him and that she had memory of people who were there.

Q. Okay. Did you tell him how many people she had identified as attackers or potential attackers?

A. Yes.

Q. How many people did you tell him?

A. Three. (3) And we also, I know we had discussed the part about looking like someone but not him or not sure.

Q. All right. Was there any discussion about the people that she had identified in that procedure compared with what she had done in the photographic arrays?

A. I'm sorry, say that again.

Q. Let me give you more specific. Was there a discussion at that meeting with Mr. Nifong about the fact that she had identified Reade Seligmann as a potential attacker when she had previously looked at his photograph, another photograph, and not identified him?

A. Not in that, no.

Q. You didn't discuss that in the meeting?

A. No.

Q. The same discussion with Mr. Evans. Was there any discussion with Mr. Nifong about the fact that she had not been able to identify him in the prior photographic arrays?

A. No. Because I was told that in the lineups prior to that no suspect was identified. I didn't ask who was in them.

Q. The identifications that she made at this April 4th photographic presentation, as you called it, were they one of the bases on which Mr. Seligmann and Mr. Finnerty were indicted?

A. Yes.

Q. In the other types of procedures that you say are not subject to this General Order, such as yearbook that you mentioned--

A. Yes, sir.

Q--have you had cases where identification from that procedure alone has been the basis for an indictment against somebody?

Mr. Hill [Gottlieb attorney]. Objection to form. Misstates prior testimony.

A. (no response)

Q. Do you understand my question?

A. Well, that wasn't the only basis. You asked me if it was one of the bases.

Q. I did.

A. Okay. Are you saying in other cases have [we] indicted someone strictly because of photographic identifications without other kinds of corroborating information? I don't know.

I know that we have indicted people by using the yearbook-style identification.

Q. After this photographic presentation, was there a discussion about whether or not to do a photographic array with Ms. Mangum?

A. No.

Q. In other cases, not this case, in other cases where you have used the yearbook procedure or some other procedure that you say isn't subject to the General Order, in your experience has any follow-up photographic array or lineup been used to identify?

A. At times, yes.

Q. But not in all cases?

A. I can't swear to it, but I don't believe in all cases.

A. Have you been involved in any cases where one of the procedures that you say isn't subject to the General Order was used and a photographic array was not done subsequently?

A. Not that I can recall.

"Whether or not the results of the six photo arrays and the photo presentation on April 4th would have ever been admissible into evidence would have to have been argued and determined by a court of law. . . They are not legally binding procedures. Any deviation from such guidelines does not necessarily mean that the eyewitness identification procedure used will be excluded from evidence or that a suspect's rights have been violated."

--Chief of Police Chalmers in his report to City Manager Patrick Baker on the conduct of the investigation by the Durham Police Department, May 11, 2007

A. . . And the indictments were done on Monday, April the 17th, and on Friday the 14th, which I just wanted to make sure of the date, was when this came up.

Q. OK. So that is when Investigator Himan came to you?

A. Yes.

Q. Tell me what were the concerns he expressed to you.

A. Well, the concerns that were expressed were basically this:

With Mr. Finnerty, we were able to show that he was at the party and that she had identified him. And we had the time cards, per se. I don't know what exactly you would call it, but each student has a magnetic card that if they go in the parking lot or dorm room or buy food, whatever, if the use that card it leaves an electronic stamp. And we had a document showing me that he arrived back at the dorm at the time as the [that] of the people who we knew were at the party.

So we were able to put together information to at least corroborate, one, he was there; two, he met the description [contradicted by Mangum's own statements; Finnerty was not short and chubby; and no person of Mr. Finnerty's description was ever described by Mangum, save in the reconstructed notes by Sgt. Gottlieb made some months after the indictment of Mr. Finnerty]; three, she was able to show him ; the SANE nurse's report was consistent with a sexual assault [contradicted by the written medical report which stated that the alleged victim had no injuries and no evidence of blunt trauma]. So we had something to work with there for an indictment.

With Mr. Seligmann, we never had anything to tie him to the party directly. . . And yes, he met the physical description. [contradicted by Mangum's own statements; Seligmann was not short and chubby; and no person of Mr. Seligmann's description was ever described by Mangum, save in the reconstructed notes by Sgt. Gottlieb made some months after the indictment of Mr. Seligmann] But strictly looking at a picture and saying, "That's the man who raped me", Ben [Himan] was very concerned. . .

Q. Did Investigator Himan talk to you about what he thought ought to happen with respect to Mr. Seligmann?

A. I told Investigator Himan that I would discuss it with the District Attorney [Nifong]...And, like I said, he said that if we believe on one, we should believe on the other.

Q. Okay. And from your previous testimony, Mr. Nifong's response was that if you believed Ms. Mangum about Mr. Finnerty, that you should also believe her about Mr. Seligmann?

A. Correct.

Q. Any other statements that he made about that?

A. That was basically it.

Q. Did he indicate that he wanted to go forward with the indictment?

A. Yes.

Q. Did he indicate why there was a need to go forward with the indictment on Monday, the upcoming Grand Jury?

A. I don't recall if it was that meeting or a different meeting, but I do know at some point, I know the indictments were being done when they were being done in order to locate the suspects.

Q. I don't understand that.

A. School was about to end.

Q. You don't recall whether Mr. Nifong had--

A. I don't recall if it was that meeting or another meeting.

Q. But at some meeting it was Mr. Nifong--was it Mr. Nifong who expressed a concern that it needed to be done because school was getting ready to end?

A. Right. People were going to be going across the country. [If suspects had to be extradited from another state, they could have fought the extradition, and in the process exposed the vacuousness of the charges against them.]

Q. The call with Mr. Nifong that you are describing, did that occur on the same day, the Friday April 14th?

A. As in my conversation with them?

Q. Yes.

A. With Investigator Himan?

Q. Yes.

A. Yes. Right after that, right after I briefed my command staff.

Q. Was the discussion during that conversation about letting the Department have some more time to develop additional facts before going forward with the indictment?

A. Well, I told him our concerns and basically he made the decision. I don't remember the exact conversation. [although he claimed to be able to reproduce 33 typed pages of notes from memory several months after the indictments]

Q. And did you keep any kind of notes of that conversation with Mr. Nifong?

A. No.

Q. To your knowledge, did anybody in the Department keep notes of that conversation?

A. I don't know.

Mr. Witt [Gottlieb attorney]. Which conversation are you referring to at that point?

Q. I'm talking about the one you've just been testifying to that I think you said occurred on Friday, April 14th, before the indictments.

A. No, I don't know.

Q. You don't know of any notes that were kept?

A. I don't.

--Deposition of Sgt. Mark Gottlieb for the Disciplinary Hearing Commission of the North Carolina State Bar April 17, 2007

Q. Did you raise the concern--at that meeting that you were present at, did you raise that directly with Mr. Nifong about a concern about going forward with indictment against Reade Seligmann?

A. Yeah, I said--I said--and I didn't--I wasn't as vocal as Gottlieb, but I said, you know, I said, we don't have him anywhere being at the party. And he--that's when Gottlieb said the same thing. I said--and there was some concern there.

And he said, "Well, if you believe one part of her story, you've got to believe the other part of her story, you can't just pick and choose what you're going to believe."

--Deposition of Investigator Himan for the Disciplinary Hearing Commission of the North Carolina State Bar May 8, 2007

It was my mom's birthday April 17 and I was sitting in a room with Julia [attorney] ...and they said indictments were going to come down, I mean, I remember , I remember exactly where I was sitting...and I was sitting in a room with... my roommate... and Julian [the attorney] had come in and said two indictments were handed down but they're sealed. I didn't know what that meant but, I didn't think that had any bearing on me, and they said they weren't going to release who it was, so it was sort of a difficult situation, you sort of wanted to know who it was... it's just that extra--it's not me, I hope it's not me...I feel terrible for whoever it is but I hope it's not me...

...and we were sort of talking and joking around, and he's sitting across the table from me, and all of a sudden his secretary comes in and says, Julian, Mike Nifong's on the phone.

....and...the room felt like it's spinning...and Julian comes in and says, she picked you...

(witness pauses to regain composure)

and... I mean, my dad just fell to the floor, and I just sat on the ground, and I said, My life is over...

(witness pauses to regain composure)

I mean, we finally got up, and me and my dad were hugging each other...and...first--the first thing I thought about was, you know, how are we going to tell my mom

(witness pauses to regain composure)

and--by the way, my dad he said he had to go out and we had to start putting together outline information, because we never thought we were ever going to be worried about it, and... a couple hours later I had to call Father Luke he is the headmaster of my school, and I told him that he was going to have to, he was going to have to be by my mom . . .

(witness pauses to regain composure)

when I called her.

(camera showing mothers of two of the accused students weeping silently in the courtroom)

So I...and I got on the phone...and I said, Mom, are you alone right now? And she said yeah, what's going on? And I said, She picked me.

(witness pauses to regain composure)

... and... I could hear her on the other end of the phone...the life was sucked right out of her

(witness pauses to regain composure)

and then ...I tried to calm her down ...and I just told her everything was going to be alright...and that we were going to prove this didn't happen, and she didn't need me to tell her that but...from that point on we just ...we had to go from there that night, we were ...we couldn't tell anybody because if we...if it got out to the press ...

(witness pauses to regain composure)

if it got out to the press... Mr. Nifong, they were going to have... Mr. Nifong wanted to come and take us out of class and arrest us... and we... if it had gotten out...we weren't going to get the privilege--we were told that we were going to turn ourselves in, for something that we didn't do ... and I had to go back ... to Duke, gather some of my stuff...I had to put a smile on my face because my roommate was in my room at the time and his girlfriend was in the room... and I had to joke around with them and pretend that everything was OK...and my girlfriend had been calling me all day, she wanted to know who, who it was... and I had to go walk into...she was sitting in a friend's room ... initially she was angry with me and she said, Why, why didn't you call me, what have you been doing all day I've been so worried. And I had to take her outside and...she was wrapped in a blanket and I had to tell her and I said, She picked me. And she just collapsed and I literally had to carry my girlfriend and it was a long walk from one of the quads all the way down to my 2007 dad's car.. and then put her in my dad's car and then my dad and I we drove her to a hotel and then the next morning we had to turn ourselves in.

We had to borrow [to pay the bond] from a friend we couldn't pay that money ...$400,000...

--testimony of Reade Seligmann before the Disciplinary Hearing Commission of the North Carolina State Bar, June 15,

Reade Seligmann and Collin Finnerty were publicly indicted on April 17, 2006. However, one week prior—on April 10, 2006-- results from the DNA tests were released, which immediately cleared them and every other member of the lacrosse team. No DNA from any member of the team was found; meaning that none of them had any physical contact with Mangum. (These results had actually been reported to Nifong on April 4, 2006.)

The players had been eager for the results of these tests. Knowing the results would show their innocence, the team expected to be cleared of any wrongdoing and that the case would be dropped. Members even joked that giving samples for the tests (which required a trip to the police station) would get them off from a day of practice. "I remember people being like 'Great, we get to go to the police station and give our DNA instead of practice.' There was nothing to hide and all of us were ready and willing to do that," said Edward Carrington. "I remember the lawyers were trying to figure out a way to get out of it. For us, it didn't occur because we wanted the truth to be known. If us giving our DNA helped that happen, then we were all for it." (Daily Progress, April 8, 2007)

But the District Attorney--who had justified the judicial order to test all the lacrosse players by saying that it would immediately rule out the innocent--now backtracked and dismissed the results, saying that he would solve the case "the old-fashioned way", as such cases were solved before DNA testing. He was not challenged about either his reversal, nor about his challenge to the reliability of DNA as evidence, by the media.

DNA testing has been the catalyst for freeing more than 200 wrongly-accused persons from prison; but apparently it was not to be allowed to prove innocence in a case where public opinion had been so effectively targeted against the defendants.

Nifong made a second attempt to find DNA evidence linking the players, by hiring a private lab in another county to perform more delicate tests. By April 21 the results had again come back negative. There were no matches to any lacrosse players.

Unusually, this time Nifong elected not to receive the results of the testing by phone, fax, or email. Instead he personally traveled to the private lab, taking the chief investigators on the case, officers Gottlieb and Himan, with him. All three made this journey on three separate occasions. Contrary to standard procedure, no notes were kept on any of these occasions, either by the police investigators, or by Nifong, or by the lab staff, which failed to draw up any memoranda about the meetings.

The lab had discovered DNA from at least four additional men, and possibly from as many as a dozen, none of whom were Duke students. Had Nifong been pursuing a genuine rape case, a logical step would have been to drop the charges against the lacrosse players and investigate these men. Instead he and the lab agreed that the lab would formally report only the absence of DNA from the players, and not mention the additional men. This would permit Nifong to short circuit the discovery rules, which required him to report to the defense lawyers all information he uncovered. If he was not formally "informed" of the presence of DNA from additional men, he could legally attempt to keep that information from reaching the defense team.

(It is doubtful there could ever be a better example of the ability of DNA testing to exonerate the innocent than the case of the accused lacrosse players--three defendants accused of a violent gang rape in a tiny space, with a half-hour struggle, where no condoms were used and where two of them were said to have ejaculated. Modern DNA testing is so sensitive that it can detect even a single cell from an individual. In the lab which conducted a second test on the lacrosse DNA, a single cell from an examiner was discovered to have contaminated the samples. This occurred under laboratory conditions with the strictest standards and safeguards. For a gang rape to have occurred at the Buchanan house under the alleged conditions, and for no DNA to be left behind by anyone--not so much as a single hair, not a single cell containing DNA (nor even a single fingerprint left by Finnerty, who had never in his life been inside the specified bathroom)--is impossible in the universe we know.)

> The DNA evidence requested will immediately rule out any innocent persons, and show conclusive evidence as to who the suspect(s) are in the alleged violent attack upon this victim.
>
> --Application for judicial order requiring lacrosse team members to submit samples for DNA testing

> [Defense attorney] Cooney said while not a single trace of DNA was left on Mangum by any of the accused men...yet BM [Brian Meehan, the lab technician] left DNA despite his best and trained efforts not to.
>
> "These [lab technician] guys are dressed up in space suits," he said.

...And for all the DNA[of as many as another dozen men] to survive and for none of it to be from the accused men, was, Cooney said, "impossible."

--"Lawyer gives inside look at Duke lacrosse case",
Statesville, North Carolina Record and
Landmark, February 14, 2009

"DNA results can often be helpful, but, you know, I've been doing this for a long time, and for most of the years I've been doing this, we didn't have DNA. We had to deal with sexual assault cases the good old-fashioned way. Witnesses got on the stand and told what happened to them."

--District Attorney Nifong at a forum on the NCCU campus
April 11, 2006, one day after it became publicly known
that there were no DNA matches to any lacrosse players

Standard 3-3.11 Disclosure of Evidence by the Prosecutor

(a) A prosecutor should not intentionally fail to make timely disclosure to the defense, at the earliest feasible opportunity, of the existence of all evidence or information which tends to negate the guilt of the accused or mitigate the offense charged or which would tend to reduce the punishment of the accused.

(b) A prosecutor should not fail to make a reasonably diligent effort to comply with a legally proper discovery request.

(c) A prosecutor should not intentionally avoid pursuit of evidence because he or she believes it will damage the prosecution's case or aid the accused.

-- American Bar Association Criminal Justice Standards

Standard 4.1 Disclosure

(a) The prosecutor should be required, within a specified and reasonable time prior to trial, to make available to the defense the following information and material relating to DNA evidence:

———

(xi) material or information within the prosecutor's possession or control, including laboratory information or material, that would tend to negate the guilt of the defendant or reduce the punishment of the defendant.

-- American Bar Association Criminal Justice Standards

MOTION TO COMPEL DISCOVERY: EXPERT DNA ANALYSIS

13 December 2006

. . . this [DNA] evidence was submitted [by the District Attorney] to two different labs: first the State Bureau of Investigation, which found no DNA link between the accuser and any of the suspects; and then to DNA Security, a private laboratory in Burlington.

. . . DNA Security identified DNA from multiple males [but] . . .Enough of that DNA existed for DNA Security to conclude that none of it matched the defendants, their teammates on the 2006 Duke University Men's Lacrosse team, or anyone else who submitted a DNA sample in the investigation.

This is strong evidence of innocence . . . in short, these discoveries by DNA Securities show that male DNA was discovered, on multiple rape kit items, which did not match any defendant in this case or their lacrosse teammates.

There is not a single mention of this obviously exculpatory evidence in the final DNA Security report. Indeed, had defendants [counsel] not undertaken an exhaustive examination of the underlying materials, which DNA Security objected to providing, this evidence would have remained unidentified in the mass of documentation underlying DNA Security's work in this case.

———

On April 8, 9, and 10, 2006, DNA Security analyzed the DNA profiles extracted from the cheek scrapings, oral swabs...and panties from the rape kit items taken from the accuser at Duke Hospital in the early morning hours of March 14. While DNA Security's final report would not reflect the findings from that analysis, underlying documents provided to the defendants on October 27, 2006, reflect that DNA from multiple male sources was discovered on the ... swabs and panties from the rape kit; it was all compared to the known reference samples from the lacrosse players; and none of it matched any of the players.

———

Thus, by April 10, 2006, DNA Security analysts had apparently discovered multiple male source DNA on the ... swabs and panties of the rape kit; had compared it to the lacrosse players' DNA; and had concluded that none of it matched the lacrosse players, including the defendants. However, none of those findings would be included in DNA Security's final report.

———

Additionally, the United States Constitution requires the disclosure of any evidence tending to negate a criminal defendant's guilt and/or affect the credibility of any

> prosecuting witness(s). See Brady v. Maryland 373 U.S. 83 (1963)...[etc.]. These materials, as the Court is well aware, have become known in criminal law practice as "Brady materials", and they include any information gathered in the course of an investigation or prosecution that tends to impeach the credibility of a prosecution witness.

Because the lacrosse team had submitted to a court order requiring them to furnish their DNA for tests, they were entitled by law--each and every member of the team--to the complete results of those tests; not only the result of whether or not there was a match to their own DNA; but to all the results of all of the testing.

> TRANSCRIPT hearing Sept. 22, 2006
>
> NIFONG: . . . It [the letter from DNA Security's Brian Meehan to District Attorney Nifong] says, 'Dear Mr. Nifong, We have received your request for additional documents for defense discovery related to the Duke case. . . a blanket discovery of the entire case file, including all records and related materials, could jeopardize the privacy of these same [other] individuals. We at DSI [DNA Securities] feel that this matter should be considered...'
>
> . . . as indicated, there are copies in the files. And I gave that to the Court. I take no position on that. But again, these are [defense] attorneys who are already on record as saying that these tests cleared their clients. And now they want to spend an additional $4035 of the state's money to investigate further.
>
> MR. BANNON: [defense counsel] I've been doing my best, Your Honor, but the district attorney's office represented the SBI lab DNA testing would clear innocent people. And then he went on to indict and prosecute

them. So I don't want to talk anymore about what defense lawyers have been saying and what district attorneys have been saying about what the DNA evidence in this case is. It's irrelevant to this exchange.

The State of North Carolina chose after the State Bureau of Investigation lab made conclusions in this case about DNA testing to go out and hire its own private lab to do additional testing. It is extraordinarily noteworthy that those tests were done in the same manner that the SBI [State Bureau of Investigation] does its tests. DNA Security didn't just do YSTR DNA testing. They also did autosomal DNA testing and made conclusions in the case that the State Bureau of Investigation did not make. That makes their case file even more important for the defense than the State Bureau of Investigation's case file is.

We did not make the choice to do a second round of DNA testing in this case. The state did. And I understand the issue of cost. Believe me, I understand the issue of cost for people who have to deal with litigation like this. But the bottom line is the state chose to pursue this evidence. It has chosen to give notice that it is going to introduce this evidence. We are entitled to the information that we're asking for no matter how much it costs. It's not, you know, you can't say that the Sixth Amendment and the Fifth Amendment have a price and that we should be able to sort of price ourselves out of getting background information that we're entitled to under statute and under constitutional law for a fair trial.

Transcript of Hearing, December 15, 2006

State's Witness Brian Meehan, Ph.D of DNA Securities [private DNA testing lab], testifying

---

Q. Do you keep communication logs at DNA Security [private testing lab]?

A. No.

Q. You don't?

A. No.

Q. Whenever you have a meeting with somebody about the testing you're doing, you don't keep notes of that?

A. There are some meetings we keep a note of and we note that on our paperwork in our case but we don't necessarily keep notes at every meeting, no.

Q. So if you had any meetings in this case, it would be noted in the paperwork you provided to us back in October?

A. If we kept any notes of the meetings, it would be in there, yes.

Q. Well, let me make sure we understand it correctly because I thought you said if you had a meeting at all, you kept a log of that meeting?

A. No. I said we don't keep logs.

Q. You don't. Okay. What about telephone conversations about this case? Do you keep logs of telephone conversations about cases you work on?

A. No, we don't.

Q. Do you ever, for instance, in your agencies e-mail each other about cases you're working on?

A. You mean from our agency to another agency? When you say, in our agencies . . .

Q. Sure.

A. We only have one company.

Q. Sure. Or within, internally, within your agency. In other words, whatever, one lab technician e-mail another, I've done this or --

A. Sure, we do that, yeah.

Q. And, of course, getting to what you just said, do you ever e-mail people outside of your agency about testing you might do, like clients --

A. Sure.

Q. -- or others that you consult about these things?

A. Yes.

Q. Did you have any such communications in this particular case either with someone outside your agency or internally?

A. Did I send any e-mails to anybody?

Q. Yes.

A. I don't think that I exchanged e-mails with anybody in this case, meaning, really, our client, Mr. Nifong, or his staff. And I doubt that I e-mailed anybody internally.

Q. If you had e-mailed anyone internally, would those have been materials that you provided to us when you provided your entire case file?

A. Only if that e-mail was something that whoever sent it or received the e-mail felt it was important to the case and made it a record in the case. In other words, they would have had to have printed it out and included it in the case file. And that happens sometimes.

Q. Does it also happen sometimes that a person might send an e-mail or a communication about a case that for whatever reason they don't put inside what you're characterizing as your file?

A. Sure. We could get an e-mail that says, I would like to have my results by next Wednesday. Or, you know, How is everything going? Are you having any problems with our specimens? And one of our analysts would just e-mail them back and say everything's fine.

Q. Okay. And where are those e-mails kept?

A. We don't, we don't catalogue them or do anything to keep them. If the individual analysts have saved them on their computers, that's where they would be. Or if I had saved them on my computer, that's where they would still be.

Q. So you find in a rape case where male DNA [not from the suspects] is found on multiple items from a rape kit not probative evidence?

MR. NIFONG: Objection, argumentative. He's explained.

THE COURT: Overruled.

THE WITNESS: No, that's not a general rule, okay. This report was a specific report at the request and in discussions with Mr. Nifong that we would report only specimens that matched evidence items [from the players]. Only, we would only disclose or show on our report those reference specimens that matched evidence items. So that's all that's here.

Q. But of course, you discussed all the results of your tests?

A. Yes.

Q. Correct?

A. Yes.

Q. But you only wrote a report about some of those pieces of evidence, correct?

A. That's correct.

Q. And is that because Mr. Nifong told you to write the report that way?

A. I don't think he told me specifically to write it that way. I think we were in agreement that the alternative would have been, as I said earlier, to produce names and profiles of everybody in the case. And I do believe it initiated with me, not with Mr. Nifong, the concern that -- we had evidence coming in, reference specimens. I had no idea who these people were, where they were coming from. They could have been the bus driver, okay. And so my concern was that that's going to come out and get available to the media and just being associated by name and that a DNA profile was done, I expressed that concern. And Mr. Nifong agreed with me that it was okay to do this.

Q. So Mr. Nifong agreed with you that it was okay to not report male DNA findings [from persons other than the players] on multiple rape kit items?

A. No. Mr. Nifong agreed that it was okay to report the evidence items and reference items that matched [the samples from the players being tested].

Q. But at the same time, he knew that there were male DNA characteristics on some of those rape kit items that didn't match reference swabs [from the players], correct?

A. I would have to assume that he did know that, right.

Q. And he asked you to create a report that didn't show that; is that correct?

A. Well, those weren't his words. He didn't ask me specifically to exclude those, okay. And I think what, we're splitting hairs and you're looking for language. He did not, Mr. Nifong did not request that I exclude data from evidence specimens specifically.

Q. Okay. Let me ask you, whose privacy would it have violated if you had simply reported the male DNA characteristics found on multiple rape kit items from multiple different males who you didn't have reference swabs for? Whose privacy would it violate?

A. That, that wouldn't have violated anybody's privacy. But it got enveloped into that whole process of just limiting the report to those matches. And I think from my point of view -- and I'm not a lawyer in the case -- from my point of view, if there's no match found, then it's a strong implication of an exclusion.

Q. How long have you been conducting forensic work in criminal cases, Dr. Meehan?

A. Since 2003.

Q. Have you ever worked on any rape case before?

A. Yes.

Q. Do you know what exculpatory evidence is?

A. Yes.

Q. What is exculpatory evidence?

A. It's evidence that would provide information that would release a person as a suspect, so to speak in lay terms. Evidence to indicate that you were not party to that.

Q. So it's evidence that tends to negate the guilt of a person charged with a crime; is that correct?

A. That's correct.

Q. I'm trying to determine whether the standard that you developed for writing this report, which is a standard that allowed you to not provide these profiles [of males other than the players], I want to know the reason for that. I'm getting different kinds of answers. I'm getting it's privacy. I'm getting it didn't match a reference sample. I'm getting it's conversations with Mr. Nifong. And I'm getting this was sort of us together. I don't really understand why it is that you chose to write a report in this case, in a rape case where you found male DNA characteristics all over the rape kit but you didn't report that those male DNA characteristics didn't match the people who have been indicted for that rape.

Can you explain that to me in a way that comports with your understanding of what exculpatory evidence is and negating the guilt of the accused?

A. Well, I explained how that process evolved, that we limited the scope of this report to only that evidence that, in my words, in my terms, was probative. All right. That being the evidence, as it says on the report, that matches suspects to evidence. Now, we would be glad to provide a more thorough report, a report of every single profile upon the request of our client as was indicated on this report. Explicitly says this information was retained pending notification of the client. So, and Mr. Nifong is our client and had he said, listen, I want a report on everything, that's what we would produce.

Q. Let me direct your attention to what is exhibit Attachment No. 15 of Defendants' Exhibit No. 1. The bottom number is 3883.

A. I'm there.

Q. Does that appear to be the protocols for your lab --

A. Yes.

Q. -- on how you run your lab?

A. Yes.

Q. Do you rely on those protocols routinely to maintain your accreditation with ASCLD/LAB?

A. Yes.

Q. I'd like to direct your attention to standards for reports. It says, No. 4, item reports shall include . . .

A. I'm there.

Q. Doesn't it say, Results for each DNA test?

A. Yes.

Q. You didn't include the results for each DNA test in your report dated May 12; is that correct?

A. That's correct.

Q. So you violated this protocol of your own lab?

A. That's correct.

Q. And there's a handwritten note on the top that says, Could be B.M.

A. That's correct.

Q. Is that you?

A. Yes, it is.

Q. What does that notation mean?

A. It means that from the characteristics within this Y profile, my Y profile is consistent with those characteristics. So in other words, if we were to use this profile, I would not be excluded from it.

Q. Does it also reflect there could possibly have been contamination in the testing that got your profile into that particular testing?

A. Well, of course. That's what, that's what that means. That means that somehow a small amount of my Y DNA could have been on this specimen.

Q. How on earth could that happen?

A. Well, actually today, it's a very simple process. I'll just point out something to you so that you understand what we're talking about. . .

A. ...Our systems are so sensitive it's just one or two cells, sometimes not even a whole cell and that could have been the case here because there's missing markers. So some extraneous DNA possibly from me, not conclusively from me because it's only six markers out of the bunch, so but it could possibly be from me. Now, do I doubt that it's from me? To be honest with you, no, I don't. This could have been -- you know what a piece of dander looks like. Right there on your table, you can probably see a piece of dander. We're talking about the amount of DNA that might be 1/20 of that piece of dander, okay. That happens. And we have systems in our lab that protect ourselves from that. There are procedural systems. We also have computer systems that monitor profiles that are produced all the time. And my profile is in our system; every analyst that's worked in our lab is in our system; police officers we regularly work with are in our system so that any time their profile comes up, we identify that. And that's what happened in this case. Somebody, one of the analysts, identified that with this limited amount of information here it is possible that that could be DNA that got there from me. It's not, it happens in every lab. It's not unusual -- I shouldn't say -- it is unusual. But it does happen in every lab and it could possibly be here.

Q. Okay. So despite all the precautions that you take that you just talked about, sometimes you still can identify DNA on an item from even a small piece of dander or one cell; is that correct?

Q. And those identifications can be made from even one cell, one human cell --

A. That's correct.

Q. -- is that correct?

A. That's correct.

Q. Now, when you produced your report in this case -- first of all, you reviewed, with respect to 3387, you reviewed and I think if I'm correct, you reviewed most of the documents that were in this file when you produced your report, correct?

A. Yeah, I may have reviewed everything in it.

Q. But your initials are on the top of this particular document that's dated, is that May 3 that your initials are?

A. That's correct.

Q. So on May 3, you reviewed these documents that showed that this could have possibly been your DNA on this item?

A. Yes.

Q. Why didn't you report that in your final report in this case?

A. There was -- I don't see any basis for reporting it.

Q. Well, would you agree that the location of your DNA characteristics on an item -- I think you would because I think you just said this could reflect contamination, correct?

A. This, this could be, these characteristics are consistent with my Y profile, yes, which would mean that if it is me, it would be a contaminant me gotten on the specimen.

Q. And, of course, that's happened in your lab before, correct?

A. Yes.

Q. Wouldn't you agree that potential contamination in your lab really goes to the credibility of the findings of your lab based on your testing?

A. Absolutely.

MR. NIFONG: Objection.

THE COURT: Sustained.

Q. What is transference, Dr. Meehan?

A. Transference. Not sure.

Q. Well, is it appropriate to say that in your line of work whenever DNA -- I think you just used the example of a piece of dander and one or two cells. And the fact that a piece of dander could perhaps get on an evidentiary item or get sort of in one of these tubes, that would then be itself part of the DNA analysis of an evidentiary item? Is that correct?

A. Can that happen? Is that a question?

Q. Yes.

A. Yes, that can happen.

Q. But even on these weak profiles, when you can exclude somebody, you can exclude them with a hundred percent certainty?

A. That's correct. That's absolutely correct.

Q. So when you say, for example, that none of the subjects or none of the players match a profile, that's with a hundred percent scientific certainty?

A. That's correct.

Q. So as I understand it, and I'll not have you turn to each attachment, but in Attachment 3 where you identified two males as contributing, potentially contributing DNA, we are a hundred percent certain it was not Reade Seligmann?

A. Well, I don't know who was on what you're reading but if he's not one of those two, then that's correct.

Q. And the same would hold true for Attachment 5 and Attachment 6 and Attachment 7 and Attachment --

A. Oh, so you're talking about, like, on the top of the page where it says --

Q. Right.

A. -- they're -- yes. They're not there.

Q. With a hundred percent certainty?

A. That's correct.

Q. Even though there are -- but there are multiple males and we just don't know who they are other than we do know who they aren't?

A. That's correct.

Q. And from what you've told me, even the smallest cell, a single cell would be enough to generate perhaps a very weak DNA finding?

A. That's right. With a few cells, you get a pretty nice profile. A single cell, you could get sporadic DNA.

Q. So it would be fair to say at least on the items that were tested by your lab, there wasn't even a single cell from Reade Seligmann on any of those items?

A. For the items that we said he was not present on. I think we're talking about the panties and the sexual assault kit.

Q. Yes.

A. There were other items tested, as well.

Q. Right. But you didn't find Reade Seligmann anywhere in any of those items?

A. I'd have to go to the report and check.

Q. If you'd like to do that, go ahead.

A. Okay. That's correct.

Q. In fact, there was more of your DNA in that than there was Reade Seligmann's?

MR. NIFONG: Objection. I believe he's already testified he could not say it was his DNA, just that it was consistent with his DNA.

THE COURT: Sustained.

MR. COONEY [attorney] : I'll withdraw, Your Honor.

BY MR. COONEY:

Q. Now, for Mr. Finnerty, who's sitting over here, again, he would have been excluded with a hundred percent certainty on each of those items in the attachments that you've been through with Mr. Bannon?

A. That's correct.

Q. And, in fact, you didn't even, you didn't find any DNA from even a single cell from Mr. Finnerty on any of the items that you subjected to testing?

A. Let me check his numbers. That's correct.

Q. Now, the date of your report is May 12, 2006?

A. That's correct.

Q. And as of May 12, 2006, both Mr. Finnerty and Mr. Seligmann had been indicted in this case. Were you aware of that?

A. I haven't been following the case but, I mean, I'm sure -- they're sitting there so I guess they have been.

Q. Well, and I -- let me put a finer focus on it. I wasn't clear.

A. All right.

Q. I apologize.

A. All right.

Q. As of the time you wrote your report, Mr. Seligmann and Mr. Finnerty had already been charged with rape and kidnapping and sexual offense. Were you aware of that when you wrote your report?

A. No.

Q. Did any representatives of the state inform you about that before you wrote your report?

A. Not that I recall.

Q. Okay. And what you're telling -- and I want to make sure I'm understanding this. You were concerned that if you put a sentence in your report saying that Reade Seligmann is excluded from all DNA analyzed under these items as a sentence in your report, that would have violated his privacy rights?

A. If we included it in our report, if I can answer more than just a yes or no --

Q. Well, you --

A. If we included it in our report, it would have been --

MR. COONEY: I'll be happy to let him explain. If I could get a yes or no and then --

THE COURT: If you can answer with a yes or no, do so and then explain. If you cannot, start with the explanation.

THE WITNESS: I can't answer with a yes or no because we would not have reported with a single sentence like that. Now --

BY MR. COONEY:

Q. Why not?

MR. NIFONG: Objection, again, for his interrupting the answer.

MR. COONEY: I apologize.

THE COURT: Go ahead and finish your answer.

THE WITNESS: A typical report, and this was not a typical report, but a standard report will reflect all the DNA profiles of that, all the DNA data from that information, from that person, and it would not just be a single little line. And again, you know, it was just a simple me trying to do the right thing saying, well, let's not put that information out there for the public because it's my experience that it will get out there and I can't, who knows what's going to happen with that information. So could we have said that? Could we have done that? Yes, perhaps we could have. Perhaps we could have sat down if we had more forethought and said, well, look, let's just, we could have said something like all the reference specimens with these numbers were not, were excluded and their names weren't even there. But it certainly was not an intention to withhold information. It was a failed attempt to provide the minimal amount of information to the public in a case that's going to be just out there and they'll be undressing people. So at the expense of talking too much, maybe it could have been done better a different way. But we were trying to do the best we could and respect everybody that was involved in this case and only release information that really felt like it had to be released because of the potential probative value of it. So that's why I couldn't answer no, or yes.

BY MR. COONEY:

Q. Is that your explanation?

A. Excuse me?

Q. Is that your explanation?

A. Yes.

Q. I appreciate that. This was not your standard report?

A. It was not a standard report. It was a report where we were trying to -- yes, it's not, it's not the typical standard report.

Q. And as of the date you wrote your report, were representatives of the State of North Carolina aware that none of the DNA you had found matched Reade Seligmann?

A. I believe so.

Q. Okay. Were they aware that all the testing that you had done excluded Reade Seligmann with a hundred percent scientific certainty as of the date you wrote your report?

A. I believe so.

Q. Did you have a specific discussion with them about whether that information excluding Reade Seligmann should be included in the report?

A. Not with that specific name, no. We never mentioned that specific name.

Q. How about any defendant?

A. We never, I actually don't recall using any defendant's names.

Q. Would you agree, then, that your report did not fully report on the results of any examinations or tests conducted by you?

MR. NIFONG: Objection.

THE COURT: Overruled.

THE WITNESS: I don't understand the question. I'm not sure was raised correctly because of the word "any."

BY MR. COONEY:

Q. Would you agree that your report, that your report did not report the results of any examinations or tests that were conducted by you in these cases?

MR. NIFONG: Objection.

THE COURT: Ask that question again.

MR. COONEY: Sure. I'll put a finer point on it.

BY MR. COONEY:

Q. Are you aware that we have laws governing --

THE COURT: Just ask the question.

MR. COONEY: Okay.

BY MR. COONEY:

Q. Did your report set forth the results of all of the tests and examinations that you conducted in this case?

A. No. It was limited to only some results.

Q. Okay. And that was an intentional limitation arrived at between you and representatives of the State of North Carolina not to report on the results of all examinations and tests that you did in this case?

A. Yes.

THE COURT: Sheriff, I'll ask you to be looking for people that are giving visible or audible reactions to anything that takes place in the courtroom. If you detect who it is, bring it to my attention. They'll be excluded from the courtroom.

BY MR. COONEY:

Q. I've just got a couple more questions, Dr. Meehan. Is that one notebook in front of you or two notebooks?

A. This is one.

Q. About how high is that? Six inches? Five inches?

A. Yeah, five or six inches.

Q. Five or six inches. And those represent the underlying data that was produced by you on October 27, 2006?

A. As well as chain of custody documentation and stuff, yes.

Q. And in order for Reade Seligmann or Collin Finnerty or Dave Evans to have found the results of the tests that excluded them, they needed to go through those six inches of paper to find them; isn't that correct?

A. That is correct.

Q. Because you hadn't put them in the report; is that fair?

A. That is fair.

Q. If you had been requested by representatives of the State of North Carolina at any time after May 12 to prepare a report reporting on the results of all of your tests and examinations, would you have done so?

A. Certainly.

MR. COONEY: I have no further questions.

On April 19, 2006, two days after he was indicted for a crime DNA tests proved he could not have committed, the press obtained photos showing Seligmann making a withdrawal from an ATM at the time the supposed rape was taking place; plus Duke entry-card records; cell phone records; and statements from the driver and a fellow passenger in the cab he used; all of which placed him far away from the scene of the alleged crime.

On April 24, 2006, Investigator Himan questioned the taxi driver on the instructions of Nifong. The driver, Moezeldin Elmostafa, was an immigrant from the Sudan who was awaiting citizenship. He confirmed his statements that he was driving Seligmann at the time of the alleged crime. When Nifong was informed of this, he ordered Elmostafa's background to be investigated. An expired warrant from 2003 was discovered, involving shoplifting, in which the shoplifter had fled in Elmostafa's taxi. Elmostafa had been instrumental in apprehending the shoplifter and had been thanked by the department store which had been victimized. Nevertheless, an old warrant still remained unpurged from the system.

> Q. --- you have a note in there that Investigator Clayton and Himan came to you about information that the cabdriver, who was the short-term alibi witness for Mr. Seligmann, had an active arrest warrant outstanding?
>
> A. Yes, sir.
>
> Q. Tell me about that.
>
> A. They came into my office early in the morning the day -- I mean, -it was as busy as could be. They basically said the DA'S office located a warrant for him and they wanted the man picked up. And I just said, "Get it done quickly and get back here." I didn't care, it was a warrant for the man's arrest. Go pick him up.

Q. Do you know how long that warrant had been outstanding?

A. From my understanding, it was out, and this is after the fact, a couple of years. And the reason it didn't show up when people were checking for warrants was there was a letter spelled different in his name. But the other information--Social Security number, things of that nature--matched, but we don't check the warrants based on that.

--Deposition of Sgt. Mark Gottlieb for the Disciplinary Hearing Commission of the North Carolina State Bar
April 19, 2007

Mr. Nifong wanted to know when we picked [Elmostafa] up.

--Inv. Himan's notes

On May 9, 2006, Himan and another officer visited Elmostafa and asked him if he had anything to add to his testimony about Seligmann.

"The detective asked if I had anything new to say about the lacrosse case," Elmostafa said. "When I said no, they took me to the magistrate."

--News and Observer

When he refused to change his testimony, Elmostafa was handcuffed, arrested, and taken into custody. After the arrest, he was again asked if he wanted to add to his testimony. Again he refused. An arrest and conviction would have destroyed his chances for citizenship, most likely have resulted in his deportation back to Sudan, and prevented him from bringing his wife and children to the United States.

Nifong declaimed any involvement in Elmostafa's arrest, saying be "I would be very surprised if the officers even thought about using that as an opportunity to ask him something"; or that the discovery of the outdated warrant was anything but routine."

At the time Durham had a backlog of 60,000 unserved warrants, many of them more recent and involving more serious crimes than that for which Elmostafa was accused.

> The prosecutor's office or police collected evidence on Elmostafa that included his insurance and driving history, several years' worth of drug tests -- all of which were negative -- and a criminal record check.
>
> --News and Observer August 15, 2006

At Elmostafa's trial a security guard testified that he had seen a woman shoplifter race to his waiting taxi, jump into the back seat and that the taxi then sped off while the door of the taxi was still open--clear evidence, it was alleged, of the driver's knowledge of and cooperation with the crime. Investigators Himan and Clayton--another officer working on the Duke case--prominently attended the trial, although they were not involved in any way with investigating the shoplifting case. However, the defense produced a security tape which showed the shoplifter calmly approaching the cab and getting in the back seat and closing the door, with the taxi driving off at normal speed--thus refuting the security guard's testimony.

> "[It was like] going live with Geraldo Rivera when he opened Al Capone's vault: there was nothing there."
>
> --Ruth Sheehan, News and Observer.

Elmostafa was promptly acquitted.

> By a wide margin, readers chose Moezeldin Elmostafa of Durham, North Carolina, as the Reader's Digest 2008 Hero of the Year. . .
>
> Despite intense pressure from the prosecution, Elmostafa agreed to appear as a witness and helped exonerate the trio. Having recently passed his U. S. citizenship test, the Sudanese immigrant says he did only what all citizens should do --- tell the truth.
>
> –*"Plum Innocent",* Reader's Digest April 2008

> "I thought they were going to deport me, take away my green card and end my life here. . . I thought about that. [But] I tell the truth. . .so jail doesn't matter."
>
> -- Moezeldin Elmostafa

Although Elmostafa received a Hero of the Year award, and appeared on the Today show to discuss his experiences, he has never been recognized or honored as an exemplary citizen by either the city of Durham or the state of North Carolina. Neither has any civil rights organization, nor the Justice Department, ever exhibited any interest in his case.

Elmostafa was not the only potential witness to whom the police applied pressure.

At the end of March, with the investigation yielding no evidence, Nifong ordered his investigators to search through the players' emails. On the night of the party, after the players had returned to their dorms, one of them sent a gag email to his teammates intended to parody a text which was required reading in some courses at Duke: *American Psycho.* The lead character in *American Psycho* is a young executive on Wall

St., a graduate of Harvard, who at night becomes a mindless killer--dispatching various people in bizarre fashion--women, escort dancers, girlfriends, business rivals, the homeless, ethnic minorities, and others.

The email read, in part:

Tomorrow night, after tonight's show, I've decided to have some strippers over to Edens [dormitory address]. All are welcome. However there will be no nudity. I plan on killing the bitches as soon as they walk in and proceeding to cut their skin off...

That this was immediately recognized as a parody was shown by the first response to this email : *"I'll bring the Phil Collins"*. The music of Phil Collins was used as part of the soundtrack for the movie version of *American Psycho.*

"I start by skinning Torri a little, making incisions with a steak knife and ripping bits of flesh from her legs and stomach while she screams in pain, begging for mercy in a high, thin voice, and I'm hoping that she realizes her punishment will end up being relatively light compared to what I've planed for the other one. I keep spraying Torri with Mace and then I try to cut her fingers with nail scissors and finally I pour acid..."

--*American Psycho*

"Do you like Phil Collins? I've been a big Genesis fan ever since the release of their 1980 album, Duke."

-- *American Psycho*

In the full context of the email conversation, it was obvious satire.

> "Ryan McFadyen knows the e-mail was a wretched thing to write. That's why he wrote it, to get a yuk out of what he thought was a private audience by quoting a book (and movie) whose protagonist makes Marilyn Manson look like Mother Theresa – shock value."
>
> -- *"No Longer Villain, McFadyen Fires Up Duke 'D'"*, Lacrosse Magazine, Feb. 10, 2009

The Durham investigators, who had access to the entire email conversation, found another use for it. They separated it from its context and called in McFadyen to ask if he had any additional information to give them about the party. Like cabbie Elmostafa, McFadyen was not going to lie for the prosecutor. The investigators did not consider McFadyen a suspect in the rape case. Neither did their subsequent actions make it seem they believed he could be involved in a murder plot: they did not question any of the recipients of the email, nor search their rooms, nor prepare conspiracy to murder charges against any of them. After McFadyen's refusal to assist them all they did was add the extracted email quote to a request for a search warrant for McFadyen's room; and then in addition they appended the email to their request for an order requiring the lacrosse team members to provide DNA samples (though the email was irrelevant to the DNA issue). Doing so meant that the email would become part of the public record, accessible to the press.

In the first week after the quotes were published--breathing life into an expiring case, and fueling public indignation to an even greater level--McFadyen reportedly received over 1000 death threats. No professor at Duke, not even those who had made *American Psycho* required reading, made the effort to explain the source of the satire.

> It is the standard practice of the Durham Police Department to not release criminal investigative files for a variety of reasons including. . . protecting the reputation of persons who may be investigated but are never charged.
>
> ----Report of Durham Police Chief Chalmers to City Manager Patrick Baker on the Duke lacrosse investigation, May 11, 2007

Even earlier, in 2005, one of the defendants in the case, Collin Finnerty, was caught up in a minor student confrontation involving some friends and some patrons of a bar, outside an eatery in Georgetown. He was charged with yelling obscenities, some of which contained homophobic slurs (although his "victim" was not alleged to be homosexual), and waving his fists in the air (but not with hitting anyone) after he was struck from behind and knocked down. By some accounts his involvement began with no more than an attempt to separate two quarrelers, after which he found himself attacked. When police arrived he was cited but given a diversion agreement--meaning his citation would disappear in six months if he did not get into any further trouble; Initially he wanted to fight the citation and plead not guilty, but was persuaded to just accept it as a minor annoyance and simply move on.

> [Witness G] said that he saw the first blow, which was Mr. Herndon hitting Mr. Finnerty in the back of the head. [Witness B] said he had not seen it but had looked up and seen Mr. Finnerty sprawled on the ground with Messrs. Bloxsom and Herndon standing over him. [Witnesses D and B] hastened to help Mr. Finnerty, [witness B] punched Mr. Bloxsom, the fight petered out, and Messrs. Finnerty, [witnesses D and B] went down N Street.
>
> --*"Collin Finnerty's D.C. Assault Conviction Is The Disgrace",* Michael Gaynor, July 14, 2006

Approximately a dozen such student altercations occur each weekend night in Georgetown, and most are settled with nothing more than a citation. Many of these involve students who are drunk, and in some instances property damage or injury results. Students punching bouncers or other revelers are not unknown. In 2000, a student punched another student, who died after his head struck the pavement.

> Georgetown junior David Shick was punched in the face on Feb. 18, 2000, and hit his head on the concrete sidewalk in the Lauinger Library parking lot, dying four days later from injuries sustained by hitting the ground. While his death was ruled a homicide by the D.C. medical examiner, the influence of alcohol in the case led the U.S. Attorney's Office to believe that there was not a "reasonable likelihood of obtaining a conviction," and the case was never prosecuted.
>
> -- Georgetown *Hoya* April 20, 2004

Shick's assailant was ultimately ordered to write a ten-page paper about the incident by his university.

When Finnerty was indicted in Durham, his diversion agreement in Washington was revoked because one of its conditions was that he not violate any law. This was done even though he was only the passive object of another's accusation. The Washington court was asked to delay action until the outcome of the Durham allegations was resolved, but refused. Instead the court placed Finnerty under a 9:00 PM to 6:00 AM curfew until trial and imposed a prohibition against his being in any place where alcohol was sold or consumed; which included restaurants, gas stations with convenience stores, and commuter trains with bars.

By July 2006, when Finnerty came to trial for his Georgetown charges, it is more than likely the DC court knew that the

Durham charges were false. DNA testing had cleared all the lacrosse players in April. Hence, it followed that the accusation which resulted in his arrest was fraudulent (and thus, he was not in violation of his original agreement, save perhaps in a technical sense). In fact, because the American legal system is built on the presumption of innocence, the court was required to consider that he was innocent, until he might be proven otherwise. **A judge in DC could not decide that Finnerty had violated the law (and hence violated the terms of his agreement) unless he was ruling on the issue of guilt or innocence in Durham.**

But by then the media had been aroused, and the Durham case had become the reverse of the Scottsboro Trials--a paradigm of race, class, and gender inequalities.

Hordes of press descended on the DC courtroom; and the US Attorney, who is the prosecutor for the District of Columbia, assigned eight federal attorneys, assisted by nine additional staff, to pursue the case. A two-day trial ensued. (The O. J. Simpson murder prosecution team generally used only thirteen attorneys and staff, for a case which involved complicated evidence and lasted several months.)

The US Attorney at the time, Ken Wainstein, was awaiting confirmation by the Senate to be Assistant Attorney General for Counter-Terrorism. He had just adroitly avoided having to prosecute congresswoman Cynthia McKinney for striking a Capitol police officer, by passing the decision on whether or not to charge her to a Grand Jury--which chose not to indict. He also avoided having to prosecute Congressman Kennedy for running his car into a street obstruction while under the influence of medication.

According to the police report, Kennedy drove his car into a security barrier near the Capitol building. When questioned by the police, he told them that he was "headed to the Capitol to make a vote," when no votes were scheduled for that time of the morning [approximately 2:45 a.m.]. (Wikinews)

Kennedy was also ordered to pay a $250 donation to the Boys and Girls Club of Greater Washington and a $100 donation to the Victims of Crime fund. Judge Melendez also ordered Kennedy to serve a 10-day jail sentence, but said if he followed the terms of his plea, then he won't have to serve the time. Kennedy is also on a one-year probation and must seek drug treatment.(Wikinews)

Coz Carson, a spokesman for McKinney, said the requested warrant should be dismissed if "this is a prosecutor who's not a politician."

--The Atlanta Journal-Constitution, April 4, 2006

Washington – The grand jury investigation of 4th District Congresswoman Cynthia McKinney enters its third month today with no hint from the federal prosecutor about how much longer it will take to settle a case that legal experts said should have been wrapped up in a matter of days.

--Atlanta Journal-Constitution June 2006

> In legal terms, McKinney's case "is as simple as you can get," said George Washington University legal expert Jonathan Turley. Usually anyone who hits a police officer is immediately arrested on felony charges, police and legal experts said.
>
> --Atlanta Journal-Constitution June 2006

As an example of the sentiment prevalent in Washington, in mid-May 2007 the Rev. Anthony Evans, president of the D.C. Black Church Initiative, roundly criticized Wainstein in a letter circulated to the press, for devoting too little effort in trying to solve crimes against blacks, while at the same time appearing to focus excessively on solving crimes against whites (citing as an example, the efforts to solve the murder of New York Times reporter David E. Rosenbaum: "From our vantage point there were three mitigating factors why you did this: 1) he was a white male, 2) he was a prominent journalist and 3) he was Jewish.")

Evans also scolded that Wainstein observed "a double standard when it comes to race. . . you have demonstrated that you devalue the deaths of those individuals by the scant amount of resources that you have devoted to solving those cases."

Wainstein, as U.S. Attorney for the District of Columbia, therefore found himself under constant and intense political scrutiny.

On the second day of the trial, a British tourist (and political activist) was murdered during a mugging in DC while trying to protect his woman companion. The Chief of the Metropolitan police thereupon declared a "crime emergency".

Washington DC Police Chief Declares Crime Emergency

Led by the Metropolitan Police Department, the FBI's Washington Field Office and the US Attorney's Office, the task force will investigate pending cases and dedicate increased resources to identify and apprehend persons responsible for robberies and other violent crimes in the District.

--American Chronicle, July 25, 2006

Yet the U.S Attorney evidently did not feel it was impossible, or imprudent, to devote the services of seventeen personnel and tie up a court for two days for a common misdemeanor assault (in which it was not even alleged that anyone had been struck).

"Justice is simply the advantage of the stronger."

--the Greek philosopher Thrasymachus

I spoke to US Attorney Ben Curtis [in DC]. He spoke to me about the case in reference to Collin Finnerty gave me information on the case. He stated he could send info but would need a letter on letter head from Durham PD and then permission from his boss. I faxed a letter at 1551 hours.

---Gottlieb's reconstructed notes for April 13, 2006

In urging the judge to order Finnerty to trial, Assistant U.S. Attorney Ben Curtis said there were "similarities" between the two cases. Both happened late at night with other lacrosse players and while consuming alcohol, Curtis said.

--USA Today April 25, 2006

Earlier this year, prosecutors agreed to dismiss Finnerty's misdemeanor assault charge if he stayed out of trouble and completed 25 hours of community service. But yesterday they revoked that deal in light of the allegations at Duke and said they plan to take the case to trial.

"The dynamics of the case have changed drastically," said Assistant U.S. Attorney O. Benton Curtis III.

--Washington Post, April 25, 2006

The two asserted victims of the alleged assault testified in their own behalf. Four witnesses testified for Finnerty. The two police officers who issued the citations "remembered" things about that night which were not in their notes; even though this was months later. The chief defense witness--and a man who was a member of neither party, but was the bartender/ bouncer for a local eatery--took the stand only to be ordered immediately to step down again. For reasons not made public, he was not allowed to testify.

[Arresting officer] Wright said Bloxsom also told him that Finnerty was the instigator. Defense lawyer Steven McCool questioned why Wright never put that fact in any of his reports. Wright responded that police reports do not include all the information he collects at a crime scene.

--WRAL, July 10, 2006

The result was that the judge (there was no jury) convicted the Finnerty of assault, sentenced him to thirty days in jail (suspended); six months' probation; six months' banning from Georgetown; a fine; counseling; required him to be at work or at school (although he couldn't attend Duke because Duke had suspended him; nor would Duke at this time permit a transfer of credits from other schools); and strict adherence to a curfew.

The media responded as primed :

"[Finnerty has] a demonstrated history of picking on disenfranchised people, whether it's race, gender, or sexuality... Obviously this is a guy who thinks wealthy white boys are better than the rest of the world."

(Wendy Murphy, "Rita Cosby Live & Direct," MSNBC, 25 April 2006)

Probation rendered him liable to incarceration at any time, at the behest of the judge, should be he found in violation again. That this was no idle threat was demonstrated more than once; as when, for example, an anonymous blog-posting falsely claimed that Finnerty had been seen partying in Georgetown; and when he missed a curfew check once because he was away from home--in Durham, preparing for his defense--with the permission of the court's own monitoring agency. Nevertheless, the first reaction of the judge on learning of these two instances was to immediately and publicly threaten him with being jailed for violating the conditions of his probation.

The strong inference assumed by some observers was that he could avoid the close monitoring (and the constant threat of being incarcerated in the racially-tensioned District of Columbia jail) if he would cooperate with the Durham prosecutor and testify against his fellow defendants.

After the Durham case was finally dismissed, and there was talk that the two asserted victims in the DC case might have changed their stories and perjured themselves while testifying, and thus should be prosecuted, the U.S. Attorney for the District (successor to Wainstein) honored some two dozen witnesses for coming forward to testify in District cases.

Among those whose heroism was recognized was a woman who witnessed a street killing and willingly testified against the murderer (though knowing she might face retaliation from him); a woman who saw a drug-related murder and then the murder of another witness, and who and was herself threatened more than once with death if she testified; and three children whose mother was killed while they slept, but who still managed to help police solve the crime. Included also were Jeffrey Bloxsom and Scott Herdon.

> U.S. Attorney Recognizes 25 Heroes
> Award Honors Those Who Help Nab Criminals
>
> ———
>
> "You are the how and why of our criminal justice system," U.S. Attorney Jeffrey Taylor told the crime victims and survivors who attended the ceremony at the U.S. Attorney's Office. "We celebrate heroes who know that without their assistance, we can't make these cases."
>
> --Washington Post,
> May 2, 2007

The witnesses in the lacrosse case who refused to be intimidated—Elmostafa, McFadyen, and Finnerty; as well as the other members of the lacrosse team who were threatened by Nifong with arraignment for "aiding and abetting"—were never honored by either law enforcement or the judicial system.

FOR IMMEDIATE RELEASE For Information, Contact Public Affairs
Thursday, July 13, 2006
Duke lacrosse player convicted of assault for unprovoked attack on Georgetown resident

Washington, D.C. A Duke University student and lacrosse player, Collin H. Finnerty, was convicted of assault for an unprovoked attack in Georgetown, United States Attorney Kenneth L. Wainstein announced today.

Finnerty, 19, was found guilty on Tuesday, July 11, 2006, after a two-day trial in the Superior Court of the District of Columbia, of misdemeanor simple assault by the Honorable John H. Bayly, Jr. The Court subsequently sentenced the defendant to 30 days of incarceration, but suspended the sentence and put the defendant on six months probation, with requirements that he participate in drug and alcohol counseling, as necessary, and pay $500 in costs. The Court also ordered the defendant to stay away from the Georgetown area of the District of Columbia and any establishments that sell or serve alcohol during the course of his probation.

In announcing the court's verdict and sentence, United States Attorney Wainstein praised the outstanding efforts of Metropolitan Police Department Officer Vincent Wright and Crime Scene Search Officer Israel Ruiz. He also commended the efforts of the United States Attorney's Office Criminal Investigation Unit, specifically Investigator Melissa Matthews and Special Agent Alan McDonald of the United States Secret Service. Mr. Wainstein also acknowledged Ray McCallister, of the U.S. Attorney's Office's Intelligence Unit, Jennifer Clark and Dr. Lorraine Chase of the U.S. Attorney's Office's Victim/Witness Assistance Unit, Assistant United

States Attorneys Elizabeth Trosman, David Goodhand, Tom Tourish, Roy McCleese and Valinda Jones of the U.S. Attorney's Office's Appellate Division, Litigation Support Technician Ronald Royal, Support Staff members Shirrell Jackson and Agnes Heard, and Legal Intern Anna Scanlon, for their invaluable work and support on this case. Finally, Mr. Wainstein praised the work of Special Assistant United States Attorney O. Benton Curtis, who investigated the case, and Assistant United States Attorneys George Varghese and Rhonda Redwood who prosecuted the case.

FOR COMPARISON: A PAIR OF OTHER DECISIONS BY THE SAME JUDGE

Cop Busted in D.C. Police Week Rape

A New York City police officer was charged with rape yesterday after he allegedly forced a woman to have sex in a Washington hotel room during National Police Week, authorities said.

——

He was part of a contingent of city cops in the nation's capital for National Police Week.

In 1995, several NYPD officers attending the event engaged in rowdy behavior, including stripping in a hotel lobby and spraying a fire extinguisher in the hallways.

(New York Daily News, May 17th 2003)

——

Wednesday, 10/13/04

Fired Cop who raped woman gets felony, fine and probation

New York - A former New York City police officer charged with raping a woman in Washington, D.C., was sentenced to 24 months probation and a $2,000 fine yesterday under the terms of a plea bargain.

[.....] who was fired by the NYPD on Aug. 20, will not spend any time in jail for the felony conviction on fourth-degree sexual abuse. District of Columbia Superior Court Judge John Bayly suspended the sentence of 12 months in prison. "I think that the sentence was a very just sentence, and justice was served," said defense lawyer Marybeth Manfreda.

The victim in the case, a woman who was a police cadet in Virginia at the time of the incident, testified on videotape that [.....] attacked her in a hotel bathroom after they met at National Police Week events in May 2003. She said she was too intoxicated from a party earlier in the night to resist. "I will never forgive him for what he did to me," the woman said in her taped victim statement.

After media coverage of the case, a second woman in Queens reported she had also been sexually assaulted by [.....]

WASHINGTON -- A man who claimed to have a cellphone implanted in his head was convicted Friday of jumping a White House fence in a bid to meet former president Bill Clinton's daughter Chelsea.

[.....] was sentenced to 150 days in jail but a District of Columbia Superior Court judge suspended the sentence -- with the stipulation [.....] stay at least one block away from the executive mansion. He also was fined $50.

Judge John Bayly rejected a prosecution request for a stay-away order covering the Capitol and Senate office buildings.

In 2007 a student from Georgetown University was accused of assaulting someone who was gay and denigrating him with epithets. The local gay community was in an uproar, as there had been several such incidents recently which had gone unsolved. The police were under great pressure to find the assailant--any assailant, quickly. They identified a possible suspect on the basis of a third-party partially overhead conversation, and some initials on the backpack of one of the speakers. The accused was never questioned by police himself and was unable to present his alibi, he was simply arrested in class during an examination. "The police investigation was nothing," said his attorney. After it was discovered that he was the son of a former Bush administration official, the media touted his arrest and his guilt was presented in many media outlets as though it were an established fact. Months passed; the person who overheard the conversation now denied having heard anyone discussing the gay bashing incident. The accused passed a lie-detector test given by a retired FBI expert. The DC prosecutors pressured the accused to accept a plea deal; if he would plead guilty he would just receive probation. If not, he would be liable to 270 days in jail if convicted. He refused the plea offer. In hearings, his attorney seemed to know more about the case than the prosecutor. For nine months the US attorney let the prosecution simmer, before finally dropping the case for lack of evidence. The emotional and financial cost to a student of being kept under suspicion and the threat of jail for the length of a school year evidently was not figured into the accounting.

> Meet Jeffrey Taylor. He is the United States Attorney for the District of Columbia, and he is a prime example of one of the principal rules of the politics of prosecution: *public perception, combined with the overwhelming need to cover your butt, creates a strong incentive for a Prosecutor to ignore his duty to fairly and impartially administer the law.*
>
> ---
>
> With the pressure of *appearing* to do something about attacks on gays and lesbians in Washington, D.C., it is apparent that United States Attorney Jeffrey Taylor does not want to *appear* to give [______] any special treatment by dismissing his case, even though his prosecutors would do so in any other case with similar facts.
>
> --Politics of Prosecution, Dec. 2, 2007

Meanwhile, there were more arrests in Durham. The former husband of the accuser, Kenneth McNeil; her boyfriend, Matthew Murchison; and another close friend were jailed on various charges, with the disposition of their cases entirely in the hands of District Attorney Nifong. While jailed, they were unable to be contacted by the press, give statements, offer opinions, or sell their stories to the media.

> DURHAM -- Durham police served two [past] criminal summonses on Police Chief Steve Chalmers' daughter Friday, saying it hadn't been done before because nobody knew they existed.
>
> --News and Observer Jun. 24, 2006

Amazingly, the Chief of the Durham Police Department would absent himself from his office for most of the duration of the lacrosse case; it was Nifong, not the Chief, who appeared before the media to make announcements. In the biggest case of his career; in Durham's history; and in the history of his department; with satellite trucks lining the curbs and a full panoply of international coverage--the Chief became "the invisible man".

> DURHAM -- The panel looking into the Police Department's handling of the Duke lacrosse case has many questions for law enforcement officers. At the top of the list is: "Where was Chief Steve Chalmers when Mike Nifong took over the investigation?"
>
> --News and Observer, July 21, 2007

On May 15, a third lacrosse player, David Evans, was indicted. The grand jury hearing his case heard 82 other cases the day it considered his. Again, no records were kept of its proceedings. The day before Evans had graduated from Duke, but had to miss the graduation ceremony because of publicity surrounding the case. Before being formally arrested, Evans addressed the media in front of the courthouse.

> **David Evans Press Conference**
> May 15, 2006
>
> My name is Dave Evans, and I'm the captain of the Duke University men's lacrosse team...
>
> First I want to say that I am absolutely innocent of all the charges that have been brought against me today; that Reade Seligmann and Collin Finnerty are innocent of all the charges that were brought against them. These allegations are lies, fabricated, and they will be proven wrong.
>
> ——

Over the past several weeks I have repeatedly through my lawyers tried to contact the district attorney. All of my attempts have been denied. I've tried to provide him with exculpatory evidence, showing that this could not have happened. Those attempts have been denied.

And as a result of his apparent lack of interest in my story — the true story — and any evidence proving that my story is correct, I asked my lawyer to get me a polygraph. I took that polygraph, and it was administered by a former FBI top polygrapher with over 28 years of experience. He's done several hundreds of sexual cases, and I passed it absolutely. And I passed that polygraph for the same reason that I will be acquitted of all these charges, because I have done nothing wrong and I am telling the truth, and I have told the truth from day one.

I'd like to say thank you to my friends and family, my coach and members of the community who have stood by us, through everything from the initial weeks to now. Their support has given me the strength to come through this. But the thing that gives me the most strength is knowing that I have the truth behind me, and it will not faze me...

If I can clear things up and say this one more time, I am innocent, Reade Seligmann is innocent, Collin Finnerty is innocent. Every member of the Duke University lacrosse team is innocent.

You have all been told some fantastic lies, and I look forward in watching them unravel in the weeks to come as they already have in weeks past and the truth will come out.

Thank you for your time.

From Scottsboro:

SCOTTSBORO PETITION

SMASH LYNCH JUSTICE!

Demand the unconditional and safe release of the Scottsboro boys!

The Scottsboro boys are innocent…The lynchers do not give up their victims easily. Ruby Bates, whose forced testimony was partially instrumental in bringing them to within the shadow of the electric chair, now testifies to the boys' innocence. But the Scottsboro boys remain in jail, and Thomas E. Knight, for the State of Alabama, is again preparing a legal lynch trial for them.

Forced by mass protest, Judge Horton's decision broke down the false testimony of Victoria Price, yet the State of Alabama still continues to prosecute the boys. Judge Horton stated that the "weight of the evidence" is in their favor, and the law of the State of Alabama holds that where the weight of the evidence favors the defendant, bail must be granted. The innocent boys have not been granted bail and are being tortured in jail.

WE, THE UNDERSIGNED, THEREFORE, DO MOST VIGOROUSLY PROTEST AGAINST THE CONTINUED PERSECUTION OF THE NINE SCOTTSBORO BOYS, AND DEMAND THAT THEY BE IMMEDIATELY RELEASED ON BAIL.

WE, FURTHER, DEMAND THEIR UNCONDITIONAL AND SAFE RELEASE.

PETITION FOR JUSTICE IN THE DUKE LACROSSE CASE

Martin Luther King said," Injustice anywhere is a threat to justice everywhere". The current prosecution in the Duke Lacrosse case and its examples of prosecutorial abuse are a matter of concern for all of us. They decrease public confidence in the reliability of our judicial system. We believe that prosecutors are not appointed to represent only one side of a case, but that they represent the State. Their obligation to the court is nonpartisan, it is colorblind, it is nondenominational; it is an obligation to Justice and all have an equal right to it, including defendants.

In examining the current Duke Lacrosse case to determine whether it should be prosecuted, any prosecutor must be aware of the fact that his complaining witness has committed to ever-changing stories that are a series of fabrications. That prosecutor therefore ethically cannot proceed with putting that witness on the stand. He must also be aware of the scientific evidence presented by the negative DNA results. It is abundantly evident that he cannot pursue this matter further, and that it must be dismissed for want of any corroborating evidence.

As with all defendants, the defendants in the Duke Lacrosse case are entitled to justice, and they are entitled to it swiftly; any further delay is a simply a continuation of the injury done them already. Moreover, in some quarters, delay may even be seen as providing some type of legitimacy for originally bringing the charges against them in the first place. That would be yet another egregious affront to Justice.

We therefore join in calling upon the Attorney General of North Carolina to bring this matter to a swift and just resolution, through a dismissal with prejudice of all charges, and to do so without concern for public pressure or opinion; but solely with the intention of seeing, as Justice Horton advised, that justice be done, 'though the heavens fall.'

Hearing May 18, 2006

JUDGE RONALD STEPHENS [former District Attorney of Durham Co.] DURHAM CO., N.C. SUPERIOR COURT: Gentlemen, remove your hats.

OSBORN: [defense counsel] ... And actually, there's a notice of hearing as to some particular matters we'd like to get heard today. They're very brief. But they are necessary in order to prevent the spoilization of evidence.

STEPHENS: Right. Well, I understand your notice of hearing. But I'll determine what's heard today. Obviously, you understand that. . .

STEPHENS: Let me talk. That's fine. Let me ask -- Mr. Nifong, I mean, I'm assuming this phone you're talking about was the one seized in the search warrant?

NIFONG: Yes.

STEPHENS: And seized at the residence?

NIFONG: Yes. Found outside by the boys, and they gave it to the...

OSBORN: Well, objection to that.

STEPHENS: Well, wait a minute. I'm going to let you both talk.

NIFONG: It was -- it was found outside the next day by the boys. They brought it inside. And the cops showed up with a search warrant. They said, look, we found this outside. Her purse as well. And then, of course, led them to, you know, fingernails they'd thrown in the trash can.

NIFONG: I would wonder what evidence he thinks that he's entitled to would be on that telephone.

STEPHENS: Well, frankly, if you have your folks do that, and the court can truly review that in camera, then I can determine whether or not there may be something there that may or may not be otherwise discoverable.

NIFONG: Mr. Osborn seemed to think that we could not do this in such a way that it would protect the integrity of the telephone's contents. And that seems to be why he filed this motion.

STEPHENS: Well, frankly ...

OSBORN: Why wouldn't we be entitled, Your Honor, to find out if she were calling people from the house? Why wouldn't we be entitled to that? Why wouldn't we be able to know last 10 calls that she made? And the important thing is -- and I've been through this, Your Honor.

If it is not done properly and if it not done now, the battery loses its charge and when the battery loses its charge, the data in the phone itself disappears. And so -- and if it's started up without being charged, if there's -- if it's not handed properly ...

STEPHENS: I hear you.

OSBORN: You could lose the information.

NIFONG: Well, Your Honor we have our own, dare I use the term, expert, at the police department who is reviewing the cell phones that were seized, computer disks and things of that nature. And he has not processed this yet, to my knowledge.

STEPHENS: Well, it's my understanding that this may be a phone that actually was a third party's phone or could -- or was it -- do you know whether or not it was her cell phone or ...

NIFONG: I do not know right off hand.

STEPHENS: So we may have third, or fourth parties who have some privacy interest in this themselves.

NIFONG: Conceivably.

STEPHENS: Whatever comes from this, the court would like to review that in chambers to make sure that, frankly, something that should not -- has no reason to be made public unless there's some need for it or some legitimate reason for it to protect the interests, privacy interests of others who are not involved in this.

[The judge appears to be very solicitous of protecting the names and privacy--and perhaps identity--of any persons who might have been in phone contact with the accuser.]

OSBORN: Yes, sir. Are you prepared to hear a bond reduction motion?

STEPHENS: No, sir.

OSBORN: Could we get a date for it?

STEPHENS: Well, your client's out on bond.

OSBORN: Yes, but he's out on bond on, you know, money that's borrowed from the family. And, you know, we have submitted, you know, what we think is a pretty clear alibi defense that's, you know, air- tight. And we have a box of material from, you know, senators, congressmen, friends, you know, that say that he's not a flight risk. And we think that $400,000 is ...

STEPHENS: $400,000 is within the guidelines for the nature of this charge.* And that's -- this court set that bond. Is it right, frankly, in the guidelines. That's what the bond would generally be, initially. [*The bond of $400,000 was actually almost unprecedented in the history of Durham up until that time.] I'm not going to hear your bond -- since he's out on bond, not going to hear your bond request today. . .

———

OSBORN: And then, your honor, I understand that it is custom at least in this county that we would be permitted to actually go over to the law enforcement officer's agency and actually go through their files, all their files, all their notes and so forth, personally.

STEPHENS: Well I'm not aware of that custom. I believe perhaps maybe that's your take on the custom. I'm not aware of that custom. I mean you surely have the discovery process and you have what you're allowed by statute and then, frankly, whatever else the D.A. allows is his call.

OSBORN: Yes, sir.

STEPHENS: And so whatever he otherwise allows, voluntarily is his call. If you find something that you think that you need and that he's not allowing, then again, this court is the place to come to ask for that. No, sir, I'm not going to sign an order allowing you to go over and rummage through the law enforcement officer's files.

OSBORN: Would you sign an order requiring the law enforcement officers to turn over all of their notes, memoranda, reports, documents, data compilations, tape recordings and so forth to the district attorney?

STEPHENS: No, sir. I'll allow him to proceed as he normally does in the compilation of his information. And if thereafter for some reason you believe that you have not received everything, then we'll address that with the court order. Right now I'm not going to order things that I believe will be done voluntarily. There's no reason for me to believe as they always generally have been, they won't be done voluntarily.

OSBORN: Yes, sir. This is a serious case.

STEPHENS: I deal with serious cases every day, and frankly I respect the seriousness of this case. But this case is not going to jump ahead of the line of all the other cases that we have here or be handled in any other way. I surely respect everyone here and the seriousness of this.

But frankly, it takes priority, but we have other cases that take priority, too. And we're not going to stop what we're doing to make sure that we accommodate everybody inappropriately.

OSBORN: Well we just want to make sure, your honor, that all of the things that have been generated be preserved and that we get a chance to see them pursuant to statute, we're entitled to look through all of the law enforcement files and we just want to make sure that nothing disappears. And I think you can assure that with our order that nothing be destroyed. And I will get an order to you in that regard.

—

OSBORN: We want to -- I want a trial as fast as we can. This young kid wants to go to school in the fall.

STEPHENS: OK.

OSBORN: And he can't until this is resolved.

STEPHENS: Well I mean, I understand and appreciate that. But again, given the number of cases that we've got in front of it and everything else, I can't surely can't assure you of that. All I can do is comply with your requests if they're reasonable. . .

From Scottsboro:

Third Scottsboro Trial, November 1933, Judge William Callahan presiding

LIEBOWITZ [defense counsel] : [Who accompanied you (Victoria Price) on the train?]

JUDGE CALLAHAN : I can't allow the time of the court [to be] wasted on matters so immaterial. You mustn't ask that question again.

—

LIEBOWITZ : Had you had sexual intercourse with any man the night before you left Huntsville?

JUDGE CALLAHAN: [The witness is instructed not to answer.]

LIEBOWITZ: May I state the reason for it [the question]?

JUDGE CALLAHAN: No, sir. I think I know.

—

LIEBOWTIZ: [asks about the hobo encampment at Chattanooga]

JUDGE CALLAHAN: That is far enough for me to know all I want to know, to know that the question is illegal.

—

JUDGE CALLAHAN : Let's don't take up time on that; that is a waste of time.

—

JUDGE CALLAHAN : That's enough of that.

LIEBOWITZ: No, your honor, I want to ...

JUDGE CALLAHAN: You are mistaken, that is enough of that; go on to something else.

Almost no records were retained of the lacrosse investigation. Some relevant police tapes from the night of March 14 were destroyed ("routinely") by the Durham police department even though the defense had filed a motion asking that they be preserved. When the defense asked that the officers involved be called to testify as to what was said that night, Nifong asserted that he did not believe they would be able to accurately remember their conversations. (In August, six months after the event, Gottlieb claimed to be able to recreate from memory 33 typed pages of notes.)

No photographs were kept of daily blackboard or other board charts noting the progress of the investigation.

Almost no notes were kept by investigating officers. During three separate visits to a private DNA testing lab in another county, in which officers Himan and Gottlieb accompanied District Attorney Nifong, neither the lab, nor the District Attorney, nor the officers, kept any notes. There was, in effect, little preserved by way of a paper trail.

Standard police procedure calls for the making and retention of notes during any investigation. Officers carry log books (or field note books) in which they record every significant event of the day. Books are to be open to inspection by superior officers during random checks and signed off at the end of each watch.

> 1. The pages of an officer's log should be consecutively numbered and the log should be bound together so individual pages cannot be removed. All entries should be in ink.
>
> ———
>
> 3. Skipping lines should be prohibited.
>
> 4. Erasures should be prohibited. Errors should be corrected by drawing a line through the incorrect entry, initialing it, and writing the correct information
>
> --*Police Sergeant Exam*, by Donald J. Schroder, Frank A Lombardo, p. 292.

> Using the notebook (Notetaking)
>
> 1. Number the pages of your notebook.
>
> ———
>
> 4. No erasures; Stroke through a mistake and initial it.
>
> 5. Do not rip out or skip pages. Do not skip lines
>
> 6. Do not destroy notes.
>
> ———
>
> Last entry followed immediately by officer's signature
>
> -- *"Code of police practice: A guide for first line officers"*, The Canadian Association of Chiefs of Police

Details regarding the times of arrivals and departures, the names of persons contacted, their identifying characteristics, evidence discovered, and how and by whom that evidence was handled, are all essential parts of record-keeping. Sketches and charts may be added when useful, and distances should be measured. If possible, the exact words used by witnesses and suspects should be retained.

CT = Clear throat   DB = Deep breath or sigh...
DII = Direct eye to eye contact

! = Loud or emphasized   Lgh = Laugh (erasure)
SIC = Shift in chair

--*Possible Note Taking Abbreviations for Nonverbal Behavior*
(John E. Reid & Associates)

Q. Going back to the type written notes, first tell me other than the three pages of handwritten notes here, were there other notes that you prepared in the Duke lacrosse cases?

A. I believe I had wrote like a date or a time on different documents. But as far as me taking notes, I really wasn't doing an investigation. So, no, I didn't take handwritten notes. I was acting as a supervisor just trying to coordinate things.

Q. I take it then there are not separate notes like you'd have, for example, a legal pad where you had written out things that happened?

A. No, sir.

Q. Okay. So, for example, if you were participating in an interview with Ms. Mangum with Investigator Himan, you didn't have a separate pad where you kept notes of what she said or questions that were asked? You had no handwritten notes of that type of -- in that situation, for example?

A. Absolutely not. Investigator Himan was keeping the notes. I wasn't there as an investigator. I was there, one, as a witness because we did it in her house; two, to give him advice if there were something that he needed advice on. It was his investigation. And for anything else that happened to come up.

———

Q. Let me see if I am understanding you. From the 15th of 2006, March 15, 2006, through this meeting on April 4th [the first two weeks of the investigation] where you were asked to prepare a time line for the City Manager, you had not kept typewritten notes of the investigation up to that. The ones that we now see here they didn't exist on the 4th.

A. No, not to my knowledge.

———

A. The case -- I never took handwritten notes, per se. I kept track of my activities by radio log. Meaning, if I stopped at somebody's house, I called in to police dispatch. If I was doing something, I called in to police dispatch for that. If I went out to Duke to assist them, I would call in to police dispatch, keeping track of that. Again, this --is Ben's [Himan's] operation. This is pretty much something that Ben is responsible for keeping up with the case. I'm there as his supervisor, and I wasn't keeping up with the notes as far as that goes.

———

A. Sir, we had meetings every day with command staff, the District Attorney's office. And I'm not saying that we met with him every day. But if I kept track of meetings, I would probably have thousands of pages.

Q. Was there any discussion during that conversation about letting the Department have some more time to develop additional facts before going forward with the indictment?

A. Well, I told him [Nifong] our concerns and basically he made the decision. I don't remember the exact conversation.

Q. And did you keep any kind of notes of that conversation with Mr. Nifong?

A. No.

Q. To your knowledge, did anybody in the Department keep any notes of that conversation?

A. I don't know. . .

Q. You don't know of any notes that were kept?

A. I don't.

Q. Okay. Did Mr. Nifong ask any questions during any of these meetings with Dr. Meehan about the results?

A. Not that I recall. It is always possible, but I just don't recall.

Q. Did Mr. Nifong take notes of any of the meetings or during any of the meetings with Dr. Meehan?

A. I don't know. I'm sorry, I don't know.

Q. And in your other meetings, not the ones with Dr. Meehan, but the other meetings that you would have with Mr. Nifong, would it be his practice to take notes if you were sitting down and having conversation with him?

A. Just very casual. No, not that I recall.

Q. I take it from your previous answer that you didn't take any handwritten notes of the meetings that you had with Dr. Meehan?

A. Oh, no, not with Dr. Meehan.

Q. And did you . . .

A. I really didn't take notes like that. . . would get information and put it in later.

Q. And did Investigator Himan, do you recall if he took notes at the meetings?

A. I don't recall. Investigator Himan was very -- I was very impressed with him. He was very meticulous in what he did, and that's all I can remember. [Investigator Himan took no notes.]

--Deposition of Sgt. Mark Gottlieb for the Disciplinary Hearing Commission of the North Carolina State Bar April 19, 2007

Q. I think I know the answer, but let me make sure. Did you keep any kind of log or record of what you provided to Mr. Nifong during the course of the investigation, documents that were provided?

A. No, there was no log. I know when discovery came, basically he said, basically around every other week or every near the end of the month, he would ask for anything new, and that is when I would update him.

Q. Okay. And how often would you say that you met or spoke with Mr. Nifong about the investigation?

A. I would say probably every other day to daily. I don't know if it was directly with him or not. It may be--some of the things there was just nothing happening so I wouldn't go up and tell him nothing was happening. I would just--just if something came up, I would go up and tell him what we had.

--Deposition of Investigator Himan for the Disciplinary Hearing Commission of the North Carolina State Bar May 8, 2007

96. Police Videotaping of Suspects

1. The . . . Regional Police Service should amend its operational manual to provide that all interviews conducted with suspects within a police station be videotaped or audiotaped, absent truly exigent circumstances. Any practice of interviewing a suspect off-camera before a formal videotaped interview undermines this policy. Similarly, a practice of encouraging suspects to speak off the record or off-camera during an interview undermines this policy. Videotaping or audiotaping ultimately narrows trial issues, shortens trials, protects both the interviewer

> and the interviewee from unfounded allegations and encourages compliance with the law; such a policy also enables the parties and the triers of fact to evaluate the extent to which the interviewing process enhanced or undermined the reliability of the statement.
>
> --*Report of the Kaufman Commission on Proceedings Involving Guy Paul Morin*:
>
> The Honourable Fred Kaufman CM QC 31 March 1998

Officers did not re-interview the accuser when evidence was presented which conflicted with her stories. According to Nifong, he never personally spoke with the accuser about the case until January, more than ten months after the case began.

> [After earlier stating her belief that the rape allegations were "a crock"] Roberts later told NEWSWEEK she believed a rape could have happened. In the meantime, Nifong, who declined a request for comment, had approved a motion to eliminate Roberts's bond payments stemming from a prior conviction.
>
> --Newsweek, June 19,2006

Key witnesses who might have contributed vital information were not interviewed until months into the case. The security guard at the Kroger's who had called the police on March 14 was not contacted until December 7. The co-workers of the accuser at the Platinum club, who could have testified that she was working as usual within days after the purported rape, were not interviewed until November, if at all.

From the first it was clear that this was not going to be a routine case. It was arguably the biggest case in Durham's history and in the history of the department. The city and its police would be under a spotlight as never before. And yet it was a case in which the most common police procedures were not followed; in which notes were not retained; in which evidence was allowed to degrade or was erased; in which defense witnesses were arrested while others went uninterviewed; and from which the chief of police absented himself for months.

By way of contrast, in 2009 when four persons were accused of gang-raping a student at Hofstra university, the District Attorney examined a cell phone video of the event and determined the accuser was lying. The accused were immediately released from jail. There were two cell phone videos made of the lacrosse party; Nifong refused to look at them, or at any of the other evidence offered him by the defense counsel. To many observers it seemed that he wanted to avoid having to see evidence of innocence, in order to be able to deny later that he was aware of it.

In July 2006 two of the police investigators were allegedly involved, at least on the periphery (although by some accounts their involvement was more direct) in "Rodney King South", an incident in which some off-duty drunken police officers knocked a black cook to the ground at an eatery and then allegedly kicked him in the head, while deriding him with racial epithets. The ramifications for the lacrosse prosecution of having some of its of investigators caught up in a racially charged incident could have been severe. In the opinion of some observers, the charges against the police investigators were adroitly steered through the North Carolina judicial system, in such a way as to avoid harm to the lacrosse investigation. There was very little publicity given to the incident; and unlike the Los Angeles case, the federal government exhibited no interest.

During Fiscal Year 2005, the FBI investigated more than 1,100 *color of law* cases. Most of these crimes fall into five broad areas:

———

Fabricating evidence against or falsely arresting an individual also violates the color of law statute, taking away the person's rights of due process and unreasonable seizure.

———

Civil Applications

Title 42, U.S.C., Section 14141 makes it unlawful for state or local law enforcement agencies to allow officers to engage in a pattern or practice of conduct that deprives persons of rights protected by the Constitution or U.S. laws. This law, commonly referred to as the Police Misconduct Statute, gives the Department of Justice authority to seek civil remedies in cases where law enforcement agencies have policies or practices that foster a pattern of misconduct by employees. This action is directed against an agency, not against individual officers. The types of issues which may initiate a pattern and practice investigation include:

Lack of supervision/monitoring of officers' actions;
Lack of justification or reporting by officers on incidents involving the use of force;
Lack of, or improper training of, officers; and
Citizen complaint processes that treat complainants as adversaries.

---FBI website

U.S. CODE TITLE 18, PART I ,CHAPTER 13 , section 241

§ 241. Conspiracy against rights

If two or more persons conspire to injure, oppress, threaten, or intimidate any person in any State, Territory, Commonwealth, Possession, or District in the free exercise or enjoyment of any right or privilege secured to him by the Constitution or laws of the United States, or because of his having so exercised the same...

They shall be fined under this title or imprisoned not more than ten years, or both...

U.S. CODE TITLE 18, PART I, CHAPTER 13, section 242.

242. Deprivation of rights under color of law

Whoever, under color of any law, statute, ordinance, regulation, or custom, willfully subjects any person in any State, Territory, Commonwealth, Possession, or District to the deprivation of any rights, privileges, or immunities secured or protected by the Constitution or laws of the United States, or to different punishments, pains, or penalties, on account of such person being an alien, or by reason of his color, or race, than are prescribed for the punishment of citizens, shall be fined under this title or imprisoned not more than one year, or both...

U.S. CODE TITLE 18, PART I, CHAPTER 73, section 1512

§ 1512. Tampering with a witness, victim, or an informant

(2) Whoever uses physical force or the threat of physical force against any person, or attempts to do so, with intent to—

- (A) influence, delay, or prevent the testimony of any person in an official proceeding;
- (B) cause or induce any person to—
  - (i) withhold testimony, or withhold a record, document, or other object, from an official proceeding;
  - (ii) alter, destroy, mutilate, or conceal an object with intent to impair the integrity or availability of the object for use in an official proceeding;

or . . .

- (C) hinder, delay, or prevent the communication to a law enforcement officer or judge of the United States of information relating to the commission or possible commission of a Federal offense. . .shall be punished as provided [by law]

- (C) Whoever corruptly—
  - (i) alters, destroys, mutilates, or conceals a record, document, or other object, or attempts to do so, with the intent to impair the object's integrity or availability for use in an official proceeding; or

(2) otherwise obstructs, influences, or impedes any official proceeding, or attempts to do so, shall be fined under this title or imprisoned not more than 20 years, or both.

In June, 2007, when Deputy Police Chief Ron Hodge stated at a public forum that he was not aware of any major mistakes made by the department in the preceding five years, the response of the audience was laughter.

Calls for federal intervention in and investigation of the lacrosse prosecution were numerous. The lacrosse defense lawyers themselves repeatedly urged federal investigators be assigned to the case. (This would be unusual if they had any doubt whatever about their clients' innocence; but they wanted more, not less, "eyes on the ground"; and more, not fewer, investigators. (*"It is error only, and not truth, that shrinks from inquiry.",* said Tom Paine*).*

But these requests were to be frustrated.

> The state attorney general has asked federal prosecutors to help conduct a criminal probe into former Durham District Attorney Mike Nifong and other government officials involved with the Duke lacrosse case, according to a lawyer representing one of the three exonerated players.
>
> --News and Observer, October 31, 2007

> In September, Jim Hardin, the acting district attorney appointed to succeed Nifong, asked the State Bureau of Investigation to consider a criminal probe.
>
> --News and Observer, October 31, 2007

Similar requests were made by nine members of the United States House of Representatives (but perhaps significantly, not by the House member for Durham).

All were rebuffed.

In January 2007 some Palestinian students at Guilford College in North Carolina alleged they were the victims of a hate crime when they were beaten up by some football players at the school. FBI agents arrived and interviewed the alleged "victims" even before the local police. (The charges were later dismissed for lack of evidence and were considered by some to have been a hoax.)

Yet despite death threats made against a defendant inside a courtroom by a uniformed member of an extremist racial-based group; despite allegations of witness intimidation, evidence tampering, denial of due process, and attempts at stirring up racial animus during an election campaign; the federal government exhibited no interest in the lacrosse prosecution. No FBI agents were dispatched.

> RALEIGH, N.C. -- The Department of Justice will not investigate former Duke lacrosse prosecutor Mike Nifong for his handling of the case, a spokesman for the federal agency said Wednesday.
>
> --ESPN, December 5, 2007

> [U.S. Attorney Christopher] Christie had a couple of his assistants fly to North Carolina in early September to confer with [North Carolina Attorney General] Cooper's staff and in-state federal prosecutors. . . The meeting was canceled [at Washington's behest] and Christie's assistants "were directed not to meet with" Cooper's staff.
>
> --Herald Sun, December 6, 2007

I've often said that if we could die our skin color the way we die our hair, we'd come to understand pretty rapidly that we're all just alike regardless of color...In the old South, a pot-bellied sheriff would believe any lie told about a black man and a jury would convict, with the press and the pastors of the community chiming along in righteous concert. In the new South, exactly the same thing happens--it's just that the colors have been reversed.

--blogger

...career lawyers in the Voting Section [of the Justice Department's Civil Rights Division] made it abundantly clear that they didn't want to use the Voting Rights Act to protect white voters, no matter how egregious the violations. . . One who went to Noxubee County [Mississippi] as an observer admitted to another lawyer that if he had seen the same type of illegal behavior being committed against black voters, he would have been outraged. But he wanted nothing to do with a suit filed on behalf of white voters.

--"*A Leadership of Cowards?*", National Review Online, by Hans A. von Spakovsky March 16, 2009

The government they had been led to believe was powerful and essentially just was proving itself to be cowardly and amoral in its dealings with segregationists...By its timidity and reluctance to aggressively prosecute civil rights violations [in 1964], the Justice Department earned the enmity of many volunteers ..."there were certain feelings of betrayal...the feeling that you couldn't count on your own government. A sort of suspension of values, almost, that the things I had grown up believing were constants, were just of dust."

--*Freedom Summer*, by Doug McAdam, pp. 130-131

CASE NARRATIVE: How a University Responded

A university is many things; it has many loci of power. For some, the university exists for the sake of the faculty. It provides them a place to do their research and write their books and push their ideas into the public forum. For others, the university is an industry, sometimes the only industry in a town of modest size; and its most important goal then must be maintaining good relations and contributing to the local community. This is especially true when the faculty and staff have resided in the community for years and become, in effect, locals. The most transient members of university--the students--are the most necessary component, and often they have the least power. And so they get the least attention. And for too many universities, the most urgent task in resolving a crisis involving students is to avoid bad publicity.

Let the honor of your student be as precious to you as your own. Avot 4.15

A teacher in an Orthodox Jewish school in Brooklyn would write the name of misbehaving students on the blackboard. By the end of the day there might be a list of such students visible for all in the class to see.

One day the principal of the school entered the classroom unexpectedly. While he addressed the class, the teacher went over and stood in front of the blackboard; and then carefully rubbed against the blackboard with the back of his jacket, erasing the names of the "offenders". The back of his jacket became covered with chalk; but thus he preserved the dignity of the 10 year-old students in his charge and saved them from shame in the presence of their principal.

(adapted from Reflections of the Maggid by Rabbi Paysach J. Krohn pages 81-82)

Consider a turkey that is fed every day. Every single feeding will firm up the bird's belief that it is the general rule of life to be fed every day by friendly members of the human race "looking out for its best interests" as a politician would say. On the afternoon of the Wednesday before Thanksgiving, something unexpected will happen to the turkey. It will incur a revision of belief.

The Duke lacrosse team was just like that turkey. The team, for years, had gone along thinking that their friendly faculty was looking out for their best interests and feeding them knowledge. The lacrosse players had no idea a false gang

> rape accusation would turn the faculty (and many of their own classmates) into a lynch mob that wanted to wring their collective necks. Or castrate and flunk them as the case might be.
>
> The jolting display of hatred towards the players by the infamous Duke Group of 88, their supporters, and campus radicals, all tacitly approved by the Duke administration, signaled that something was seriously wrong with higher education.
>
> --The Johnsville News blog, November 11, 2007

Duke University administrators were first informed about the rape allegations from their own Duke University police officers, who were at the hospital and had participated in the early questioning of Mangum. These officers reported that Mangum's claims were not believable and that the case was likely to fade away. Dean Wasiolek, Assistant Vice President for Student Affairs, spoke with the lacrosse team captains by phone and repeated that assumption. Though she was a lawyer herself, she told them that they did not need lawyers and that they should not tell anyone, including their parents, about the allegations. The police, she said, would be coming to search the Buchanan St. house, and they should cooperate fully. Had she suggested that they obtain lawyers and not speak to officers without counsel present, the three team captains would not have voluntarily submitted to hours of questioning by Durham police; and perhaps the entire case, for want of probable cause, might have been halted at the start.

At the same time, Duke was preparing a dossier on all the team members, to include their team photos, along with key-card information detailing when they had entered their dorms, in answer to a police request. This was in violation of the Family and Educational Privacy Act (FERPA); and the students were not informed beforehand, thus depriving them of their right to object. The keys to the Buchanan St. house were also provided by Duke, the landlord.

The house was searched on March 16, and the captains interrogated all that night and into the following morning of March 17. Later that day the captains met with their coach and an associate Duke athletic director; the associate athletic director, contradicting Dean Wasiolek, advised the players both to tell their parents and to retain counsel.

The lacrosse captains and the coach met with Duke Executive Vice President Trask, and Duke Athletic Director Joe Alleva, on March 24. Trask became angry when he learned that the captains had secured counsel; he wanted them to tell him what had happened at the party, and promised them that anything they told him would be protected by "student-administrator privilege". Although having been instructed previously by counsel not to say anything, the captains went ahead and repeated their accounts of what took place at the party, insisting that nothing had happened. Trask told them he believed them, and that they should now concentrate on winning their upcoming lacrosse match game against Georgetown. Trask shortly thereafter participated in Duke University President Brodhead's decision to cancel the Georgetown game; and he offered and gave to Durham police what he had been told "in confidence" under the rubric of "student-administrator privilege".

Later that day, President Brodhead held a meeting with Duke faculty, in which the more radical members demanded that he punish the entire lacrosse team and their coach, and end lacrosse as a sport at Duke. Two days later Duke administrators met at President Brodhead's home and decided that they "needed to send a signal that [they] took seriously what happened in the house." Instead of stating their belief, based on what the police had reported to them and what they had heard from the lacrosse captains, that nothing had happened, they decided to cancel the next two lacrosse games. Athletic Director Alleva later informed lacrosse coach Mike Pressler that no further action was contemplated by Duke unless police decided to file criminal charges.

Many of the parents of lacrosse team members--about fifty--were in town for a (now canceled) game with Georgetown and they requested to meet with President Brodhead. Brodhead, who was to commonly meet with protesters, faculty members, Durham city leaders, reporters, and others who wanted to voice a protest against the alleged "rape" or obtain an interview, adamantly refused. (Similarly, he refused to meet with the players' attorneys, who offered to provide him with evidence of the players' innocence.) The parents were instead permitted to meet with Athletic Director Alleva, Dean Wasiolek, Vice President Trask, and Larry Moneta, Duke Vice President for Student Affairs.

The parents were assured that Duke's administrative leadership did not believe the charges; but Duke would not make a public statement to that effect. Later the same day, however, President Brodhead made his first public remarks :

"Physical coercion and sexual assault are unacceptable in any setting and will not be tolerated at Duke. As none of us would choose to be the object of such conduct, so none of us has the right to subject another to such behavior. Since they run counter to such fundamental values, the claims against our players, if verified, will warrant very serious penalties, both from the university and the courts."

The effect of his remarks, even though he made a passing reference to the presumption of innocence, was to infer that the players were guilty. Brodhead also stated : *"I urge everyone to cooperate to the fullest with the police inquiry while we wait to learn the truth."* Again, this gave the public the impression that the players had not been cooperating when in fact they had cooperated fully from the start.

HOW BRODHEAD HANDLED ANOTHER CRISIS

In 1998, a Yale student was found murdered half a mile from the home of her senior essay advisor, James Van de Velde. There was no evidence liking Van de Velde to the crime; DNA of an unknown person was found beneath the student's fingernails, but not the DNA of Van de Velde. Fingerprints of an unknown person--not Van de Velde's--were also found at the scene. Some evidence suggested that the victim might have been forced into a vehicle and them dumped where she was found--further distancing, literally, Van de Velde from the crime. Like the lacrosse players, Van de Velde, when questioned by police, willingly offered them DNA samples, to let them search his home, and to take a lie-detector test. None of these offers were accepted at the time.

Richard Brodhead was then a popular professor and Dean at Yale. Responding for the university Brodhead cancelled Van de Velde's spring lectures after he was cited by police as being in "a pool of suspects". While asserting that *"the cancellation of the course doesn't follow from a judgment or a prejudgment of his hypothetical involvement in the ...case,"* nonetheless his actions left the opposite impression. Van de Velde's contract was permitted to lapse, and he was forced to leave Yale, under a cloud of suspicion.

In the opinion of some observers, perhaps what was important was that the story of a murder at Yale be swept from the front pages, before it could further damage the institution's reputation; a goal which a prolonged investigation, or championship of an accused's rights, would necessarily imperil.

Meanwhile, demonstrations against the lacrosse players began on the campus, aided, sometimes organized and attended, by Duke faculty. Off-campus housing rented by lacrosse players was surrounded by demonstrators. Stilt walkers and the Cackalack Thunder Drum Corps (who beat in time with the protest chants) joined the demonstrators; and a handout sheet provided the crowd with prepared slogans:

"Who's being silent?	*They're being silent!*
Whose protecting rapists?	*They're protecting rapists!*
So, who are the rapists?	*They must be the rapists!"*
"Out of the house!	*Out of the town!*
We don't want	*You around!"*

When defense counsel asked that some kind of security be provided for the players, or that at least they be permitted excused absences from classes, Larry Moneta refused: "Well, frankly, I don't believe you ." Lacrosse players were forced to move out of their homes and stay with friends; and one ended up temporarily living out of his car.

From Scottsboro:

On the night of the first day's trials we could hear a band outside. It played "There'll Be a Hot Time in the Old Town Tonight" and "Dixie".

--Scottsboro Boy, by Haywood
Patterson and Earl Conrad, p. 10

"Castrate!" "Give Them Equal Measure!"

--banners paraded in front of the
Buchanan St. lacrosse house

> But less than a week after the party, Thomas said, the woman [Mangum] seemed fine, and weeks later, he realized a friend of his had a video of her dancing at the club in the early hours of March 26.
>
> --News and Observer, November 4, 2006

> Thomas said dancers must sign in when they take guests into the club's VIP room. He said those sheets show that the woman [Mangum] had signed in March 17 and 18. He said she also danced the following weekend.
>
> --News and Observer, November 4, 2006

(Some commentators questioned whether the accused players would have been treated the same if they had been black. In fact, stereotypes about their race, gender, and class only seemed to work against them. In "the other Duke rape case", in what might have been considered a reverse-image of the lacrosse case, early in 2007 a white Duke student alleged she was raped at an off-campus party at a house rented by a black Duke fraternity member, and at which some black Duke athletes were also allegedly in attendance. News reports said that drugs and a gun were found in the house. Larry Moneta's comment in this instance was that the incident and its circumstances were only *"part of the reality of collegiate life and of experimentation and some of the consequences of students not necessarily being in the right place at the right time. This happens around the country. Duke is no different in that respect."* Some observers considered this "blaming the victim".

(There were no ramifications for the fraternity, there were no vigils, no faculty open letters; and President Brodhead issued no statements. In June of that year, the alleged suspect, who was not a Duke student, and who had been released on bond--which was 1/8 of the bond originally set for the indicted lacrosse players--was accused of a second rape after his release. No 'wanted' posters were issued for him and he was not arrested until November. The national media did not cover the story, the local press barely mentioned it, the district attorney did not go before the cameras even once, and no national magazine ran a cover story about the charges.)

APPLICATION FOR SEARCH WARRANT
Feb. 19, 2007

On 02/12/2007 I, Investigator A.J.Simmons...was briefed on the incident ... and I was given the following information :

A party was being held at the residence and approximately 75-100 males were at the party.

The victim was sexually assaulted in a bathroom at the residence.

—

There was an invite list of approximately 300 individuals and it was posted on www.facebook.com

On 2/12/2007 Investigator Guardino and I met with the victim at the Durham Police Substation number three... She made us aware that she had previously danced with the suspect and when she went to use the bathroom he came in behind her and closed the door. Once inside of the bathroom the suspect forced her to the ground causing her to hit her head on the sink, he then sexually assaulted her. The victim stated that she would be able to identify the suspect if she saw him again.

—

> The person of the intended search warrant is [__________] and he is described as a black male with the date of birth of [________]. ..He is approximately 6 ft. in height 170 pounds in weight; he has black hair and medium brown skin.

Note that the application for search warrants in the lacrosse case did not contain any physical descriptions of the suspects, although the accuser had provided those descriptions—"short", and "chubby".

> Police Investigate Alleged Assault of Duke Student
>
> "A neighbor told WRAL that Duke and Durham police broke up the party around the same time as the alleged attack. Sources tell WRAL both drugs and possibly a gun were found inside the home by authorities." WRAL TV Feb 11, 2007

The response of Duke, however, was quite tranquil compared to its response to the lacrosse case:

> NBC17 Reporter (Costello): "No matter what colleges do, incidents like this are inevitable"
>
> Duke VP Larry Moneta: "It's part of the reality of collegiate life and of experimentation and some of the consequences of students not always being in the right place at the right time."

And in this case, the District Attorney had no comments to make, and did not take over the investigation:

> Man charged with raping Duke student at party
>
> In the latest case, police have said the district attorney's office would not be involved until after charges were filed.
>
> --News and Observer Feb. 20, 2007

> Man out on bail charged in second rape
>
> DURHAM--Police say a man free on bail in the alleged rape of a Duke University student attacked another woman is now in the Durham County jail.
>
> --WTVD November 25, 2008

Eventually this man accepted a plea bargain in which he confessed to the two rapes; and, with time off for good behavior and time served in jail, would conceivably be able to gain his freedom with a little more than two additional years served.

It would have been impossible, politically, for such leniency to have been shown to convicted lacrosse players, who were members of groups which the public had been conditioned to dislike; or for their case to be similarly ignored by the media and civic leaders.

The extent to which the players were demonized by virtue of their backgrounds can be illustrated by the remarks of some Duke professors. Professor Tim Tyson, for example, the author of various works about race relations in the South, declaimed on National Public Radio:

"I think the spirit of the lynch mob lived in that house on Buchanan St., frankly, and I think that we prefer to think of white supremacists as ignorant, pot-bellied, tobacco-chewing sheriffs and Ku Klux Klan members from Mississippi; but here we have the sons of power and privilege, the wealthy and well-educated among us, who are acting out this history."

Another professor, Houston Baker, authored an open letter:

MARCH 29, 2006

"...Young, white, drunken men among us--implicitly boasted by our athletic directors and administrators--have injured lives. ..

"All of Duke athletics has now been drawn into the seamy domains of Colorado football and other college and university blind-eyeing of male athletes, veritably given license to rape, maraud, deploy hate speech, and feel proud of themselves in the bargain...

"How many mandates concerning safe, responsible campus citizenship must be transgressed by white athletes' violent racism before our university's offices of administration, athletics, security, and publicity courageously declare: enough!

"How many more people of color must fall victim to violent, white, male, athletic privilege...?"

Professor William Chafe, a well-known history professor and former Dean of Duke's Arts and Sciences faculty from 1995-2004, wrote in an article for the Chronicle ("Sex and Race", March 31) :

"So sex and race have always interacted in a vicious chemistry of power, privilege, and control. Emmett Till was brutalized lynched [sic] in Mississippi in 1954 [sic] for allegedly speaking with too easy familiarity to a white woman storekeeper...What has all this to do with America today, and with Duke? Among other things, it helps put into context what occurred in Durham two weeks ago. "

Many saw in the lacrosse case a chance to push larger agendas. Sexual Assault Awareness Week at Duke had long been scheduled for March 27 through March 31. With the charges against the lacrosse team, the Week took on a new focus. Many who were regular organizers and activists on the campus and in the community now emerged to take an active part in shaping campus response.

"Manju Rajendran is a 25-year old artist, activist, and biologist. She is on the Future 5000 team of the League of Young Voters, which means she is part of creating an incredible online directory of dope progressive youth organizations across the country. She has worked with Hip Hop Against Racist War, NC Lambda Youth Network, Youth Voice Radio, Movement Rising, National Child Rights Alliance, and more."

--CampusProgress.Org: Speaker

"Well, I feel like this rape is an outrage, the racist attack is an outrage. But I feel like this is much bigger than Duke and Durham. I feel like we, as a nation, are wrestling with a long legacy of institutionalized racism and a whole culture of sexual violence. We're trying to undo a long legacy here, with centuries of oppression."

--Manju Rajendran, MSNBC

"There is a sense that Duke students need to be protected from Durham, but rapes are happening off East Campus at the hands of Duke students," said Manju Rajendran, an organizer of the event. "We are here to break the silence around sexual assault and violence."

--Manju Rajendran, CSTV.com

From a false claim of rape, the case was now morphing into a case about institutionalized racism and unreported "rapes [that] are happening off East Campus at the hands of Duke students".

"The fact is there are many people who desperately want this to be true, because it reinforces their preconceived notions."

--Duke student

Rann Bar-On, a Duke graduate student and veteran of peace demonstrations on the West Bank (where he was struck by an Israeli rubber bullet); and co-organizer of the Palestine Solidarity Movement Conference at Duke, appeared at demonstrations and later issued calls for the institution of additional mandatory diversity programs at Duke to confront racism at the university.

Duke Senior Shadee Malaklou penned a guest editorial for the Herald-Sun, "*"Lacrosse Players Far From Innocent" :*

"...Much of this emphasis on 'innocence' has ignored the gender and racial prejudice of the March 13 party...Nifong might not be in the right legally, but that doesn't mean he's not doing the right thing."

The case was now supposed to focus on gender and racial prejudice. For activists, the case had become an opportunity. The world was listening; the red lights of the TV cameras were on; the satellite trucks had arrived. The truth about whether three accused students had actually committed a rape was to be subsumed into larger statements about the guilt of society in general.

In her columns last year and this fall, sophomore Shadee Malaklou encouraged her peers to embrace their sexuality and have as much fun as the guys. Malaklou taught a student-led, half-credit house course last spring titled "Dating and Mating: The Hook-Up Culture at Duke" and is teaching it for the second time this spring.

--Duke Magazine

Dating and Mating: Hookup Culture at Duke.

Course Syllabus:

Section 1: Classes 1-3. "Framing the Conversation"-- What do we mean by "hookup culture"? What are the overarching issues to be addressed by this class? We are trying to define 'the big picture' here.

Section 2: Classes 4-5. "Situations Conducive to 'Hooking up" -- What kind of environment fosters and is conducive to a "hookup," looking at college campuses specifically.

Section 3: classes 6-8. "The Before and After"--What are the expectations before a hookup, what happens afterwards?

Section 4: Classes 9-11. "Identity"--How are one's sexual encounters shaped by that person's upbringing and social identity?

Section 5: Class 12. "What Now?"--Where do we go from here to create constructive sexual encounters between college students (at Duke especially)?

The reality of the meta-narrative of racism was all well and good, but racism did not force Tawana Brawley to jump into a bag and smear s--t on herself and dupe the world.

---*Letters from Camp Tawana*, by Brian Mahoney

The university itself had maintained an uneven record with regard to issues of sex and exploitation on the campus.

Duke bans strippers from campus — again
Sept. 21, 2006

"It's a moral choice. ... We made a decision that a stripper at a campus event is something that we don't want to support" [said Stephen Bryan, Associate Dean of Students and Judicial Affairs Director]. "

-- (AP)

SEX WORKERS' ART SHOW

Arts/Music/Theater

Date: Sunday, February 3, 2008 - 8:00pm - 10:00 pm

Sponsor: Duke Student Health & Duke International Women's Health Alliance

Where: Reynolds Theater, West Campus

Why: SEX WORKERS' ART SHOW

Sunday, February 3 at 7:00pm

Reynolds Theater, West Campus

The Sex Workers' Art Show is a cabaret- style performance done by workers in the sex industry--phone sex operators, prostitutes, strippers--to express their creativity and genius; the show's topics vary from prostitute\'s rights and the humor to be found in the work to the dark side of the industry and in history.

Come out and join the Healthy Devils for this great performance!

Tickets are FREE, so bring your friends! We will be handing out tickets at the door, but please email so that we can get an estimate of numbers.

The show was sponsored by the following official university departments, centers and student organizations: the Duke Women's Center, the Duke Student Health Center, the Healthy Devils, the Program for the Study of Sexualities, the Campus Council, the Women's Studies Department, the

University and Cultural Fund, Students for Choice, Students for Choice and the Sexual Assault Support Services.

--Jay Schalin, February 4, 2008

The performances also included a male stripper who crouched on his hands and knees in a kiddie pool and appeared to put a lit sparkler in his rear end.

--ABC, Feb. 7, 2008

A stripper. . .yanked a string of dollar bills out of her posterior as the sound system played Dolly Parton's version of "God Bless the U.S.A." . . .

A dominatrix . . .

----Jay Schalin, February 4, 2008

"The Sex Workers Art Tour was suggested and driven by student interest and was sponsored by numerous campus groups. It dealt with controversial areas, but hopefully gave viewers an understanding of an industry which most students know little about. It is hoped this was a worthwhile experience for those who chose to attend."

-- William Purdy, executive director
of Duke University Student Health

Larry Moneta, Duke's vice president for student affairs, said the performance "raised issues for discussion." Asked about the difference between the art show and the lacrosse team's hosting strippers, he said, "one served the purpose of personal gratification and the other had educational value."

--ABC, Feb. 7, 2008

Chief Justice Durham of the Utah Supreme Court,
[and member of the Duke University Board of Trustees]

concurring in part and dissenting in part:

IN THE SUPREME COURT OF THE STATE OF UTAH

American Bush v. City of South Salt Lake
July 28, 2006

—

I do not believe that nude dancing performed in private establishments for paying customers constitutes an abuse of the right of free communication.

—

117 With this framework in mind, I now address whether nude dancing is communicative in nature. In considering

this question, I first inquire whether dance in general is a form of expressive activity that is entitled to constitutional protection. If it is, the inquiry then becomes whether dancing done without clothing likewise imparts a particular message that is stifled when nudity is banned.

---

121 It is beyond debate that the musicals, ballet, and modern dance described above, which often include nude and erotic dancing, are communicative. The dancers in such performances are engaged in an expressive exhibition, the point of which is to entertain the audience; this conduct conveys a variety of messages. Accordingly, such forms of nude and erotic dancing are also communication under the plain language of the Utah Constitution.

---

122 Nude dancing performed at sexually oriented establishments is conceptually indistinguishable from nude dancing performed in musicals, ballet, or modern dance, and therefore is communication within the meaning of the Utah Constitution. Concluding otherwise is to disregard what it is that nude dancing communicates. Like in all commercial dance performances, the nude dancing at issue in this case is performed for entertainment purposes to paying customers. As with the other forms of dance described above, a nude dancer communicates a message to her audience through her movements and appearance. The message of the nude dancing at issue is presumably one of sexuality. Much as the expressive nature of modern dance or ballet would be muted if the dancers were required to wear everyday clothing, the message of the nude dancing at issue is distorted or diminished by banning nudity. In other words, these dancers are simply not able to communicate

> their message as effectively when they are clothed, however scantily.
>
> [footnote 13] Nor is simple disapproval on moral grounds a sufficient justification to allow regulation of such conduct, a point which is discussed further infra at paragraph 145. Justice White gave an excellent analysis of this very issue in Barnes v. Glen Theatre, Inc., 501 U.S. 560 (1991), stating:
>
> *The purpose of forbidding people to appear nude in parks, beaches, hot dog stands, and like public places is to protect others from offense. But that could not possibly be the purpose of preventing nude dancing in theaters and barrooms since the viewers are exclusively consenting adults who pay money to see these dances. The purpose of the proscription in these contexts is to protect the viewers from what the State believes is the harmful message that nude dancing communicates.*
>
> *It is only because nude dancing performances may generate emotions and feelings of eroticism and sensuality among the spectators that the State seeks to regulate such expressive activity, apparently on the assumption that creating or emphasizing such thoughts and ideas in the minds of the spectators may lead to increased prostitution and the degradation of women. But generating thoughts, ideas, and emotions is the essence of communication.*

Animus against the lacrosse team (and perhaps all sports teams at Duke) continued to grow. In a March 30 meeting with the Academic Council, incensed faculty members railed at President Brodhead and demanded that the lacrosse season be canceled and the team disbanded, if not permanently, than at least for the next three years. One (chemistry) professor was shocked at the vehemence : *"I have never heard presumably intelligent, careful, balanced people being so completely over the top... It was the most disgusting display I've ever seen in my life."*

Two players who had been receiving passing grades were suddenly flunked in one class (meaning that one of them, a senior, would no longer be able to graduate). A player in another class was told by a professor that she might feel sorry for the team if they were really innocent (implying they were not). Other players had to sit in classes and hear professors denigrate them.

On April 5, following the release to the media of a player's email parody of *American Psycho,* Brodhead announced that he was canceling the rest of the lacrosse season. He also announced the resignation of lacrosse Coach Pressler:

"Allegations against members of the Duke lacrosse team stemming from the party on the evening of March 13 have deeply troubled me and everyone else at this university and our surrounding city. We can't be surprised at the outpouring of outrage. Rape is the substitution of raw power for love, brutality for tenderness, and dehumanization for intimacy. It is also the cruelest assertion of inequality, a way to show that the strong are superior to the weak and can rightfully use them as objects of their pleasure. When reports of racial abuse are added to the mix, the evil is compounded, reviving memories of the systematic racial oppression we hoped to have left behind us."

These words, though feebly tempered with a reminder about the concept of innocence until proven guilty, and coupled with the dismissal of a veteran coach, virtually convicted the lacrosse players of an event which never happened.

Mike Pressler had been coach of the Duke lacrosse team for 16 years. He was a thrice ACC Coach of the Year, and had led his teams to within a hairbreadth of national championships. He owned a home in Durham and raised his family there, and expected to retire in the city. Abruptly he was told to resign. He was not provided with a process or a forum in which to defend himself. Unique in the history of NCAA athletics, an entire season was to be canceled and a coach dismissed; and this only upon allegations, not proven facts. When Pressler begged Duke Athletic Director Joe Alleva at least to wait a few days until the DNA results could come back, Alleva answered, *"It's not about the truth anymore. It's about the integrity of the university, it's about the faculty, the city, the NAACP, the protesters, and the other interest groups".* Pressler became a pariah and experienced great difficulty finding further employment; while the Duke athletic deparment largely remained aloof from their former colleague.

The adroit manipulation by the Durham police department of a player's email parody of American Psycho had done its job, and raised a new firestorm in the community and nationally. To many there appeared to be no will at Duke to officially question any of the charges.

In discussing the university's handling of the charges against the lacrosse players, Robert K. Steel, Chairman of the Board of Trustees, told the New Yorker in an interview that *"we had to stop those pictures [of the lacrosse team at practice]. It doesn't mean that it's fair, but we had to stop it."* With regard to the firing of coach Pressler, he explained to the mother of a player, *"Life sucks. Bad things happen to good people and you better get used to it."* And later, in September, he asserted to Jason Trumpbour, the spokesman for Friends of Duke University, that it wouldn't matter if the players were convicted because the convictions could be reversed through appeals in the coming years.

In July Brodhead would privately admit to a lacrosse parent that *"recent stories have offered extensive evidence exonerating the indicted students and questioning the legitimacy of the case."* Yet he still refused to make any kind of public statement acknowledging this; or in support of his students' right to a fair due process.

HOW ANOTHER UNIVERSITY RESPONDED IN A CRISIS

"I believe that the young men we have recruited for our football team are young men of great character, but they did a very bad thing. . . It's time for me to say publicly that I believe in them, that I believe that they did something awful, but that I want them to continue at the University of Miami. And it's time for me to say to the community and to those that have been sending me e-mails that this university will be firm and punish people that do bad things.

"But we will not throw any student under the bus for instant restoration of our image or our reputation. I will not hang them in a public square. I will not eliminate their participation at the university. I will not take away their scholarships. . .

"It's time for the feeding frenzy to stop. These young men made a stupid, terrible, horrible mistake and they are being punished. They are students, and we are an educational institution and we will act like an educational institution, not like a PR machine trying to spin and restore an image that we worked so hard to put in place. . .

--Donna Shalala, President,
University of Miami, October, 2006

"If our students did what is alleged, it is appalling to the worst degree. If they didn't do it, whatever they did is bad enough."

--President Brodhead addressing the Durham
Chamber of Commerce, April 20, 2006

"There has not been a single note, card or other expression of kindness from anyone in the Duke administration to any of the three accused students."

--Jason Trumpbour, spokesman, Friends of Duke University October 25, 2006

The day after Coach Pressler was fired, a group of 88 Duke faculty members published a full-page advertisement in the university newspaper. The ad said, in part :

"We are listening to our students...What is apparent everyday now is the anger and fear of many students who know themselves to be objects of racism and sexism; who see illuminated in this moment's extraordinary spotlight what they live with everyday...

The ad quoted Duke students as saying :

"We want the absence of terror."

"I can't help but think about the different attention given to what has happened from what it would have been if the guys had not been just black but participating in a different sport, like football, something that's not so upscale."

"And this is what I'm thinking right now--Duke isn't really responding to this. Not really. And this, what happened, is a disaster. This is a social disaster."

The ad closed with :

"The students know that the disaster didn't begin on March 13th and won't end with what the police say or the court decides... We're turning up the volume in a moment when some of the most vulnerable among us are being asked to quiet down while we wait. To the students speaking individually and to the protesters making a collective noise, thank you for not waiting and for making yourselves heard."

The ad listed its sponsors:

"We thank the following departments and programs for signing onto this ad with African and African-American Studies: Romance Studies; Psychology; Social and Health Sciences; Franklin Humanities Institute; Critical US Studies; Art, Art History, and Visual Studies; Classical Studies; Asian and African Languages and Literature; Women's Studies; Latino/a Studies; Latin American and Caribbean Studies; Medieval and Renaissance Studies; European Studies; and the Center for Documentary Studies."

> The haste and vehemence with which scores of Duke University professors publicly took sides against the students in this case is just one sign of how deep the moral dry rot goes, in even our most prestigious institutions.
>
> ——
>
> We have become a society easily stampeded, even by the unsubstantiated, inconsistent and mutually contradictory statements of a woman with a criminal record.
>
> --Thomas Sowell, Feb. 1, 2007

> The humanities professors who persecuted Duke lacrosse players had acquired their jobs through force — through protests and demands that began in the 1960s. By the 1980s, Duke University had succeeded in filling its ranks with professors . . . who fit the new gender, race, and left-wing ideological categories.
>
> ——

> "Critical race theory" is one label for such an anti-Western notion of justice; its ideas seep into the humanities. . . Its promulgators. . . insist that long-held beliefs that underpin our legal system be replaced by a "justice" that takes into account past and current racial discrimination — however subjectively determined it may be. . .
>
> The lacrosse players' presumed guilt, based on their white race, their male gender, and their class, followed lock-step.
>
> --Mary Grabar, Pajamas Media, October 29, 2008

> They could not see the facts of this specific case because maintaining the legitimacy of their generally cynical and destructive world view took precedence. . .
>
> Criminal cases should rest on their specific merit and nothing more, not serve to promote a political agenda.
>
> --Brian Garst, "A Year Late, Duke Case Finally Dismissed", April 12, 2007

On April 10, 2006, DNA tests results from the State Bureau of Investigation were made public, revealing that there was no match to any lacrosse players. Yet a week later, the Durham county Grand Jury indicted two lacrosse players for rape. There had, as yet, been no convictions, nor was there any evidence to support the accuser's accusations; yet the university, speaking through its President, its faculty, its departments, and the Chairman of its Board of Trustees, had seemed in the eyes of many to be ready to announce the verdict first and dispense with the cumbersome bother of a trial.

At the same time as Brodhead announced the firing of Pressler (April 5), he simultaneously announced the establishment of a committee to investigate the disciplinary problems of the lacrosse team. On May 1, the committee released its report, which came to be known as the "Coleman Report", from its chairman, Professor James Coleman of the Duke Law School. At a press conference a speaker summarized the players' conduct with words such as "deplorable", and this was thereafter the focus of press accounts of the report.

In fact, however, the Coleman Report was largely positive in its findings, and drew conclusions opposite to those suggested by the media.

REPORT OF THE LACROSSE AD HOC REVIEW COMMITTEE

TO :
Richard H. Brodhead, President of Duke University
Paul H. Haagen, Professor of Law and Chair of the Duke University Academic Council

---

a. Academic and athletic performance.

... In 2005, twenty-seven members of the lacrosse team, more than half, made the Atlantic Coast Conference's Academic Honor Roll, more than any other ACC lacrosse team. Between 2001 and 2005, 146 members of the lacrosse team made the Academic Honor Roll, twice as many as the next ACC lacrosse team. The lacrosse team's academic performance generally is one of the best among all Duke athletic teams.

Team members had been involved with the Durham chapter of the Special Olympics; the Hurricane Katrina Relief Fund (raising more than any other Duke sports team); mentoring programs at elementary schools; Verizon Read with the Blue

Devils; lacrosse clinics and camps for the Durham community; and the North Durham Little League.

School groundskeepers and the equipment manager described the team as respectful and appreciative; and as among the best or the best athletes they have worked with. Team members cleaned the team bus on trips; and were complimented by airline personnel.

Scholastically, the team had a 100% graduation rate; and former team members contributed loyally as alumni. However, members who were freshmen and sophomores broke the law against underage drinking (age 21); but in this they were no different from university freshmen and sophomores everywhere. No lacrosse team member was involved with an alcohol incident requiring hospitalization.

> Their reported conduct has not involved fighting, sexual assault or harassment, or racist behavior.
>
> --Report of the Lacrosse Ad Hoc Review Committee

> A single incident in the Fall of 2001 involved ten students in a dorm room playing a drinking game; three of the players received disciplinary citations. The players apparently were entertaining a high school student the team was trying to recruit.
>
> ----Report of the Lacrosse Ad Hoc Review Committee

Other reported infractions included the theft of a pizza, the possible theft of a banner, assorted noise violations (hitting a golf ball against the wall of a building), and "suspicion of throwing water" in a water fight. (This must be the only instance where mere "suspicion" of throwing water in a dormitory water fight rated mention in a formal committee report.) There were no reported instances, other than of one student smoking marijuana in his dorm room, of drugs, or of weapons. In short, these were typical of the sort of violations which might be found on any college campus on any random weekend.

Statistics, however, were manipulated. Information furnished to the committee asserted that lacrosse players were responsible for 50% of the student body's noise violation citations; and for one-third of the Duke student body's open container violations--surely much out of proportion to their numbers. What was not explained was that the sampling size for the first statistic consisted of exactly two students (one of whom was a lacrosse player); and for the second statistic, of three Duke students (one of whom was a lacrosse player). The committee was also not informed of a later incident in the fall of 2006 (not involving lacrosse players) in which seven students received seven noise and seven open container violations in a single night. Hence, Disraeli's dictum remains valid; and the source of the "deplorable" description.

> 4/18/06
>
> 1420
> Inv. Himan and I discussed the possibility that some evidence may still be at one or the other individual's [the two students indicted on April 17] room on Duke Campus. We spoke to Capt. Lamb about our concern and he agreed. I spoke to District Attorney Nifong and he stated write up search warrants for both rooms. Inv. Himan and I placed our names on the warrants so the search warrants could be executed simultaneously.
>
> 1646
> Search warrants for [dormitory room] (Collin Finnerty)and [dormitory room] (Reade Seligmann) were signed off after they were reviewed by District Attorney Nifong.

1735
Duke Police and Durham Police briefed outside of [dormitory room]. Inv. Himan would execute the Search Warrant on Rm. ___ and I would execute the Search Warrant on Rm. ___. Duke had pass keys in the event no one was home to make non forced entries.

1755
1 arrived outside of the room ____ with Duke Inv. Rush and CSI Sale. I began to knock and announce in a normal tone of voice. There was no answer. After the official with the pass key completed his assignment on Rm. ___he arrived at my location. Three loud knock and announcements were made, no answer, and a soft entry was made using the key. No one was home. There were no computers in the room, only evidence that they were recently there. The wires for Internet access, etc.

I read the search warrant to the vacant room. About 10 minutes into the search [the roommate] arrived. He was on his cell phone with a family member. I went ahead and read the search warrant to him also. The search began inside the room. [The roommate] chose to sit on his sofa during the search. I located a letter addressed to Collin Finnerty from what appeared to be his girlfriend. In the letter she discussed how good it was to visit, and she thanked him for allowing her to use his ATM card as usual while she was there. A news article about some problems Mr. Finnerty was having was discovered, and his lease for the Duke Dorm Room was located. I asked CSI to photograph it. Inv. Himan called me and asked me to come to room ____. I told him I would be there after [the roommate] signed the inventory form. Robert Ekstrand, his Attorney, was there as a witness.

> 1840
> I left the room in the custody of Inv. Rush while CSI Sale completed her collection of evidence. The inventory form and return of service was done later at the Magistrates Office before Chief Magistrate Chet Dobies.
>
> 1844
> Went up to room ___ and met with Inv. Himan. He stated there was a printer on the floor next to [the roommate's] bed, but the owner's manual was in Reade Seligmann's Desk drawer. He asked if he should seize it. Mr. Ekstrand [attorney] was standing outside of the room with [the roommate]. I asked [the roommate] whose printer was the item on the floor. Mr. Ekstrand pulled his client aside and returned and stated it was [the roommate's] printer. Neither person knew the owner's manual was in the other person's desk, so when I posed the question Mr. Estrand pulled [the roommate] away again. He stated it was his, that he bought it. Even though it is in the scope of the search warrant, I told Inv. Himan we could charge [the roommate] for lying if we discovered he was making something up possibly hiding evidence and have something to hold over him at a later time. It was photographed and left. I went into the drawer to locate the owner's manual to seize it.
>
> --Sgt. Gottlieb's reconstructed notes for April 18, 2006

Apparently at some point it was realized that Duke had violated the Family and Educational Records Privacy Act (FERPA) by handing over to Durham police private key-card and other information about its students without their consent. A sham process was then initiated. Nifong obligingly issued a subpoena for the same information--information he had already received from Duke. Duke thereupon informed its students on June 2 :

"Duke University has received a subpoena requiring us to produce certain information regarding use of your DukeCard. If you wish to object to the release of these records by the University, your attorney must file a motion to that effect. If we have not heard from you by Monday, June 12, 2006, at 9:00 a.m., we intend to comply with the terms of the subpoena. If you file a motion to quash or otherwise object to the subpoena please send up copies of the relevant papers at your earliest convenience."

Late in July a judge ruled that Nifong was not entitled to the information requested:

"The request for key card information for all listed students without any showing of materiality or necessity does not rise to the level required to overcome the confidentiality of student information assured by FERPA."

Thus, Duke and the District Attorney cooperated in an attempt to provide cover for Duke's violation of FERPA; and both lied to the court about the process, engaging in a pretense that the information sought had not already been handed over weeks before.

In the meantime, various faculty members continued their denunciation of the players. This was not matched by any corresponding faculty defense of the accused, nor even by support for their right to a fair legal process.

"I understand the impulse of those outraged and who see the alleged offenders as exemplars of the upper end of the class hierarchy, the politically dominant race and ethnicity, the dominant gender, the dominant sexuality, and the dominant social group on campus."

--*"Perfect Offenders, Perfect Victim: The Limitations of Spectacularity in the Aftermath of the Lacrosse Team Incident"*, Wahneema Lubiano, April 13 online article

> "Judgments about the issues of race and gender that the lacrosse team's sleazy conduct exposed cannot be left to the courtroom."
>
> -- *"Coda: Bodies of Evidence"*, Karla FC Holloway, The Scholar and Feminist Online, Summer 2006

Professor Grant Farred was to say at a public forum in September 2006:

"...the secret of Duke's lacrosse . . . continues to be burdened, arguably (overly so, we might argue) with its own history...A tendency toward misogyny and arrogant sexual prowess."

And he would later add: *"At the heart of the lacrosse team's behavior is the racist history of the South."*

Professor Houston Baker followed up his open letter with an email on June 10, in which he asserted the possibility that "46 white guys on the lacrosse team at Duke may well have raped more than one woman." On New Year's eve, he was to answer an email from one of the (non-indicted) players' mothers :

You are just a provocateur on a happy New Year's Eve trying to get credit for a scummy bunch of white males! You know you are in search of sympathy for young white guys...live like a bunch of farm animals near campus...Unhappy new year to you...and forgive me if you really are, quite sadly, mother of a farm animal." [spelling errors corrected]

The case for some faculty members had long since ceased to be about a particular woman making accusations about specific students; for those with agendas, she became a representative of an oppressed class; and the defendants, stereotypes without names. *("A case too important for innocence to be allowed as a defense.")*

CHANGE OF VENUE MOTION

41. Since that time, members of the Duke faculty have written numerous editorials and letters in the Herald-Sun, in which they have congratulated the District Attorney for indicting the players. "Don't be too Quick to Toss Lacrosse Case," November 12, 2006, claimed that there is "secret racism" underlying the claimed actions of the Defendants...

42. The Canon of the Duke University Chapel published an editorial --based upon a sermon preached in the Chapel-- in which he said facts of this case were the "disturbingly extensive experience of sexual violence, of abiding racism, of crimes rarely reported and perpetrators seldom named, confronted, or convicted, of lives deeply scarred, `of hurt and pain long suppressed." ("A Time to Talk at Duke," April 9, 2006.) He concluded that "the last week has exposed the reality that sexual practices are an area where some male students are accustomed to manipulating, exploiting and terrorizing women all the time --and that this has been accepted by many as a given."

43. The Website of the Department of Women's Studies at Duke University now features an article written by Prof. Karla Holloway entitled: "Coda: Bodies of Evidence," In it, she wrote, in part:

". . .At Duke University this past spring, the bodies left to the trauma of a campus brought to its knees by members of Duke University's Lacrosse team were African American and women. I use the kneeling metaphor with deliberate intent. It was precisely this demeanor towards women and girls that mattered here. The Lacrosse team's notion of who was in service of whom and the presumption of privilege that their elite sports' performance had earned seemed their entitlement as well to behaving badly and without concern for consequence. . . "

Thus, probably uniquely in the history of American education, a university's faculty and administrative staff were cited in a change of venue request as being a part of the reason some of its accused students could not receive a fair trial.

"We're sensitive to the fact that [defense counsel] and others believe that an apology is appropriate. That has not yet been determined to be the position of the university."

-- John Burness, Duke University Senior Vice President for Public Affairs, Daily Progress interview, April 8, 2007

Burness said there is a segment of the population that has asked him if Duke will apologize to the players if their legal problems disappear. "I said," Burness replied, "for what?"

--John Burness, Duke University Senior Vice President for Public Affairs, Newsday interview, April 9, 2007

What President Brodhead really needs to take responsibly for and has yet to do so are the selfish motives that drove the administration's policies. The administration wanted the case to go to trial. It believed that, if the case were dismissed before trial for whatever reason, people would say that Duke used its influence to have it dismissed. Robert Steel, the Chairman of the Board of Trustees told me that a year ago. . .

Steel told me that it did not matter if they were convicted because all the problems with the case would be sorted out on appeal. That is not the way the appeal process works and I told him that, but that was still his plan.

—

In the end, the administration's policies were never about ignorance of the facts or credulity concerning the motives of public officials. The facts were irrelevant. It was all about keeping up appearances.

--Jason Trumpbour, Friends of Duke University spokesperson

We have an autocracy which runs this university. It's managed. We were told the following: "If President Kerr actually tried to get something more liberal out of the Regents...why didn't he make some public statement to that effect?" And the answer we received from a well-meaning liberal was the following: he said, "Would you ever imagine the manager of a firm making a statement publicly in opposition to his Board of Directors?" That's the answer.

I ask you to consider: if this is a firm, and if the Board of Regents are the Board of Directors, and if President Kerr in fact is the manger, then...the faculty are a bunch of employees and we're the raw material. But we're a bunch of raw material that don't mean...to be made into any product, don't mean to end up being bought by some clients of the university...We're human beings.

--Mario Savio, Berkeley Free Speech Movement, 1964

CASE NARRATIVE: How the Media Responded

> *"The media's the most powerful entity on earth. They have the power to make the innocent guilty and to make the guilty innocent, and that's power. Because they control the minds of the masses."*
>
> --Malcom X

Durham's principal local newspaper is the Herald-Sun. In the first six months after the charges were made, it published approximately 300 articles about the lacrosse case, including twenty unsigned editorials, plus a large number of guest opinion columns. Almost without exception these appeared to assume the guilt of the players; and, as a consequence, deprived the city's readership of ready access to all of the facts and set the tone for much of the subsequent public discourse.

CHANGE OF VENUE MOTION

48. In its first significant editorial on these cases, the Herald-Sun stated that not only had a crime occurred, but that those present during the crime were guilty of an additional "outrage" by not confessing to the crime:

Outrage at Duke Lacrosse Players

"Get a conscience, not a lawyer," read signs waved in front of the house [610 N. Buchanan] on Sunday. We agree that the alleged crime isn't the only outrage. It's also outrageous that not a single person who was in the house felt compelled to step forward and tell the truth about what happened. And these are our best and brightest, America's future leaders? When did we stop teaching right from wrong? (March 28, 2006.)

———

50. The Herald-Sun has further editorialized that the Lacrosse team was "out of control," April 12, 2006, that it had a reputation for "loud, obnoxious partying and belligerent behavior" and only had "themselves to blame for the current trouble," (March 30, 2006.) that the Lacrosse team threw "drunken parties" and that "obnoxious behavior [was] favored by the lacrosse team," (April 16, 2006.) that the Lacrosse team had a history of "loutish behavior," (April 27, 2006.) that if the "rape allegations had not been acted on . . . would the lacrosse team have faced any serious discipline," (May 10, 2006.) and that the rape allegations are a "throwback to a bygone era" of a "culture of alcohol abuse and an arrogant, macho attitude among some male students," (May 18, 2006.)

51. The Herald-Sun has also repeatedly claimed that the District Attorney must have compelling evidence that has not yet been revealed, evidence that justifies its positions:

"But even in the wake of compelling DNA evidence, those who would echo team members' attorneys and declare the case shut would be smart to wait to see what District Attorney Mike Nifong has up his sleeve, Nifong was convinced early on that a crime occurred and he has not ruled out filing charges." (April 12, 2006.)

"Nifong is a prosecutor with 27 years of experience in Durham. As such, we imagine he knows when evidence supports an accusation and when it doesn't. We also imagine there is evidence he hasn't revealed yet. And we have to assume that Nifong believes the case is strong enough to pursue. In that case, what choice does he have?" (May 19, 2006.)

---

52. In contrast to its position concerning the evidence possessed by the State, the Herald-Sun has consistently and openly mocked any claim of innocence made by the Defendants and repeatedly claimed they are privileged persons with expensive lawyers:

"The players were white and privileged. The alleged victim was black and less well-off...

"... We may have been angry about the drunken parties and obnoxious behavior favored by the lacrosse team. But that doesn't mean we want players to be wrongly convicted of rape. Nor, if the allegations prove to have substance, do we want the guilty to get away with it because they can afford expensive lawyers." (April 16, 2006.)

"It's not difficult to conclude that indictments against two Duke lacrosse players were sealed as a courtesy to the players and their families that other defendants would not normally receive...

"It's true that the media circus often casts Durham and Duke University in an unflattering, unbalanced light. That's no reason to add more fuel to the fire by giving credence to the charge that these defendants, due to their economic status, are getting preferential treatment." (April 20, 2006.)

"Evans seemed sincere and steadfast, and we felt sympathy for him, as did many others. Unfortunately, one strong speech and claims of passing a polygraph test aren't proof of innocence. Nor are many statements by defense attorneys that, unsurprisingly, portray the defendants as blameless and play down anything damaging." (May 19, 2006.)

"Many TVs in the Triangle will be tuned to "60 Minutes" Sunday when correspondent Ed Bradley will report a segment about the infamous Duke lacrosse case. That doesn't mean well learn much that has not already been explored in the intensive nationwide coverage of the case. The three defendants will be interviewed and, we're sure, will profess their innocence." (October 14, 2006.)

"The players maintained an aura of sweet innocence with reporter Ed Bradley either downplaying or ignoring conflicting evidence.... Most of Durham knew the lacrosse players were no choirboys, as "60 Minutes" tried to portray them...

". . . Roberts was separated from the accuser for at least two periods of five to 10 minutes. We still haven't heard why an assault couldn't have occurred during those gaps." (October 17, 2006.)

53. Finally, while paying lip service to the fact that the Defendants should only be convicted in a courtroom based

upon evidence that proves guilt, the Herald-Sun editorial position has been clear that it is only "possible" that the crimes did not occur and that it is up to the Defendants to prove their innocence:

"We acknowledge that there certainly exists the possibility that the alleged victim, who was hired to strip at a wild lacrosse party, isn't being truthful about what happened in the bathroom. (She contends that she was raped, robbed and beaten that regrettable night.) But how anyone who was not present in the bathroom can claim to know for certain that the three lacrosse players accused of rape are innocent isn't being honest." (May 26, 2006.)

"Furthermore, with an upcoming trial that is sure to draw major media attention, it would be better for the players to have an opportunity to prove their Innocence at trial." (November 9, 2006.)

[It should be noted that in the American judicial system, the default position is that a defendant is innocent, and it is the job of the prosecutor to present convincing proof that he is guilty; an accused person is not presumed to be guilty and tasked with offering convincing proof he is innocent.]

The Opinions of Columnists in the Herald-Sun

54. The themes and attitudes expressed in the unsigned editorials of the Herald-Sun have been reflected and often magnified by the "opinion" columns that the Herald-Sun has chosen to publish.

55. On April 17, 2006, the Herald-Sun published a column written by the pastor of St. Peter's United Methodist Church in Morehead City. It began by claiming: "At the end of Lent 2006, the Duke University lacrosse team's disgusting behavior

and alleged crimes have forced the entire Duke community into the difficult Lenten practice of self examination." It continued:

"This university-based self-examination started with questions: How could these sordid incidents have happened? Why did they occur? What personal and social harms did they inflict? First, there is the dimension of personal morality and immorality. The personal immorality of the lacrosse players --the drunkenness, the sexual degradation, the racism, the violent threats, the conspiratorial silence -- deserve decisive denunciation by leaders within the Duke community. These were not trivial, little mistakes. They were gross immoralities."

56. A week later, the editor of the Herald-Sun wrote in his opinion column that "many are frustrated with the off-campus reputation of some students, including without dispute many member of the lacrosse team, for whom late parties and disdain bordering on contempt for the neighbors is common."

57. Following the indictment of Dave Evans, the Herald-Sun chose to publish an opinion column on May 17, 2006, in which the author, commenting on Evans' statement that he was innocent, wrote:

"We'll see what David Evans does, along with the other two rape suspects, should the case make it to trial. We'll see how brave they are then. If they are innocent of any crime, perhaps each should sit down in the witness box, raise the right hand and swear to tell the truth, and then tell all of it. I hope all three suspects will be as outspoken before a jury as their lawyers will be. These children of apparent privilege will certainly have the privilege to decline, but let's just see if their confidence extends to cross-examination. The victim will have no choice but to speak if she wants to make her case and win it."

58. On May 31, 2006, in another opinion column, the author asked what the Defendants will be doing until a trial, noting that "maybe the cynics are right in saying anybody whose mama and daddy can keep them out of jail on a $400,000 bond doesn't have to worry about a job." The columnist then noted:

"But that's what can happen when you don't keep your nose clean. Whether or not he's [Dave Evans] shaved his would-be incriminating mustache in the days since a stripper claimed he attacked her...But I have to ask: What if the accuser's lying? Wait a minute, now! Don't throw a brick at me. The operative word here is "if." I can just as easily ask, "What if the white boys did do it to her?" It cuts both ways. The lacrosse boys brought it on themselves, though -- even if the accuser's lying."

59. Subsequently, on July 23, 2006, the editor of the Herald-Sun wrote that barely a day goes by that we don't worry about the impact of the coverage that is, after all, being driven by events. We've tried to consistently remind that all the facts aren't out, and that the defense attorneys are releasing just fragments of the total evidence they choose to make public." On August 20, 2006, the editor wrote in another opinion column that "Students at Duke will be watched" and went on to add that "the Duke students' return is watched with particular wariness this year."

60. On November 1, 2006, the Herald-Sun chose to publish a "guest" editorial column entitled, "Give Nifong Credit for Believing Accuser." (November 1, 2006.) The columnist, a resident of Durham, wrote:

". . .In fact, most of the town and most of the Duke campus were entirely ready to believe that these young men had done such

a thing. They were notorious for their drinking, their sexual excess, their arrogance. They were literally a public nuisance -- the source of many neighborhood complaints. When the DA indicted them, it would have been quite accurate to say 'they asked for it.' Because they had, for years.

"If you are one who is sorry for the laxers, ask yourself how we all, through our treatment of athletes, our embrace of out-of-control behavior, our deathly notions of proving manhood, contributed to their upbringing. Don't blame the DA because he believed her. I promise you that it is a whole lot better than what happened in the good old days."

61. In the weeks since the election, the Herald-Sun has published "guest" columns entitled, "Don't Be Too Quick to Toss Lacrosse Case," (November 12, 2006.) and "Lacrosse Players Far From Innocent," (November 19. 2006.) Both columns are riddled with hearsay, innuendo, and factual inconsistencies -- yet were published apparently without even a minimum of "fact-checking" by the Herald-Sun.

62. For example, the column published by the Herald-Sun on in its Sunday issue on November 19. 2006, purports to "rebut" statements made by the attorney for Dave Evans. It begins:

"For every smug remark by a smug, white attorney representing a smug, white lacrosse player, there is a woman cringing."

The "columnist" [Shadee Malaklou] then proceeds to argue that "much of the emphasis on this 'innocence' has ignored the gender and racial prejudice of the March 13 party. If nothing else, Nifong is holding the lacrosse players accountable for that and as a woman at Duke who knows just how much these men get away with, I'm thankful." In short, the columnist published by the Herald-Sun argued that regardless of whether the Defendants are innocent of the crimes charged or not, they should be convicted of rape because of "gender and racial prejudice" and because she "knows" how much "these men" get away with.

The Herald-Sun is still dissembling as it calls for a speedy trial and it is shirking its duty. Instead of waiting for the truth, the paper should start digging into the mistakes made by the media, Nifong, and Duke. Isn't that what a watchdog press is supposed to do?The paper has no appetite for such work. Like most local media, they are loyal lapdogs for prosecutors. This is made clear by the gentle way they handle the questions about Nifong's handling of the case . . .

It is a touching to see the media place such childlike faith in a politician.

--Lead and Gold blog, July 5, 2006

Durham's other major newspaper, the News and Observer, early on carried an exclusive interview with the accuser ("Dancer gives Details of Ordeal", March 24, 2006). Many of its "details" were incorrect. The article painted a picture of a pitiable victim (never, "alleged" victim), caught in the midst of a drunken party ("A Night of Racial Slurs, Growing Fear, and Finally, Sexual Violence"), all of which were belied by the facts, and which would have fit easily into a magazine thriller *("We started to cry," she said. "We were so scared.")* In addition, the interviewer (or her editor) decided to omit a portion of the interview in which Mangum asserted her fellow dancer might also have been raped:

"She said that although she saw no proof, she believed the second dancer was also attacked, but didn't come forward because she would lose her job as an escort."

"I got the feeling she would do just about anything for money," Mangum said of the second dancer, Kim Roberts."

Including those statements might have cast doubt on the rest of Mangum's story. But they were withheld from publication. Months later, the paper's staff attempted to explain:

"...As I explained previously, two things the accuser said did not make it in to print... nothing about that information shed light on what happened that night, nor would the publication have made a difference in how this case has played out." -- (Linda Williams, Dec. 24, 3006)

Neither did the paper at first inform its readership of full details of the accuser's past police record; nor inquire why an allegedly poor woman who was trying to work her way through college had two drivers; nor interview her co-workers at the Platinum club (where it might have found out that the lacrosse party was not, as she sometimes claimed, the first time she had danced before men).

The paper was not without resources, though. It was able to investigate the backgrounds of the accused and provide the details in gushing prose *("They came from a world of hushed golf greens and suburban homes with price tags that cross the million-dollar line")* give their names (while withholding the name of their accuser), describe the high schools they attended, and their background in sports (" *Suspects in rape share background of privilege*", April 19).

Media coverage outside of Durham was not much better.

On March 31, 2006, Selena Roberts wrote in the New York Times (*"Bonded in Barbarity"*), of *""a group of privileged players of fine pedigree entangled in a night that threatens to belie their social standing as human beings."*

"At the intersection of entitlement and enablement, there is Duke University, virtuous on the outside, debauched on the inside..."

On April 11 she mused further that *"Duke's lacrosse members established a Lord of the Flies ethos in Durham."*

In the Washington Post, for April 25 (two weeks after it was publicly known that DNA testing had cleared all the lacrosse team members), Eugene Robinson wrote, *"The master-slave relationship, the tradition of droit du seigneur, the use of sexual possession as an instrument of domination--all this ugliness floods the mind, unbidden, and refuses to leave."* A full month later--by which time there should have been little doubt about the players' innocence, and a great deal of skepticism about Nifong--Lynne Duke was writing for the same paper (May 24), that *"In the sordid but contested details of the case, African-American women have heard echoes of a history of some white men sexually abusing black women--and a stereotype of black women as hypersexual beings and thus fair game."*

Even worse were television personalities Nancy Grace and Wendy Murphy (an adjunct law professor who made over 30 appearances on the case and at one point affirmed, "I never, ever met a false rape claim, by the way. My own statistics speak to the truth")

> "I'd even go so far as to say I bet one or more of the players was, you know, molested or something as a child."
>
> --Wendy Murphy, CNN Live Today, May 3, 2006

The day after the April 4th ID session (during which Crystal Mangum identified four persons as her attackers, three of whom were to be indicted), but a week before that information was made public, the New York Times ran what some have called a "hit piece" on Collin Finnerty. There was no particular reason why at that time Finnerty should have been singled out for attention from among all the other lacrosse team members; and after he was indicted there was speculation that the Times had been fed inside information from the Durham investigation, designed to create a brushfire of public opinion against him in preparation for his being charged.

For the month of April, Network newscasts devoted almost as much, and in some cases more, to coverage of the lacrosse case as they did to the Iraq war. (*"Justice Delayed",* by Rachel Smolkin, American Journalism Review, August/September 2007) Much of that coverage dovetailed around the issues of race, gender, and class; depicting an elite university with a student body that was an alien implant in the South; "privileged" rich white athletes; and an accuser who was portrayed as a poor working mother of two, a Navy veteran, and a victim of the upper class's disdain. This story line, though false, nonetheless was to prove resilient as it was the perfect vehicle for the energizing of many activist agendas.

And in April, an Internet search for "Duke Lacrosse" would have resulted in over 12 million hits.

In late August, the New York Times published a lengthy article which asserted its own examination of some 1800 pages of discovery items indicted there was ample evidence to support Nifong's prosecution.

"...an examination of the entire 1,850 pages of evidence gathered by the prosecution in the four months after the accusation yields a more ambiguous picture. It shows that while there are big weaknesses in Mr. Nifong's case, there is also a body of evidence to support his decision to take the matter to a jury. "

There was no explanation given as to how the Times had obtained the discovery material. The Times then went on to say,

"It was 12:04 a.m. March 14. The question is, what happened in the next 30 to 50 minutes?"

ignoring the already public proof that Reade Seligmann had left the party early; and that released time-stamped photographs which showed the accuser outside the house for much of that time.

The Times also claimed that *"except in some initial contacts with the police, she [the accuser] gave a consistent account during that night and since then of how many men raped her"*; dismissing the many changes in her story, not only of how many men attacked her (three, five, twenty; or four, as she identified them on April 4) but also the explicit details of the attack (did the second dancer help the attackers? did three additional men seize and separate the dancers? were there four dancers or only two? was her money stolen by the second dancer?); and so on.

Perhaps the most blatant assertion was that Sgt. Gottlieb had been able to use his own three pages of handwritten notes to reconstruct from memory some 33 pages of typed notes, four months after the initial investigation; which were now referenced by the Times article. In Gottlieb's reconstructed notes the original descriptions given by Crystal Mangum of her attackers, as recorded by officer Himan at the time ("white male, short, red cheeks fluffy hair chubby face, brn"; "heavy set short haircut 260-270 [lbs.]"; "chubby") became transmuted into descriptions which bore an uncanny match to those who had been charged :"1) W/M, young, blonde hair, baby faced, tall and lean, 2) W/M, medium height (5'8"+ with Himan's build), dark hair medium build, and had red (rose colored) cheeks, and the third suspect as being a W/M, 6+ feet, large build with dark hair." Cleary investigator Himan, who was at the same interrogation as Gottlieb when she provided these descriptions, and who kept contemporary notes of her remarks, either misheard, or wrote down inaccurately, what she had said; or else Gottlieb's memory four months later was extraordinarily faulty.

Within four hours of the articles' publication online, it had been analyzed by bloggers and shown to be hasty, riddled with factual errors, and the "evidence" to be quite possibly fraudulent. In this new age of the Internet, not even the Grey Lady could expect to publish online and not be fact-checked. Nor would it--or any other press source-- be able to posture as the final unquestioned authority on any subject.

(Left unanswered was the question of whether an investigator would be permitted to present to a court notes "reconstructed from memory" months after the events in question. Were that to be allowed, there would be no bar to police "creating" notes to fill in holes in a prosecution's case, tempered to fit whatever evidence investigators have discovered.)

From Scottsboro:

All Negroes Positively Identified by Girls and One White Boy Who Was Held Prisoner with Pistol and Knives While Nine Black Fiends Committed Revolting Crime

--Jackson County Sentinel headline about
the Scottsboro allegations

From Scottsboro:

How far has the community sunk when one must contemplate the frightful things that occurred in that gravel car!

--Chattanooga News, on Scottsboro, 1931

From Scottsboro:

The white girls were found in the car in a terrible condition mentally and physically, after their unspeakable experience at the hands of the black brutes...

--Jackson County Sentinel, March 26, 1931

From Scottsboro:

...details of the crime coming from the lips of the two girls, Victoria Price and Ruby Bates, are too revolting to be printed.

--The Progressive Age, 1931

From Scottsboro:

The Advertiser may be dumb, but to save itself it cannot see what the political rights and privileges of Negroes in Alabama have to do with the guilt or innocence of the gorillas who are charged with criminal assault upon two women.

--The Advertiser (Montgomery, Alabama)

From Scottsboro:

The matter [Scottsboro] is something about which... no one, perhaps, should venture to feel absolutely certain.

--Birmingham News

"...it is a crime to have relied on the most squalid elements of the press...It is a crime to lie to the public, to twist public opinion to insane lengths ... It is a crime to poison the minds of the meek and the humble, to stoke the passions of reactionism and intolerance..."

--*"I Accuse"*, Emile Zola in defense of Dreyfus

"...among the most frightening aspects of the [Duke lacrosse] case is that even after much of [Nifong's egregious] misconduct became publicly known in the spring and summer of 2006,...media organizations led by The New York Times...continued for many months to look the other way or even facilitate his efforts."

(*Until Proven Innocent,* Taylor and Johnson, p. 356).

Of course, demonizing members of an unpopular stereotype so as to make them appear somehow less than fully as human as oneself, and therefore guilty by reason of birth, is both a frequent tactic and a common psychological response :

"The season is over, but the paradox lives on in Duke's lacrosse team, a group of privileged players of fine pedigree entangled in a night that threatens to belie their status as human beings . . . Whatever the root, there is a common thread: a desire for teammates to exploit the vulnerable without heeding a conscience. "

--Selena Roberts, The New York Times, March 31, 2006

"Maybe the team used bad judgment in hiring a stripper. What is almost humorous to me is that the media and Duke faculty have painted these boys as "white, privileged hooligans." When I asked [my son] why they let Crystal in, since she was clearly impaired and not at all like the dancer they thought was coming, his comment was, "We didn't want to hurt her feelings."

--mother of an unindicted player

From Scottsboro:

You must realize these Negroes are vicious and ignorant, they are not innocent victims of a frame up, but were a gang of criminals running from the Chattanooga police when they got into trouble on the freight train... It is hard to get the truth out of them, because they belong to a low grade of intelligence and moral conception which does not know what the truth is.

--William McDowell, Episcopal Bishop of Alabama, on the Scottsboro defendants

The subhuman – [black, white male, Jew, fraternity member, or the foe de jour] that biologically apparently same shaped creation of nature . . . is only an approximation of man, with human-like facial features – spiritually, psychologically, however, standing lower than any animal. Inside this being a chaos of wild, uninhibited passions: nameless will to destruction, most primitive desires, most undisguised baseness.

--*The Subhuman*, 1935, Heinrich Himmler

For its May 1, 2006, edition, Newsweek ran a cover story on the case, featuring booking mug shots of two of the indicted players and the headline, "Sex, Lies, and Duke"--which could hardly have done more to infer the guilt of the players and convict them in the mind of the public. The accompanying article, "What Happened at Duke", spoke of "raunchy rich kids", "elite", and "privileged".

"The story has freakish turns, but it is also the product of a widespread college-age culture that proud parents do not wish to examine too closely: future Masters of the Universe who sometimes behave like thugs."

Lacrosse players at Duke were said to have a reputation for "swagger" and "rowdiness".

"Strutting lacrosse players are a distinctive and familiar breed on elite campuses along the Eastern Seaboard. . . the players tend to be at once macho and entitled, a sometimes unfortunate combination."

By contrast, in the fall of 2005, an article in Duke Magazine referenced the lacrosse team this way :

"Despite their success, Danowski and his fellow lacrosse players are largely unheard of and unheralded on a campus where high-profile sports such as basketball and football dominate the collective sports consciousness. A low recognition factor has its pluses, Danowski says. Small-sport collegiate athletes tend to be grounded by their relative anonymity and more focused on academics and life after the game. "You look at all the good lacrosse schools and you see they're also very good schools…I think the kids who play lacrosse have more of a balance between academics and athletics." ("After the ball", Duke magazine, September to October 2005)

It would be hard to find a supposedly objective news report employing in the same article, as Newsweek did, a plethora of adjectives like "raunchy", "swagger", "rowdiness", "strutting", "macho", "entitled" and "thugs".

Explaining the cover later, Newsweek editor Evan Thomas said,

"The mug shots reflected the indictments. But I had a twinge at the time, and I wish I'd had a stronger twinge. My advice at the time was we should think about this, but I did not--and I want to be clear about this--I did not bang my hand on the table and say, 'We can't do this.' It was merely, 'Are we comfortable with this?'

"…The narrative was properly about race, sex and class... We went a beat too fast in assuming that a rape took place... We just got the facts wrong. The narrative was right, but the facts were wrong."

Perhaps few would assume that the only impression the public received from the publication of mug shots was that two persons--whom the law requires be presumed innocent until they are proven guilty--had been "indicted".

> The mug shot is a common use of photography in the criminal justice system. . . The conventions of the mug shot were presumably familiar to most people who saw the [O.J. Simpson] covers of Time and Newsweek. . . These conventions of framing and composition alone connote to viewers a sense of the subject's deviance and guilt, regardless of who is thus framed; the image format has the power to suggest the photographic subject's guilt.
>
> ———
>
> In addition, because of the codes of the mug shot, it could be said that simply taking Simpson's image out of the context of the police file and placing it in the public eye, Time and Newsweek influence the public to see Simpson as a criminal even before he had been placed on trial.
>
> --Practices of Looking: An Introduction to Visual Culture, (chapter 1: Images, Power, and Politics), by Marita Sturken, Lisa Cartwright

> "These are arrest or booking photos provided by law enforcement officials. A criminal charge is merely an accusation. A defendant is presumed innocent unless proven guilty.
>
> --standard disclaimer used by Newsday

> "These arrest and booking photos are provided by law enforcement officials. Arrest does not imply guilt, and criminal charges are merely accusations. A defendant is presumed innocent unless proven guilty and convicted."
>
> --standard disclaimer used by the Chicago Tribune

A characteristic treatment by the press--a joining with the mob to endorse popular stereotypes--is nothing new:

> In story after story, the newspapers printed the most gruesome details of the St. Elmo crime. Each played on stereotypes, repeatedly referring to the attacker as a "Negro brute" and Nevada Taylor as "young white princess." . . Never did either newspaper use its pages to seek to calm the community.
>
> --*Contempt of Court: The Turn of the Century Lynching that Launched a Hundred Years of Federalism*, Mark Curriden and Leroy Phillips, Jr., Faber & Faber, 1999.

> The newspapers certainly played along. Whatever the judge, prosecutor or sheriff told them, they printed as fact. Seldom did they ever attribute information, and never did they seek a second source for confirmation.
>
> --*Contempt of Court: The Turn of the Century Lynching that Launched a Hundred Years of Federalism*, Mark Curriden and Leroy Phillips, Jr., Faber & Faber, 1999.

"There have always been people strong enough to resist the most powerful kings, to refuse to bow before them; there have been very few to resist the masses, to stand up alone to the misled multitude."

--Clemenceau at the funeral of Zola

HOW THE MEDIA MISSED THE STORY

The media with all their resources never found Mangum dancing publicly at the Platinum club.

The media with all their resources never went to find Kim Roberts and interview her.

(The media DID expend the effort to find the players' homes and spent considerable ink denigrating their presumed lifestyles.)

The media didn't ask the basic question of why Crystal Mangum couldn't drive herself but needed one (or two) drivers.

The media didn't report on the full text of what Mangum said in her interview with the News and Observer (which might have cast doubt on her story); nor did it report what her neighbors said about her (which might have had the same result).

The media didn't press Nifong on why DNA testing, which he claimed going to reveal who was innocent, was suddenly not important to the case.

The media never found out that Nifong had never interviewed Mangum.

The media didn't find out that Nifong most likely had never interviewed Kim Roberts, either.

The media didn't follow up on investigating Jarriel Johnson or Brian Taylor, Mangum's drivers.

The media didn't follow up on Mangum's sometime would-be spokesperson, her cousin Jacki; yet it reported Jacki's statements regardless of their inaccuracies.

The media didn't press Duke on why it fired veteran Coach Pressler and canceled the lacrosse season before any guilt was established. (Where were the sports writers?)

The media didn't hard questions about "Rodney King South" or how the incident was handled afterward by Durham police and Raleigh courts.

The media didn't ask how a police chief can be absent from his department for months and yet still claim to be running his department (on full salary).

The media didn't ask why so many potential witnesses in the case were arrested, with the disposition of their cases in the hands of Nifong. The media never commented on its inability, as a result of this, to interview Mangum's ex-husband (about her claim he had tried to drag her off into the woods and kill her); or her boyfriend (about her activities the week before the party on Buchanan St.).

*Number of additional forcible rapes reported in Durham for 2006 : 97**

*Number of forcible rapes reported in nearby Chapel Hill for 2006 : 24**

Number of satellite trucks sent to cover these additional 121 forcible rape claims: 0

Number of television programs devoted to these additional 121 forcible rape claims: 0

Number of magazine covers devoted to these additional 121 forcible rape claims : 0

Number of editorials and cartoons devoted to these additional 121 forcible rape claims: 0

**FBI crime statistics*

Democracy depends upon many things, by far not the least of which is a media watchdog on government. When the watchdog performs like a lapdog, praising its master; or is reduced to performing a secretarial function for government officials (taking down their statements and parroting them without comment to the public), then freedom itself may find itself in jeopardy.

It was like a gauntlet of people they just swarmed us everywhere we went...my mom and my father the day...the day I was indicted my mom and my brothers had to pack up and drive to a friend's house because they parked big trucks... all the trucks that you see outside with satellite dishes on our front yard and they were--from what I heard from our neighbors...they were going after every single person they could...I mean, it was just, everywhere ...after I got out I walked over to, we walked to our car...we tried come out the back entrance of the jail and...they just rushed us and we pretty much had to run to our car to get there and you know from that point on from that initial...rush to our car that was the beginning of just a media frenzy for an entire year, and it continues now.

(camera showing mothers of indicted students weeping silently in the courtroom)

We came out of the parking garage and we were--as soon as they saw us come out of a little tunnel there...a swarm of media...and when we were walking up, we were walking up towards the doors there were Black Panther representatives, or whatever you want to call them, they were dressed in fatigues, and amid all of this chaos with the, with the media, I remember I had planned on keeping my head up...I'm going to walk into this as an opportunity for people to see who I am...and...you could barely, you could barely walk, because the media was so close in front of me that you were worried about stepping on who... whatever correspondent was standing in front of you...and I couldn't see my dad...we just had to do it as fast as we could. and it was just my dad, I think it was Kirk [defense attorney] my dad, Buddy Connor and myself. . . and while we were walking the Black Panthers started screaming out, it felt like from all different angles...they kept saying, Justice will be done, rapist! They said, You're going to get yours, rapist! And from trying to hear that, and I was trying my hardest to keep a straight face ...you don't want to let people know that they're getting to you ...I mean, that was, I was terrified, I was completely terrified and I didn't' know...I mean, I didn't' know whether somebody was going to hit me from behind, or take a shot...I had no idea, I'd never been in a situation like that before in my life...and like I said before, like a gauntlet, it was, we were just tucked into this pocket of media and Black Panthers...and finally we were able to get though the doors.

...once we got in the courtroom, that was my first experience sitting in a courtroom...but we walked in, and there were tons of peoples sitting...like a cafeteria...there were people yelling, there were people shouting all different things, and I tried to ignore it, I felt like was going to be real safe because once you walk in a courtroom you know then you're safe, then...the sheriffs are going to take care of it. And we sat down in the first row...and there was a guy behind me that kept leaning up he,

he leaned up to me and said ...he sort of screamed it out ...and he goes, I don't want to sit next to this piece of_____.

...and he's screaming that out and I didn't want to turn around I didn't want to look at him I didn't want to have to deal with him ...there were comments from all over... from people sitting in there ... I don't even know who these other people were ...but someone in the back in the back corner had screamed out...but they said ...he said, You're a dead man walking! And I mean I was doing my best to try and keep it together but to hear someone--and it's behind you, you can't see it, you can't see who it is--and finally, you know, I think it started to settle down, but the entire time Mr. Nifong would be standing there in the room, and I didn't really know really what he looked like so I wouldn't have noticed him and he had been shuffling his papers around...while this was going on and finally Judge Stephens came in and sort of gave a speech saying this is my courtroom no one is going to behave like that or you'll get thrown out or something, you know, whatever he said...at that point things started to settle down.

The one thing that stuck out to me was that Mr. Nifong sort of smirked to himself at the other table ... at that point I think we sort of understood where we were headed...

--Testimony of Reade Seligmann at Bar Hearing of District Attorney Nifong, June 15, 2007

"Garbage. All of it. The hysteria, the pronouncements, the Alcohol Task Force, the new rules - a monstrous edifice of nonsense built on a foundation of lies."

--*"It Didn't Happen",* The Flat Hat, William and Mary Student Newspaper, February 2004, editorializing about a campus rape claim which turned out to be false.

CASE NARRATIVE : How a Community Responded

"It is a case that talks about what this community stands for."

--District Attorney Michael Nifong

We will have to repent in this generation not merely for the hateful words and actions of the bad people but for the appalling silence of the good people.

-- Letter from A Birmingham Jail, April 16, 1963

CHANGE OF VENUE MOTION

Community Demonstrations

12. As a result of the pre-indictment statements by the State, protests broke out across the community condemning the Defendants. Several protests were held in front of 610 N. Buchanan within the first few weeks following these

allegations. In all, approximately 10 protests have taken place at that location since late March. The "Call for Action," that organized the early protests included "facts" that were taken verbatim from statements of the District Attorney and his office--"facts" which the District Attorney has now apparently conceded are no longer correct.

"UPDATE » WAKE UP CALL AGAINST RAPE
by anonymous Saturday March 25,2006 at 10:55 PM

*"In the early hours of March 14 at 610 N. Buchanan Blvd. two black women went to work as exotic dancers for a Duke Lacrosse Team party. The women were surrounded and had racial slurs flung at them by the aggressive men. The two dancers tried to leave but were coaxed to return. One of the women was pulled into a bathroom and raped, sodomized, and beaten by at least three white men for over half an hour. The accusations are first-degree rape, kidnapping, assault by strangulation and robbery, but the members of the Duke Lacrosse Team are maintaining a strict code of silence. Y'all, a sister--an NCCU student and a mom of two--has been brutally assaulted, and we need to get together and make a big noise! A group of concerned Durham residents are planning a Wake-Up Call against Sexual Assault on AM Sunday (*tomorrow *) outside 610 Buchanan Blvd. This is a *peaceful* protest at the house where the rape occurred. Duke officials say the house is rented by three lacrosse team captains. We will not be trespassing onto the property-- we will line up along the sidewalk without blocking it. Dress warmly, bring your whole family and bring pots and pans and things to bang them with! We are having a "Cacerolazo," or a pots & pans protest, because it is a tool women all over the world use to call out sexual assaulters. Show up on time! If the police inform us that neighbors feel we are disturbing the peace, we will quietly disperse. We are hitting the ground running on this one, so please call at least one person tonight and pass the word on your neighborhood listservers."*

13. Based on media accounts, more than 250 people attended the early protests and, when protesters discovered that no one was living any longer at 610 N. Buchanan, they marched to a house rented by other members of the Duke Lacrosse team. The protesters chanted "shame" and held signs that read: "Real men don't protect rapists," "You can't rape and run," and "It's Sunday morning, time to confess."

---

14. In late March a 'Take Back the Night" rally and march on the Duke University campus included the distribution of anonymous fliers that were placed on automobiles--these fliers contained the photographs of all of the members of the Duke Lacrosse team, and, according to media reports, "urged the players to tell what they know about the incident." (News and Observer, March 30, 2006.)

The explosive nature of the charges, and their exploitation by Nifong, whose remarks served to stir up racial animus, was seen in the streets. At 3.00 AM one morning in late March two white Duke students entered the drive-through lane of a take-out restaurant. A black youth approached and said, You aren't welcome here [in Durham] because you're "going to rape our women". The driver of the car was hit in the head and knocked unconscious.

In the Trinity Park area near the 610 Buchanan Street house cars filled with black youths cruised by, their passengers mimicking shootings, or making obscene gestures and yelling at Duke students. The Chronicle, the Duke student newspaper, warned of the danger of gang violence in the area. This was followed up by a similar warning by the university administration.

CHANGE OF VENUE MOTION

Statements of Public Officials

16. At a demonstration at 610 N. Buchanan on April 1, 2006, two school board members and a former member of the City Council who was running for the State House appeared. (Herald-Sun April 2, 2006.)The two members of the school board commented:

"You've got white kids here at an elite university, and they get all the attention," [Steve] Matherly said. "Our kids are poor black kids in the Durham schools. Their lives have been ruined by years and years of being racially targeted."

The alleged victim -- like [Jackie] Wagstaff, a single mother and a "nontraditional" student going back to college at NCCU --"could have been any female," Wagstaff said.

17. On April 3, 2006, the Herald-Sun published a "guest column" by the Director of the Durham Human Relations Department. In that column, he wrote that: "I am sincerely saddened by the alleged gang rape at a Duke lacrosse team party. My heart goes out to the victim and her family. I pray for her and hope that she can begin the recovery process soon. Let's demonstrate to the world that this type of behavior will not be tolerated here in Durham. Let the media carry the message across the country."

18. At a Durham City Council meeting on April 6, 2006, members of the City Council commented that "...the allegations 'are both appalling and horrific,'" [and another] "termed them 'abhorrent and disgusting.'" Still another expressed "concern" that there would not be DNA matched to the players because others may have been at the party; he was assured that there were "experienced police investigators

who will get through the evidence." City Council members had earlier appeared at one of the many protests at 610 N. Buchanan, one stating that the "wall of silence" was "tragic and deplorable," and the other stating that "it's horrible about the incident. . . . any violence against women should not be tolerated.' (Herald-Sun March 27, 2006.)

19. On April 14, 2006, the Herald-Sun published a column written by a columnist identified as "an emergency judge throughout the state." In that column, the columnist wrote about the case that:

"We can be thankful. Thankful for the fact that we are in a society where one black woman can make her voice be heard. This huge, nationwide response has been caused by the claims of one black woman. It was not long ago that a black woman who claimed to be raped by a white male had little or no chance to proceed with her case."

---

21. On March 31, 2006, the Herald-Sun reported on the reaction of students at North Carolina Central University (NCCU). It noted that one of the students, a junior from Durham who was running for Vice-President of the student government association, was organizing a March on Duke University: "It seems like Duke is trying to sweep these things under the rug." The article noted that a member of the Durham School Board was nearby and nodded during this statement. "Both said the investigation would be proceeding differently if the victim had been white and suspects black. 'Right now, it's all talk and no action,' [the student] said-- 'I don't think true justice will come out of it." The next week, at least three separate groups at NCCU held several events in response to the rape allegations. (Herald-Sun April 1, 2006.)

---

23. On April 7, 2006, the President of the State Conference of the NAACP held a news conference in front of the Durham County Judicial Building. In it he announced that "We are in the middle of a community and legal crisis." (Herald-Sun April 7, 2006.) Speakers at the news conference "expressed concern about the truth being covered up by the lacrosse team's mass of lawyers. 'All this money, all this cover-up, that's why we're not getting anywhere.'" Another speaker declared that 'it's a hate crime and they [the players] made it a race issue when they called her what they did', she added as the audience applauded loudly."

24. Subsequently, on April 9, 2006, at still another rally at 610 N. Buchanan, Bishop John Bennett claimed that, "if truth be told, if it was another ethnic group they would have been charged and a high bond set." (Herald-Sun April 10, 2006.) During that demonstration close to 100 people "nearly all of them black and most of whom appeared to have come straight from the church, yelled along with Bennett as he pointed to the house and shouted, 'Why?'" Bishop Bennett continued, noting that "until justice is served, the house at 610 N. Buchanan will remain a symbol of a system that 'caters to and protects the rich.'"

25. In an interview on MSNBC, the assistant editor of the "Campus Echo,"--the student newspaper at NCCU--revealed that among "the people in the community, it was the belief that the entire lacrosse team should have been arrested: "the overall feel is that they want, you know, the team should have been arrested." ("The Abrams Report" MSNBC, April 11, 2006.)

---

26. On April 16, 2006, interviews with those in the African-American community conducted by the Herald-Sun included

one woman who said that "'I think something did happen in that house. As far as racial [aspects are concerned], if they don't do something about it, there is going to be a big mess. I wouldn't say so far as a riot.'"

27. On April 18, 2006, the Herald-Sun published a column by a person identified as a "scholar-in-residence" at NCCU. In that column, the author wrote that: "What happened on Buchanan Boulevard did not begin on Buchanan Boulevard. Rather, it began decades earlier in organized institutions within the lacrosse players' respective communities. What is termed 'the Duke culture' is American culture. The stereotypes and images of all minorities are indexed to words such as exotic, greasy, lazy, noble savage, smart promiscuous, crime and poverty. The words are deeply embedded into the American psyche. Sociologically, they project an image of dependency, vulnerability, cultural inferiority, and, at the same time, the exalt the sanctification of whiteness, which is power."

28. On April 19, 2006, the Herald-Sun reported on the arrests of Reade Seligmann and Collin Finnerty. In one article, it quoted from a press release issued by the Chancellor of NCCU in which he wrote: "Our hearts continue to go out to the young lady as she goes through this process. We will continue to do everything that we can to support her." In another article, the President of the NAACP announced that his group would "monitor the work of investigators and prosecutors as the case against.. . [the defendants] moves forward." He then stated: "the allegations against the pair 'suggest a downward spiral from privilege and advantage to decadence and deviance." (Herald-Sun, April 19, 2006.)

29. The next day, the NAACP sponsored a "mass prayer meeting" at the Ebenezer Missionary Baptist Church. According to an article published in the Herald-Sun on

April 21, 2006, the audience included members of 35 congregations. It noted that part of the prayer meeting included a "breakdown" of the case by the NAACP attorney. [NC NAACP President] Barber's comments followed a breakdown of the case by NAACP lawyer Al McSurely, who characterized District Attorney Mike Nifong as an 'honest' public servant, and the accused members of the lacrosse team as 'white boys mainly from the North who started drinking beer at 2 p.m.'

McSurely said the players' defense attorney would be quick to roll out complex, 'minute-by-minute accounts of the night of March 13-14, verified by ATM receipts and testimonies of cab drivers in an effort to obscure what really happened --a crime that, in his estimation, probably took only 10 minutes. "That's all it takes.... I won't say anymore on that," McSurely said. The article further noted that when a request was made for "even-handed justice," it was met by laughter and giggles.

30. The Rev. Jesse Jackson came to Durham to assist in the African- American community's response; he immediately pledged to fund a scholarship for the accuser to North Carolina Central University. (Newsweek Magazine, May 1, 2006.)

31. The New Black Panther Party for Self-Defense also led a protest march. The head of the New Black Panther Party, Malik Zulu Shabazz, spoke directly with the District Attorney and claimed that they discussed the case at "some length." (News and Observer May 2. 2006.) On April 27, 2006, the National Field Marshall for the New Black Panther Party reported that the accuser had received death threats. (Herald-Sun.) The article further noted that the New Black Panther Party was handing out brochures that asked "Had enough of disrespect and racism from Duke University?" and

showed photographs of [the defendants]. In connection with a demonstration that took place on May 1, 2006, at 610 N. Buchanan, the New Black Panther Party issued eight demands which included the demand "that defendants ... be found guilty." (Herald-Sun, May 2, 2006.) During the course of the demonstration, Malik Shabazz, an attorney, led the following chant:

"How do you find the two defendants in this case?" Shabazz shouted.

"Guilty," the crowd shouted back.

Among the demonstrators noted to be present was "activist Victoria Peterson," the co-chairman of the District Attorney's citizen's committee.

---

33. Since that time, the District Attorney has claimed that his political opponents see this prosecution "as a threat to their sense of entitlement," a theme that has been repeated by prominent members of the African-American community. One commented that the Defendants should be prosecuted "whether it happened or not. It would be justice for things that happened in the past," (Newsweek Magazine, May 1, 2006.) and that "this is a race issue . . . people at Duke have a lot of money on their side," (Newsweek Magazine. May 1, 2006.)The Bishop of the Church of Apostolic Revival International openly worried about civil unrest "if people don't think the victim is treated fairly."

34. On May 25, 2006, the attorney for the NAACP announced that he intended to seek a "gag order" in these cases, claiming that defense attorneys were violating the ethical rules of the North Carolina State Bar. (Herald-Sun May 25, 2006.) The same article quoted a journalist with a predominantly

African-American newspaper as saying that "We are seeing powerful forces trying to remove that right [to have the accuser's allegations tried] from her." This claim was repeated by the attorney for the NAACP the next day at a conference in Durham. (Herald-Sun May 26, 2006.)

35. The NAACP Chapter in Durham County has included on its website a "Duke Lacrosse Update: Crimes and Torts committed by Duke Lacrosse Team Players on 3/13 and 3/14 as Reported in the press, mainly from the Three Players' Defense Attorneys." NAACP Website. The "Update" then lists 82 separate paragraphs of "evidence" which it claims proves that the Defendants were guilty of these and other crimes. This "evidence" includes the following posted "facts":

"The satellite party houses, although owned or rented by Duke students, are not under the jurisdiction of the Duke police. Thus, if a Duke coed were to be given a date-rape drug at a party in one of these houses, and was gang-raped, Duke police and Duke would not have to report this in the annual sexual assault reports that Federal Law mandates." Paragraph 5.

"The serial killer in American Psycho followed a similar pattern with his female victims." Paragraph 52.

"The defense lawyers are paid large fees to zealously represent their clients. A tactic in every sexual assault case is to intimidate the survivor/witness of the attack into refusing to testify. As part of this tactic, they released their photos of the dancer, they have dug up old stories about how she was traumatized as a teenager, and have tried to put her past character on trial, knowing well her past sexual history is off limits before the jury." Paragraph 74.

"The strategy of the Duke 3 Support Group is as old as sex. Attack the survivors, the vulnerable women. Trash them to

re-traumatize them. First the night of the assault, and then every night after on the TV talk shows, the blogs, and on the front pages of the press --trying to bludgeon them into to being afraid to testify." Paragraph 75.

"The three defendants they have two mountains to climb. First, they must deflect public attention from their boorish, racist, and illegal behavior by mounting outlandish attacks on the survivor and the D.A. Second, they must deal with a mountain of physical evidence, that is corroborated by, we have reason to believe, accounts of some of the men who were at the party who have cooperated with the police and the D.A. from early on.' Paragraph 78.

36. Since the re-election of the District Attorney, members of the African- American community have announced: "This goes to show that justice can't be bought by a bunch of rich white boys from New York,' said Harris Johnson, a former state Democratic party official and Durham resident for 56 years. 'Duke has a habit of sweeping things under the carpet. I guess this goes to show that no matter how much money you have, Durham is owned by its citizens." (The Chronicle November 8, 2006.)

From Scottsboro:

"Now the question in this case is this: Is justice in the case going to be bought and sold in Alabama with Jew money from New York?" --Prosecutor Wade Wright addressing the jury in the Scottsboro trials.

--NY Times, 4/8/33

From Scottsboro:

"We all have a passion, all the men in this courtroom, and that is to protect the womanhood of the state of Alabama."

-- Prosecutor Knight addressing the jury in the Scottsboro trials Nov. 30, 1933

"You are the shame of the planet earth today. You are a shame to yourselves and you are a shame to the University," Shabazz said outside the [Buchanan St.] house. . .

The group leader added that the current system is one of white male supremacy, and that women--especially black women-need to be protected.

--Duke Chronicle, May 1, 2006

"[The players are] suffering from a deep sickness in their souls".

--The Rev. William Barber, president of the North Carolina NAACP

The North Carolina NAACP adopted a posture of vigorous support for the accuser. It appointed NCCU law professor Irving Joyner as a special "watchdog" for the case. It published 82 paragraphs of contention about the case on the Internet, many of which contained erroneous or false information, and which were left in place for months, despite repeated calls for them to be corrected. It reversed a decades' old policy of encouraging a change of venues for well-publicized cases and insisted that the lacrosse case must be tried in Durham.

> "A Durham jury may see things differently than would an Orange or Wake County jury because the Durham jury will probably have more African-Americans on it than would be involved in most other counties in North Carolina....This case originated in Durham and should be tried here."
>
> --Irving Joyner

In other words, an official spokesman for the NAACP, which for so long fought against the railroading of innocent defendants by racially-exclusive juries, was now insisting that race must be included as a significant factor for members of the lacrosse jury.

A jury--which was originally intended to be comprised of "peers" ("equals") of the accused, in order to prevent a prosecutor's bias from convicting an innocent person--was now supposed to be revised and be composed of representatives of local community interest. (But what if the local community itself is biased? And what protection does a jury provide if it is not crafted to be "the last bastion of refuse for the accused"?)

The NAACP also called for a gag order, which would effectively have muzzled the defense attorneys after Nifong had already flooded the media with derogatory accusations--and thus poisoned the jury pool.

By these actions it effectively threw away an opportunity to argue for reform of the North Carolina judicial system; meaning that future defendants will remain without protections which might prevent more innocent persons from being charged and convicted. It treated no other case in this way; and as far as can be noted, it had nothing to say about the other 121 rape accusations made in the Durham vicinity in 2006.

From Scottsboro:

[In the face of] one of the most atrocious crimes ever committed in this section, [the town of Scottsboro] set the rest of the South an impressive example of self-restraint and in readiness to let justice be done in a legal and orderly manner.

--Chattanooga Daily Times

From Scottsboro:

"There [is] no doubt [of the defendants' guilt among] those who are here and know the facts in the case."

--letter from Scottsboro resident
I. J. Browder in The New Republic

From Scottsboro:

[The verdict was] a natural reaction to the flamboyant attempt on the part of outsiders to take a hand in an affair that the people of Alabama would. . . properly conceive to be for their own decision.

--Charlotte Observer

From Scottsboro:

To Hell with 'em, we say. We've not asked for their advice [about Scottsboro]. Don't need it and feel that we are entirely capable of handling our own affairs without outside interference.

--Dothan [Alabama]Wireglass Journal

"I am tired of people from out of town trying to tell people in Durham what they should do in the lacrosse case. . .

--letter from Durham resident George Harris
in the Herald Sun, Oct. 22, 2007

The misguided outrage and animus against Mr. Nifong by the state, media, and public, along with the unwarranted capitulation by Duke University to the outrageous demands of the avaricious carpetbagger families of Duke Lacrosse defendants in reaching an out of court settlement, are not only responsible for the perpetuation of animalistic party behavior by Duke students in Durham neighborhoods, but are the grounds for the related legal problems that now face the city.

--Justice for Nifong

From Scottsboro:

Alabamians in general feel that a prejudice as strong as any of which they themselves may have been guilty in the past has actuated some of the committees and individuals from outside the State who have concentrated funds and legal talent at Scottsboro in efforts to undo the death sentence passed upon eight Negroes convicted of criminal attack upon two white girls... Alabama Newspaper Editorial (from 1931)

From Scottsboro:

Since taking charge of the [Scottsboro boys'] defense he had examined more than 1,000 prospective jurors from Morgan County without yet finding one who would admit that he harbored the least bit of prejudice against the Negroes or would treat them any differently than he would white defendants in a court of law, said Mr. Leibowitz.

Yet, he continued, outside the court room on the streets or Decatur white men had told him privately that a Negro did not have a chance and that his life was as worthless as a burned matchstick.

New York Times, July 24, 1937

A "town hall" meeting [about the lacrosse case] is also planned at 6 p.m. Monday at St. Joseph's African Methodist Episcopal Church on Fayetteville Street. Shabazz is set to be the keynote speaker. The Rev. Philip R. Cousin Jr., the minister of the church and a Durham County commissioner, did not return calls about the event. Representatives of the NAACP and the Nation of Islam are also expected to attend.

-- New and Observer, April 28, 2006

<u>POSTER</u>

URGENT ....Monday May 1st 6:00 pm

BLACK COMMUNITY TOWN HALL MEETING

SUBJECT:

RAPE allegations by a Black Female NCCU Student by Duke University Students

Racism in Durham North Carolina

Unity in our Community and Respect for our Black Women

Keynote Speech by Attorney Malik Z. SHABAZZ
National Chairman NEW BLACK PANTHER PARTY
National Spokesman--BLACK LAWYERS FOR JUSTICE

Panelists include:

North Carolina Central U. Student Leaders
Rev. Phillip Cousins (Host Pastor)
Dr. Bruce Bridges
NAACP
Nation of Islam
Min. N. Muhammad (NBPP)
Min. Y. Muhammad (NBPP)

"Kill every goddamn Zionist in Israel! Goddamn little babies, goddamn old ladies!"

--Malik Zulu Shabazz April 20,2002

Shabazz: Who is that controls the Federal Reserve?
Audience: Jews! (faintly)
Shabazz: What? You're not scared, are you?
Audience: Jews! Jews!
Shabazz: Who is it that controls the media and Hollywood?
Audience: Jews! Jews!
Shabazz: Who is it that has our entertainers...and our athletes in a vise grip?
Audience: Jews!'

--Malik Zulu Shabazz as a warm-up speaker for Khalid Abdul Muhammad at Howard University (February 1994)

St. Joseph's African Methodist Episcopal Church was abuzz Monday evening . . . Many in the audience cheered the new Panthers' attacks on Zionism, capitalism and white Americans.

From the pulpit, NBPP officials said they had come to Durham to share their revolutionary message and defend the accuser in the Duke rape case.

Another NBPP official, spokesman Yusuf Shabazz, expanded on his party's anti-Semitic black separatist agenda. . .

--Duke Chronicle, May, 2006

By report, a speaker mocked the name of one of the defendants because it sounded Jewish. Some in the audience snickered. (Did they also think the names of Jesus and Mary were too Jewish?) Possibly this was the first time a church, consecrated in the name of the husband of a Jewish woman-- whose image, along with the image of her infant Jewish son, it likely often displays-- has tendered its pulpit to a speaker who has urged the murder of Jewish women and children.

In Mississippi a black politician suggested that nooses ought to be brought back and used on drug dealers. Some in his audience walked out, offended by the mention of nooses.

In a Durham church meeting, an audience was made up of 1200 local civic and social leaders. They held books in their hands written by Jews. Jews were depicted in the artwork. They were from a culture which swims in bibles and knows the relationship of Jews to the bible. Yet when speakers from an organization which believes that all Jews should be killed took the pulpit and proceeded to attack Jews, no one got up and walked out.

--blogger

From Scottsboro:

"All New Yorkers do not have horns. As for the Jew money, when the hour of our country's need came there was no question of Jew or gentile, of black or white--all, all together braved the smoke and flame of Flanders Fields."

--Samuel Liebowitz, defense counsel,
summary to the Scottsboro jury

"As I returned to the top of the bank, the rabbi was kneeling and blood was streaming from wounds on his eye and the back of his head...the man raised his bar and hit the rabbi again...While helping the rabbi I noticed that he was growing weaker from loss of blood...."

--*Freedom Summer* [1964], Doug McAdam, pp. 154-155

Twenty-four hours after arriving in Mississippi, one in the first group of volunteers, Andrew Goodman [New Yorker], climbed into a station wagon with staff members James Chaney and Michael Schwerner [New Yorker] , and drove off to investigate a church bombing near Philadelphia, Mississippi. . . it was not until August that the bodies were discovered beneath an earthen dam near Philadelphia...

--*Freedom Summer* [1964], Doug McAdam, pp. 69-70

"What'd he [Schwerner] believe in?"

"He believed in you."

"In me! What the hell!"

"Yeah, I said. " He believed in you. He believed love could conquer hate. He believed love could change even you. He didn't think you were hopeless. That's what got him killed."

---William Bradford Huie speaking with one of the murderers (cited in *African-Americans and Jewish Americans*, by Hedda Garza, pp. 156-157)

"Sometimes good people have to suffer for the good of the organization."

--attributed to Robert K. Steel, Chairman of Duke's Board of Trustees, explaining why the university would not step up to defend its innocent students.

This case was generating a lot of media attention both locally and nationally, hence creating a considerable amount of local public attention. It had all the ingredients for the perfect storm with respect to race, alleged rapes involving students at our city's two prominent universities with distinct student populations of different races. If not handled properly, and carefully, it could have gotten uglier. As a responsible leader, I wanted to be sure our Police Department was conducting a thorough investigation and had the resources it needed to do so expeditiously.

As mayor, it is my responsibility to protect Durham, and, as this case emerged, I did what had to be done to keep tensions in check. It's easy for those who didn't bear the burden of leadership to be critical now. But when it came down to it, I did what I could to keep the city together while national pressure was trying to tear it apart.

--William V. "Bill" Bell Mayor, Durham, NC, October 3, 2007

When Pilate saw that he was accomplishing nothing, but rather that a riot was starting, he took water and washed his hands in front of the crowd, saying, "I am innocent of this man's blood; see to that yourselves."

--Matthew 27:24 New American Standard Bible

CASE NARRATIVE : An End and a Beginning

The trick if you are sitting at the defense table is to be patient. To wait. Not for just any lie. But for the one you can grab on to and forge like a hot iron into a sharpened blade. You can then use that blade to rip the case open and spill its guts out on the floor.

--Michael Connelly, "The Brass Verdict"

In December, 2006, did Nifong's case start to publicly crumble. At a hearing on the fifteenth of that month, which one of the defense attorneys called *"the most remarkable day in court that I have experienced in 25 years of law practice"* the defense team was able prove that Nifong had lied to the court. He had falsely asserted that he had turned over to the defense all the evidence the state had developed in the DNA testing; when in fact he and a private testing lab had colluded to withhold that evidence which tended to prove the players' innocence.

Deliberate concealment of evidence and deliberate lying to the court about such an action can be considered obstruction of justice and would be a felony in North Carolina.

For anyone in law enforcement ("under color of law") to deliberately deprive someone of a constitutional right can result in federal charges of violating their civil rights. If Nifong deliberately concealed evidence from the defendants, then he violated their right to proper due process in a fair court of law.

> North Carolina State Bar Disciplinary Hearing Committee Findings of Fact, Conclusions of Law, and Order of Discipline
>
> June, 2007
>
> The representations contained in Nifong's May 18 written discovery responses were intentional misrepresentations and intentional false statements of material fact to opposing counsel and to the Court...
>
> Nifong's response to Judge Stephens' question was a misrepresentation and a false statement of material fact...
>
> Nifong's representations to Judge Stephens at the June 22 hearing were intentional misrepresentations and intentional false statements of material fact to the Court and to opposing counsel...
>
> Nifong's statements and responses to Judge Smith at the September 22 hearing were intentional misrepresentations and intentional false statements of material fact to the Court and to opposing counsel...
>
> Nifong's representations that he was unaware of the existence of DNA from multiple unidentified males on the rape kit items and/or that he was unaware of the exclusion of such evidence from DSI's written report, were intentional misrepresentations and intentional false statements of material fact to the Court and to opposing counsel...

But Nifong was not ready to give up. Abruptly, a week after the hearing he dispatched an investigator hired by his office to interview Crystal Mangum. According to Nifong's own statements, this would have been the first time she had been interviewed by anyone from the District Attorney's office about her charges. The statement she gave to the investigator suddenly changed important "facts" about her allegations: she now asserted that she was unable to remember if she had been penetrated by any of her attackers; but claimed instead that she recalled she had been penetrated by an object of some kind.

This "new" statement by Mangum would permit Nifong to continue his prosecution but avoid both the exonerating evidence provided by the DNA tests (that no player had any contact with Mangum) and his concealment of it. (The presumption would be that a non-living object would not leave DNA.) The charge would now be "sexual assault", and not rape; but the possible criminal penalties would remain the same.

TYPED INVESTIGATIVE REPORT DATED 12/21/06 CONDUCTED BY INV. LINWOOD WILSON

December 21, 2006
1:00 PM
Interview of Crystal Mangum
Investigator Linwood H. Wilson

———

Crystal Mangum stated, "Dave Evan grabbed me by the arm, Tall one, (Collin Finnerty) grabbed me around my waist and the other one Reade was holding my legs."

[Note that Mangum is now using the actual names of the three defendants. This showed that she had followed news accounts of the case. That would invalidate any in-court identification of the defendants, since it would be assumed her memory of events could have been influenced by news coverage. Without such an in-court indentification--and assuming that the April 4th photo ID session was thrown out as invalid--there would be no basis for the case to proceed.]

There were about 20 guys in the bedroom [although the performance took place in the living room, not the bedroom] and some of them started pushing me into the bathroom while the 3 guys were holding me. Dave Evans was holding my arms and said, "Sweatheart you can't leave."

Crystal Mangum stated she was wearing a white top, red dressy undertop, white skirt and white thongs. Crystal Mangum stated, "once inside the bathroom, Dave Evans was behind me, Reade Seligmann was in front of me and Finnerty was on the floor under Seligmann."

[The small bathroom in which these events were alleged to have transpired could barely hold four persons, if at all. Neither could such gymnastics as herein described be performed.]

...Crystal Mangum stated that Dave Evans was in the rear and after a few minutes he asked one of the other guys (Seligmann) to get back behind her and Seligmann said he didn't want to because he was getting married.

[Seligmann had no plans to get married; and remains single at the time of this writing.]

Finnerty then got up and got behind her and Dave Evans got under Finnerty on the floor and Seligmann was still in front of her. . . Both Finnerty and Evans were trying to get Seligmann to "do it" but he kept saying NO. Then Seligmann got behind her, Finnerty got on the floor under her and Evans got in front of her. . .Someone opened the door and handed them towels and they started wiping me off, Dave Evans off and wiping up the floor.

[Here a towel is introduced into the story. This would later be referred to as the "magic" towel, because a towel was found outside the second bathroom in the house, used by David Evans, which had Evans' DNA on it. However, this towel--which the prosecution desired to present as the one used to wipe of Mangum--somehow managed to have none of Mangum's DNA on it (though it supposedly had been used to wipe her off).

Raising the issue of the towel appeared to many to be the a last desperate attempt by Nifong to retain some kind of DNA link to a rape, no matter how tenuous.]

Crystal Mangum stated, "When they opened the door with the towels I saw Nikki [Kim Roberts] standing in the doorway. Nikki said 'we have to go they want us to leave' and the guys were saying 'get that trash out of here' so after I sat there a few minutes I ran outside screaming trying to get away."

[The neighbors did not report hearing anyone screaming.]

Crystal Mangum stated, "I fell on the ground, they (guys) picked me up, put me in her (Kim's) car and we drove away. "They were yelling names at us and calling us 'Nigger.'"

[The neighbors did not report hearing any use of the "N" word.]

—

By asserting that other players had opened the door to the bathroom in order to hand in a towel (somehow managing to get the door pushed open when four people were inside the tiny bathroom), the story raised the issue of accomplices against whom Nifong could also bring charges.

Mangum's statement also attempted to alter the time of her arrival at the party, to get around the fact that both Seligmann and Finnerty had iron-clad alibis; and to "correct" her claim that David Evans had a mustache, by saying what she really meant was that he had a five o'clock shadow. However, time-stamped photographs (as well as watches visible in those photographs), the testimony of a neighbor who saw Mangum arrive, cell phone records of Mangum and of players, and testimony from her driver and the players, confirm the time of Mangum's arrival.

But because Nifong had never given the defense a Bill of Particulars, he was free to alter the "theory of the case" to "fit" any new developments. (To protect defendants against this kind of conduct, the 6th Amendment provides that "*In all criminal prosecutions, the accused shall enjoy the right . . . to be informed of the nature and cause of the accusation*"--a right ignored in the lacrosse case.)

I thought the hardest point was when they dropped the rape charges and people called me and said congratulations, you know, it's over, it's great, and... that was the hardest point , because these entire... this is the Duke Lacrosse Rape Case and the rape charges were thrown out and ... we continued to live this life of the cloud hanging over our head ..."sexual assault and kidnapping" and it just--at that point we felt we were just being--and it always felt that way--but at that point it felt almost like a sick joke, like we were being toyed with, like he was doing it maliciously on purpose ...

-- testimony of Reade Seligmann before the
Disciplinary Hearing Commission of the
North Carolina State Bar, June 15, 2007

"I feel like there's a mad man chasing my son down the street and there's nothing I can do to stop him."

-- mother of one of the accused

"...the kind of grief for lost ideals you're describing would burn a hole in most souls."

--Duke professor to the mother of one of the accused.

The next court hearing in the case was scheduled for February 5, 2007, to consider motions about dismissing the April 4th identifications. Yet no matter how many twists and turns the prosecution's case might take, in the end, as Nifong had earlier stated, the only twelve people he would have to convince were the twelve sitting on the jury.

An appearance by the accuser in court, reacting emotionally at the sight of her "attackers", might register with the jury more than any prolonged testimony about the nature of DNA, or the validity of time stamps on digital photographs.

It is also possible that Nifong at this point considered dropping the charges against one defendant, Seligmann, altogether, since his alibi (to the extent the abilis were known by Nifong) appeared to be the strongest. Removing him from the defendants would further ease the burden on the prosecution. Nifong curiously stated,

"[The February 5th hearing is] an opportunity [for the accuser] to say, 'Yes, I'm 100 percent certain these are the people who did it. It's also an opportunity to express doubt.

....I have told the defense attorneys that if at any time the victim in this case tells me that she thinks that one of these people who have been identified was not her assailant, as soon as she tells me that, then that case will go away. I've said I'm not interested in prosecuting somebody that's innocent. But until she tells me that, until she tells me these are not the right guys, we're prosecuting this case."

Dropping the charges against Seligmann, however, would mean that every other member of the lacrosse team who had been at the party would then once again become a suspect; meaning increased legal and emotional burdens for all of them, until the case was finally resolved.

Yet no matter what mistakes or outright misbehavior Nifong indulged in, he might have rested secure in the certainty that no intervention by the state bar would take place until after the trial was over--until after he had succeeded in obtaining convictions against the players, for at least some kind of offense. A conviction would shield him from litigation afterward, and leave the convicted unable to sue the state, even if it were overturned later.

What was unprecedented was that the state bar then decided to break with custom; it voted to begin disciplinary action against Nifong while the case was still in progress (instead of waiting until it had concluded). The vote to take this action by the bar's Disciplinary Committee was evenly split, until the chairman broke the tie; thus, by a single vote, by the slimmest possible margin, Nifong was forced to answer to the bar. Absent that, he would have continued as District Attorney, and likely have forced the lacrosse case to a (hopelessly biased) trial.

[James] Cooney [lacrosse defense attorney] said now that the case is over, people have the impression that the system worked well and as intended and there's no way Nifong could have gotten away with his massively flawed prosecution.

"The problem is that is nowhere near the truth," he said. "There are at least a dozen happenstances . . . that if we missed something by just a hair, we would be in the middle of a jury trial right now. We would be in the middle of a jury trial with three young men who were innocent."

"How did Mr. Nifong think he would get away with it? The answer is, he almost did."

-- "Duke lacrosse lawyers overcome a 'rush to judgement'"
The Florida Bar News, June 15, 2007
June 15, 2007

Q. Did you ultimately agree or disagree with the Attorney General's decision to dismiss the charges?

A. I agreed.

Q. Why did you agree?

A. There is significant evidence that proved her wrong, that she was saying. On multiple, multiple times she was contradicted with indisputable evidence, I mean, with her time line of pictures and stuff like that.

Just some of the examples : She explained that the picture that Linwood had showed her, she explained that when she arrived at the party, when if the picture is actually blown up, she is wearing only one shoe.

And we told her, "You don't arrive at a party with one shoe on, you arrived with two shoes on." And she said that it was--that the picture was made up, that it was phony, that it was a fake.

I mean, they just went through her time line of pictures and contradicted her on multiple examples, multiple times. Even when she said that the two people that assaulted her brought her out to the vehicle, well, they have pictures of the people that are putting her into the vehicle, and it is not David Evans and it's not Collin Finnerty, and it's not Reade Seligmann.

And those are the people she's saying attacked her in the bathroom and she said also brought her out to the vehicle where there's pictures of who brought her out to the vehicle, and it's not them.

Q. Did you--by the time the criminal charges were dismissed, did you come to any conclusion yourself about whether you thought Ms. Mangum was sexually assaulted on March 13th and 14th at 610 Buchanan?

A. I came to the conclusion that she--she had made up--that she was not telling the truth about anything. That she was improvising everything that she had said. That everything she was contradicted with, she would make up improvisation of what actually happened of why this happened, why this didn't happen. . .

Q. Was new information developed during the Attorney General's investigation that didn't exist prior to Mr. Nifong's recusal?

A. There was information I had never even seen before. I mean, they were able to have full cooperation with the players. They had numerous, numerous amounts of pictures, documents, alibis, receipts, I mean, it was--unbelievable how much stuff they actually turned over to the Attorney General's office.

Q. Are you talking about the defense attorneys?

A. Yes

--Deposition of Investigator Himan for the Disciplinary Hearing Commission of the North Carolina State Bar May 8, 2007

ORDER OF DISBARMENT

Thursday, July 12, 2007

Michael B. Nifong is hereby DISBARRED from the practice of law

State of North Carolina
Wake County

Before the Disciplinary Hearing Commission of the North Carolina State Bar

---

55, By April 20, 2006, from its testing and analysis, DSI [DNA testing laboratory] had determined that all the lacrosse players, including the two who had already been indicted, were scientifically excluded as possible contributors of the DNA from multiple males found on several evidence items from the rape kit.

56. On April 21, 2006, Nifong again met with Dr. Meehan and the two DPD officers to discuss all of the results of the DNA testing and analyses performed by DSI to date. During this meeting, Dr. Meehan told Nifong that: (a) DNA from

multiple males had been found on several items from the rape kit, and (b) all of the lacrosse players, including the two players against whom Nifong had already sought and obtained indictments, were excluded as possible contributors of this DNA because none of their DNA profiles matched or were consistent with any of the DNA found on the rape kit items.

---

72. The representations contained in Nifong's May 18 written discovery responses were intentional misrepresentations and intentional false statements of material fact to opposing counsel and to the Court.

---

75. Nifong's response to Judge Stephens' question was a misrepresentation and a false statement of material fact.

---

80. Nifong's representations to Judge Stephens at the June 22 hearing were intentional misrepresentations and intentional false statements of material fact to the Court and to opposing counsel.

---

83. Nifong did not comply with Judge Stephens' June 22 Order.

---

88. Nifong's statements and responses to Judge Smith at the September 22 hearing were intentional misrepresentations and intentional false statements of material fact to the Court and to opposing counsel.

---

99. On January 12, 2007, Nifong recused himself from the prosecution of the Duke Defendants.

100. On. January 13, 2007, the Attorney General of North Carolina took over the Duke Lacrosse case and began to review evidence and undertake further investigation.

101. After an intensive review of the evidence, the Attorney General concluded that Ms. Mangum's credibility was suspect, her various inconsistent allegations were incredible and were contradicted by other evidence in the case, and that credible and verifiable evidence demonstrated that the Duke Defendants could not have participated in an attack, during the time it was alleged to have occurred.

102. Based on its finding that no credible evidence supported the allegation that the crimes occurred, the Attorney General declared Reade Seligman, Collin Finnerty, and David Evans innocent of all charges in the Duke Lacrosse case. The cases against the Duke Defendants were dismissed on April 11, 2007.

---

110. Nifong's representation to the Grievance Committee that he did not realize that the existence of DNA from multiple unidentified males on the rape kit items was not included in DSI's report from May 12 until he received the December 13 motion to compel was a false statement of material fact made in connection with a disciplinary matter, and was made knowingly.

---

113. Nifong's responses to the Grievance Committee set forth in paragraph 111 concerning his representations to the Court

at the December 15, 2006, hearing were false statements of material fact made in connection with a disciplinary matter, and were made knowingly.

FINDINGS OF FACT REGARDING DISCIPLINE

1. Nifong's misconduct is aggravated by the following factors:

   a. dishonest or selfish motive;

   b. a pattern of misconduct;

   c. multiple offenses;

   d. refusal to acknowledge wrongful nature of conduct in connection with his handling of the DNA evidence;

   e. vulnerability of the victims, Collin Finnerty, Reade Seligman and David Evans; and

   f. substantial experience in the practice of law.

2. Nifong's misconduct is mitigated by the following factors:

   a. absence of a prior disciplinary record; and

   b. good reputation.

3. The aggravating factors outweigh the mitigating factors.

4. Nifong's misconduct resulted in significant actual harm to Reade Seligmann, Collin Finnerty, and David Evans and their families. Defendant's conduct was, at least, a major contributing factor in the exceptionally intense national and local media coverage the Duke Lacrosse case received and in the public condemnation heaped upon the Duke

Defendants. As a result of Nifong's misconduct, these young men experienced heightened public scorn and loss of privacy while facing very serious criminal charges of which the Attorney General of North Carolina ultimately concluded they were innocent.

5. Nifong's misconduct resulted in significant actual harm to the legal profession. Nifong's conduct has created a perception among the public within and outside North Carolina that lawyers in general and prosecutors in particular cannot be trusted and can be expected to lie to the court and to opposing counsel. Nifong's dishonesty to the court and to his opposing counsel, fellow attorneys, harmed the profession. Attorneys have a duty to communicate honestly with the court and with each other. When attorneys do not do so, they engender distrust among fellow lawyers and from the public, thereby harming the profession as a whole.

6. Nifong's misconduct resulted in prejudice to and significant actual harm to the justice system. Nifong has caused a perception among the public within and outside North Carolina that there is a systemic problem in the North Carolina justice system and that a criminal defendant can only get justice if he or she can afford to hire an expensive lawyer with unlimited resources to figure out what is being withheld by the prosecutor.

7. Nifong's false statements to the Grievance Committee of the North Carolina State Bar interfered with the State Bar's ability to regulate attorneys and therefore undermined the privilege of lawyers in this State to remain self-regulating.

8. This Hearing Committee has considered all alternatives and finds that no discipline other than disbarment will adequately protect the public, the judicial system and the profession, given the clear demonstration of dishonest conduct,

multiple violations, the pattern of dishonesty established by the evidence, and Nifong's failure to recognize or acknowledge the wrongfulness of his conduct with regard to withholding of the DNA evidence and making false representations to opposing counsel and to the Court. Furthermore, entry of an order imposing discipline less than disbarment would fail to acknowledge the seriousness of the offenses committed by Nifong and would send the wrong message to attorneys regarding the conduct expected of members of the Bar in this State.

Based upon the foregoing findings of fact, conclusions of law and additional findings of fact regarding discipline, the Hearing Committee hereby enters the following

ORDER OF DISCIPLINE

1. Michael B. Nifong is hereby DISBARRED from the practice of law.

Signed by the Chair with the consent of the other hearing committee members, this the 10th day of July, 2007.

F. Lane Williamson
Chair, Disciplinary Hearing Committee

Additional remarks by F. Lane Williamson
State Bar Disciplinary Panel Chairman

Thank you for your patience. The hearing committee has deliberated and we are in unanimous agreement that there's no discipline short of disbarment that would be appropriate in this case given the magnitude of the offenses we have found and the effect upon the profession and the public.

I do want to make some remarks as to why we reached our conclusion. This matter has been a fiasco. There is no doubt about it. It has been a fiasco for a number of people, starting with the defendants and moving out from there to the justice system in general. We've heard evidence over the last several days of how that came about. Though we are lawyers and a school administrator — we're not psychologists — you have to ask yourself, "Why? Why did we get to the place that we got?"

I want to say something about who the victims are here. The victims are the three young men to start with, their families, the entire lacrosse team and their coach, Duke University, the justice system in North Carolina and elsewhere. And indeed prosecutors — honest, ethical, hard-working prosecutors throughout the nation — as we've heard through anecdotal evidence are victims of this conduct. And in particular the justice system is a victim of the way this was taken out of — this Mr. Smith testifying — taken out of the courtroom and put in the hands of the public and not only the public in general but into a media frenzy unprecedented in anyone's experience.

But the fact that if these extraordinary [events] had not come to pass, leading to that declaration of innocence, raises another point that we should all be aware of, which is that the person who is the most powerful in the criminal justice system is not the judge and except at the end of the process it's not the jury, it's the prosecutor who makes the charging decision to start with.

The prosecutor, as any defense lawyer will tell you, is imbued with an aura that if he says its so it must be so. And even with all the constitutional rights that are afforded criminal defendants, the prosecutor merely by asserting a charge against defendants already has a leg up. And when that power is abused, as it was here, it puts constitutional rights in jeopardy. We have a justice system but the justice system only works if the people who participate in it are people of good faith and respect those rights.

When I think back to those early days in the spring of last year and we think of how public opinion was so overwhelmingly against these defendants and you think of the public aggravation that they suffered and then you look at how the truth came out slowly in small increments and look at the situation now as to what public opinion is there is a 180-degree turn. And those who made a rush to judgment based upon an unquestioning faith in what a prosecutor had told them were made to look foolish and many still do look foolish.

But we've had an opportunity over the last several days to hear additional evidence — and while it is really not within the purview of the panel to make such a pronouncement — I want to say again that we acknowledge the actual innocence of the defendants. And there is nothing here that has done anything but support that assertion.

It's been truly — a fiasco is not too strong a word. . . But I certainly hope that this process will help assuage the harm and stop the ripples that seemed to start when the stone was thrown in the pond. They just got bigger and bigger. But hopefully they will ebb from this point forward.

We expect to enter a written order in the near future. I won't put a timetable on it. It will take a little time. But again that will be a final order and I understand the defendant has waived his right to appeal.

So unless there is anything further for us to address, this proceeding is concluded. Thank you.

"You waved a petition. You waved it in the air, like a banner! . . . You were on TELEVISION. An artist drew a picture of you brandishing your petition like Robespierre or Danton, and you were on TELEVISION! You played to the mob, didn't you-- and perhaps there are those right now in this courtroom who ENJOYED that performance! Well, I got news for you! Those who come into THIS courtroom waving banners. . . LOSE THEIR ARMS! . . . DO I MAKE MYSELF CLEAR?"

--Judge Kovitscky in *Bonfire of the Vanities, by* Thomas Wolfe

Prosecutors Drop All Charges in Duke Case

RALEIGH, N.C. (April 11) -- The Duke lacrosse rape case finally collapsed Wednesday, with North Carolina's top prosecutor saying the three athletes were railroaded by a district attorney who ignored increasingly flimsy evidence in a "tragic rush to accuse."

North Carolina Attorney General's Office
North Carolina Department of Justice

SUMMARY OF CONCLUSIONS

in the investigation of the Duke lacrosse case

The State's cases rested primarily on a witness whose recollection of the facts of the allegations was imprecise and contradictory. This alone would have made it difficult for a prosecutor to prove the allegations. However with additional evidence uncovered in the new investigation, it was clear that there was no credible evidence that these crimes occurred at 610 N. Buchanan Blvd. in Durham that night.

Because of the lack of evidence and the additional affirmative proof that these crimes did not occur during this time, the Attorney General along with his special prosecutors, Senior Deputy Attorney General James J. Coman and Special Deputy Attorney General Mary D. Winstead, believed it was in the best interest of justice to declare these three individuals innocent of these charges.

The Attorney General and his special prosecutors based their decision on the totality of their review of the evidence. Primarily, their investigation found that:

The accusing witness's testimony regarding the alleged assault would have been contradicted by other evidence in the case from numerous sources;

The accusing witness's testimony regarding the alleged assault and the events leading up to and following the allegations would have been contradicted by significantly different versions of events she told over the past year;

No testimony or physical evidence would have corroborated her testimony;

The accused individuals were identified through questionable photographic procedures;

Credible and verifiable evidence demonstrated that the accused individuals could not have participated in an attack during the time it was alleged to have occurred;

The accusing witness's credibility would have been suspect based on previous encounters with law enforcement, her medical history and inconsistencies within her statements.

The Investigative Method

The Attorney General's Office special prosecutors, together with agents from the State Bureau of Investigation (SBI) and assistance from the Durham Police Department, spent 12 weeks reviewing the case files, questioning witnesses, examining evidence and collecting information. They reviewed more than 7,000 documents including the original police and prosecution investigative reports, cellular telephone records from witnesses and the accused individuals, state and private laboratory records, defense summaries, and records which remain under seal by court order.

They reviewed more than 600 photographs, including police non-testimonial photographs of Duke lacrosse players and 25 photographs and two videos of the accusing witness taken by individuals who were at 610 N. Buchanan Blvd at the time in question. They verified through expert witnesses and sworn affidavits that the metadata times reflected in the photographs and videos were accurate.

The special prosecutors and SBI agents interviewed 47 people, including 17 members of the Duke University lacrosse team, one of whom was the team's only non-white player, and two other students, all of whom attended the party. They interviewed medical personnel, police officers and attorneys for the indicted players. The special prosecutors asked Durham Police Department investigators and SBI agents to follow a number of investigative leads. The special prosecutors also consulted with SBI experts on DNA, toxicology, blood chemistry and other forensic evidence.

They visited the house at 610 N. Buchanan Blvd. The Office of the Attorney General's review of this information helped to establish a sequence of events that occurred that night.

The Special Prosecutors therefore concluded that the results of the DNA testing did not support a prosecution of any of the three accused individuals.

Credibility Issues

The special prosecutors met with the accusing witness a number of times and questioned her about inconsistencies that existed at the time the Attorney General's office accepted the case, as well as other inconsistencies that had arisen since then. This was apparently the first time these questions of inconsistencies had been asked formally. In meetings with the special prosecutors, the accusing witness, when recounting the events of that night, changed her story on so many important issues as to give the impression that she was improvising as the interviews progressed, even when she was faced with irrefutable evidence that what she was saying was not credible. The accusing witness attempted to avoid the contradictions by changing her story, contradicting previous stories or alleging the evidence had been fabricated.

She stated that they danced in a bedroom not the living room. When confronted with credible photographic evidence to the contrary, she claimed Duke paid someone to alter the photos. She routinely denied she made various earlier statements that were attributed to her by law enforcement officials. She denied that she had made statements attributed to her in medical reports both the night of the alleged attack and in the ensuing days.

The accusing witness claimed that the photograph of her on the back porch at 610 N. Buchanan Blvd., time-stamped at 12:30 a.m. and in which she is smiling broadly, is a picture of her arriving at the party. When the special prosecutors pointed out that she was wearing only one shoe, she persisted in her position that the picture was taken when she arrived at the house.

In the same interview, the credibility of the accusing witness's ability to identify the alleged attackers was further called into doubt. When asked how she could recall with such certainty who allegedly attacked her she claimed she was good at remembering faces. When the special prosecutors brought Officer Gwen Sutton of the Durham Police Department into the interview room, the accusing witness claimed she did not know Officer Sutton and had not seen her before that day. Officer Sutton had spent more than five hours with the accusing witness during the early morning hours of March 14, 2006.

When asked how she could be certain of her identifications of her attackers, she said she was dizzy when the dancing started, she "woke up" in the bathroom, and then was dizzy afterward.

In a meeting with the special prosecutors on April 4, 2007 the accusing witness demonstrated unsteady gait, slurred speech and other mannerisms that were consistent with behaviors observed by numerous witnesses who were at the party the night in question and confirmed through a video taken that night. The special prosecutors confirmed that the accusing witness had taken Ambien, methadone, Paxil and amitriptyline, for which she had prescriptions, prior to meeting with the special prosecutors that day.

The Conclusion

While prosecutors acknowledge that rape and sexual assault victims often have some inconsistencies in their accounts of a traumatic event, in this case, the inconsistencies were so significant and so contrary to the evidence that the State had no credible evidence that an attack occurred in that house that night.

Based on the significant inconsistencies between the evidence and the various accounts given by the accusing witness, the Attorney General and his prosecutors determined that the three individuals were innocent of the criminal charges and dismissed the cases April 11, 2007.

"We believe that these cases were the tragic result of a rush to accuse and a failure to verify serious allegations. Based on the significant inconsistencies between the evidence and the various accounts given by the accusing witness, we believe these three individuals are innocent of these charges."

--North Carolina Attorney General Cooper at the press conference announcing results of his investigation into the lacrosse case, April 11, 2007

In a single word [innocent], the man gave us our life back. In a single word ...everything that, everything that had happened, all the bad stuff that we had to go through... were erased when he said it...

We were sitting in the room, all of us in a hotel room, and we were watching ...and it felt like an eternity...and he was very deliberate in the way he was saying everything, and he said... there's insufficient evidence to go forward ...no one in the room reacted, no one said a word and then he kept going and he said, you know, we believe these boys are innocent....the room just erupted, just erupted. I mean that was (witness struggling to retain composure) I only. . .

My whole life turned around on that one word.

-- testimony of Reade Seligmann before the Disciplinary Hearing Commission of the North Carolina State Bar, June 15, 2007

APPENDICES

From Scottsboro:

"The whole damnable thing was a frame-up of two irresponsible women."

--Samuel Liebowitz addressing the Scottsboro jury

--NY Times, 4/9/33

From Scottsboro:

"I didn't get justice. I didn't lie in Scottsboro. I didn't lie in Decatur and I ain't lied here. I've told the truth all the way through and I'm gonna go on fighting til my dying day or til justice is done."

--Victoria Price, Scottsboro accuser, at the unsuccessful conclusion of her suit against NBC in 1977 for its portrayal of her in a TV movie

"I'm not just someone who tried to frame innocent Duke students"

--Crystal Mangum, press conference October 23, 2008

From Scottsboro:

But if she had lied about the rape, she had done so because she lived in a setting which encouraged and rewarded this monstrous lie.

--Dan T. Carter, Scottsboro, a Tragedy of the American South

About a month ago, we were sitting around talking with some friends, and my friend asked [my son] "What are some of the good times you remember from Duke?" His answer shocked and saddened me. He said, "I never think of the good times, because it brings me back to the bad times, which are just too painful to think about."

--mother of an unindicted player

DEFENDANTS' PRESS CONFERENCE

after the declaration of innocence by the North Carolina State Attorney General

April 11, 2007

JOE CHESHIRE: (David Evans' Attorney)

Let me introduce, first, the families to you all.

(APPLAUSE)

CHESHIRE: I want to make just a brief comment about these three groups of people.

I have two boys myself. Both are grown, both lacrosse players. I've said quite often that if you don't have children, you don't understand what the words love and fear and hate and joy are. You don't understand any of the emotion words. You might think you do. You might have a girlfriend you love or you might love your dad or your mom, but you don't know what love is.

And you don't know what pain is. And I want you all to know that these people have suffered as much pain as one could suffer without losing a loved one. But I also want you to know that they have done it with grace and pride, like no one you have ever seen. And I have never in my life been prouder to know mothers and fathers than I am to know these three groups of moms and dads.

(APPLAUSE)

CHESHIRE: ... I do want to remind you all of one brief thing. On March the 30th of last year, when the press was completely out of control, when these boys were the guiltiest people on the face of the Earth, when everyone in this country was pillorying them as hooligans and rapists, I called a little press conference in my office and I looked at you national media and you local media and I said --I was kind of scared when I said it -- but I said you all are wrong and when this case is over, you're going to be embarrassed if you don't open your eyes and listen to what the truth is.

Somebody in the press said to me afterward, we've never had anybody speak to us like that. That's a pretty dangerous thing to say.

Well, Roy Cooper said a word today. The word is I N N O C E N T. And I want to make sure everybody has got that and knows how to spell it. These young men were, are and always have been innocent.

CHESHIRE: I don't -- I don't-- I don't want to go on -- I don't want to go on forever about these young people. But they have been mistreated as badly as any group of young people I have ever seen. And any of you that have had a child who works 40 hours a week at their studies and 40 more hours a week at their sport and has the discipline and desire to do that and also does community service and has grade point averages above 3.0, to say that those people are not fine people and to pillory them and talk down to them is just disgusting, to put a word on it.

I'd like to call on Dave Evans, if I may.

He would like to make some comments to you all.

DAVID EVANS: Thank you all for being here.

Just as this saga is ending, I'd like to say we all got stuck on the elevator on the way down and never thought we would ever make it to here. But we finally have.

But I'd like to start out by thanking the attorney general and the special prosecutors for their diligent and professional job in reviewing the case file. It's been 395 days since this nightmare began and finally today it's come to a closure.

From the very beginning, many of the men who are sitting in this room, including myself, Reade and Collin, have said that we were innocent. And we're just as innocent today as we were back then. Nothing has changed. Facts don't change. And we have never wavered in our story.

EVANS: In addition -- I've got many other 'thank you's and I could never get to them all --but my parents and my sister-- lord knows I've put them to hell and back and their support has let me remember and stay true to who I am in the face of tremendous scrutiny, speculation and outright fantastic lies.

When things were being said about me by people who had never met me, never cared to interview me, they kept me close. And this could have separated us all, but we stayed close and we're a stronger family because of it.

I don't take lightly the fact that their hard work, their success and their sacrifice has allowed me to be represented by such fine lawyers. Many people across this country, across this state, would not have the opportunity that we did. And this could simply have been brushed underneath the rug just as another case and some innocent person would end up in jail for their entire life.

And it's just not right. And I thank God every day that my parents have worked as hard as they have.

And thank you. And hugs and kisses. I won't do it now but...

I'd like to thank all the members of the university lacrosse team, Duke's University men's lacrosse team -- men's and women's -- who stuck together. We know who we are. A great disservice has been done to the sport of lacrosse through this whole thing and the stereotypes just aren't true. They sell magazines, they sell newspapers, but they are not anything that represents us as a sport, as a school, as a university and as a team, and they are wrong.

Along those lines, I'd like to thank my coach, Mike Pressler, who sacrificed everything. Sixteen years he spent building up a team to fall on the swords so that we could continue as a team at the university he loved, and we owe him everything. And I know he's out there...

(APPLAUSE)

EVANS: I can say, over the past year, I've gotten to know Reade, Collin and their families very well, and you couldn't find two more incredible boys -- men. People don't like us being referred to as boys. We are men and we accept responsibility for that.

I could never imagine what they have gone through. I was indicted the day after my graduation. And as difficult as that weekend was, finding out on Friday before I was indicted on Monday, I reached a pass in my life where I could take some time off. I still worked through it. I didn't want to have idle hands.

But these boys were ripped out of school --the team that they loved, their friends, everything they'd ever worked for -- based on lies. And now they try to regain whatever they had before -- a university that will support them; their education, most importantly.

And I can tell you they are exceptional students, exceptional athletes and exceptional young men who are mature vastly beyond their years. . . All they want to do is go to school and graduate.

I had that honor. Let's just hope that they can, as well.

I'd like to say once again -- and I said it a long time ago -- these allegations are false. These charges were false and should never have been brought. We fully cooperated from the beginning. There was never a blue wall of silence. Look at the facts of the case and you will see that.

It --it's painful to remember what we went through in those first days and it's just a testament to all of our character that we never lashed out. We stood there strong. If you want to know what character is, walk around your campus and see signs with your photo all over it and "wanted" signs and have people in the media relating to you to Hitler and other terrible people from history when you've done nothing wrong.

That is character to sit there and take that, as the young men of the Duke University men's lacrosse team did.

I hope that something good can come from this. In this past year that was robbed from our lives, all of the men of the Duke men's lacrosse team have gone to hell and back. But I hope -- and all of us sincerely hope -- that it was not in vain.

So first and foremost, I hope that people can realize innocent people can be charged of a crime and it is up to the justice system to determine guilt or innocence, not the news, not speculators and not people with some other agenda.

That is why there is a legal system. And today the legal system has prevailed.

Secondly, I hope that the state of North Carolina can address some issues that arose from our case, most notably the grand jury procedures. They are a check on the power of the prosecutor and in this case there are no records of what was used to secure indictments against the three of us. We have no idea.

The evidence shows that exculpatory evidence was there, but we cannot go back and understand why we were indicted. There was no "there" there. There was no factual evidence. It was speculation and we do not know and how can we, as a country and a legal system, control the people who are supposed to enforce it if they can simply say whatever they want to say, produce whatever they want to produce and nobody else has an opportunity to see or ever question it.

And I hope that the state assembly can address that. I know that they're addressing other issues as it relates to this.

In closing, I'm excited to get on with my life. It's been a long year -- longer than you could ever imagine. But I hope these allegations don't come to define me. I hope that the way that I could be remembered is sticking up for my name, for my family and for my team against impossible odds, impossible odds -- the entire country against us.

And we fought back for our names. You can never tell what life is going to give you, what curve balls, but you can be judged on how you handle the situation that's brought to you. And my family and I can sleep at night knowing that I did everything that I have always been told to do.

I never lied. I went in and cooperated from a day after the party and I can walk with my head held high and sleep at night knowing that I could not have done anything else to prove my innocence. And this day has been coming for a long time.

But, again, I'd like to thank the professionalism of the attorney general's office for giving me back my life. And I look forward to leading it.

Thank you.

(APPLAUSE)

CHESHIRE: Collin Finnerty is now going to address you all and he's going to do that right here from his seat.

COLLIN FINNERTY:

There are many other people I'd like to thank for their continuing upport over the last year.

The three defense teams involved in this case demonstrated their great legal skills, their ability to work together and their commitment to exposing the truth.

My family, and especially my parents -- my mom and dad really showed their true love for each other and for their family, as they held the five kids together through so much. I know my mom is probably feeling the best of anybody in this room. She definitely deserves it. My family has always stood behind me and they were with me with, with only support from the first minute this case broke.

Although we went through many tough times, both emotionally and physically, I feel closer to them now than I ever have before. That's definitely one of the best things that I can take from this case.

Something important about these three families up here, the Seligmanns' the Evans and the Finnertys, is that we have become one big family through all this. We have a bond that will last forever. It's been a very long and emotional year for me and for all of us.

At points it was tough to see the light and even imagine the day without this weight on our shoulders. Knowing I had the truth on my side was really the most comforting thing of all throughout the past year. There were many ups and downs and points like it seemed where it would never end. . .

I now look forward to a lot of things, although I will not miss the constant attention from the media. I'm excited to return to be a college student. I hope to return to the field again to play lacrosse and I can't wait to return to a normal life . . .

Although I have not been away at college over the past year, I have learned a lot. I now understand in a way that I never did before that family and friends are what matters most.

I hope to use my experience to prevent this from ever happening again to anyone. There seem to be some flaws in the legal system that should be addressed, as Dave said, the fact that in North Carolina there are no recordings of the grand jury. And to establish checks and balances on the D.A.

In the future, I will do everything I can to help others who face a situation similar to the one I have faced in the last year.

Finally, I would just like to say thank you for everyone who supported me. This experience will be with me forever and I will never forget all of those who stood next to me throughout the whole thing. The truth finally did prevail, as everyone said it would. Thank you.

(APPLAUSE)

CHESHIRE: Reade Seligmann will now speak with you all. And he will do so from the podium.

READE SELIGMANN: Hopefully you will all bear me right now. I'm a pretty emotional guy and it's a pretty emotional day, so I'm going to do my best.

But I want to start off by saying that we are all deeply saddened by the absence of [the late] Kirk Osborn. Kirk deserved to be here and he stood by my side from the very beginning of this injustice.

(APPLAUSE).

SELIGMANN: Not only has North Carolina lost one of its finest attorneys, it has lost a man who embodied the words honor and integrity. We will never forget his sacrifices and our thoughts and prayers are with his family.

Today marks the end of the year long nightmare that has been emotionally devastating for all of our families. This dark cloud of injustice that's hung above our heads has finally cleared and now we can look forward to moving on with our lives.

I must also thank all of my attorneys --the late Kirk Osborne, Buddy Conner, Antonio Lewis and Jim Cooney, as well as all of the other men at the table. These attorneys did everything they could to ensure that three men did not spend 30 years in prison for a hoax.

This entire experience has opened my eyes up to a tragic world of injustice I never knew existed. If police officers and a district attorney can systematically railroad us with absolutely no evidence whatsoever, I can't imagine what they would do to people who do not have the resources to defend themselves.

So rather than relying on disparaging stereotypes and creating political and racial conflicts, all of us need to take a step back from this case and learn from it.

The Duke lacrosse case has shown that our society has lost sight of the most fundamental principle of our legal system -- the presumption of innocence. For everyone who chose to speak out against us before any of the facts were known, I truly hope that you are never put in a position where you have to experience the same pain and heartache that you have caused our families, where your hurtful words and outrageous lies will forever be linked to this tragedy, everyone will always remember that we told the truth.

In the words of Abraham Lincoln: "Truth is the best vindication against slander."

As the healing process begins for our families, I feel as though it is my responsibility to make sure something positive comes from this experience.

I look forward to continuing my education and pursuing the goals I have always set for myself. I greatly appreciate my educational and athletic opportunities and I look forward to continuing both in the fall.

My ultimate aspiration moving ahead is to live a life that will make all of those who stood by my side from the beginning of this injustice proud to know that they defended the truth.

Thank you.

(APPLAUSE)

CHESHIRE: Jim Cooney?

JIM COONEY, (Reade Seligmann's Attorney) :

...I got involved in this case when I was in the middle of another trial in the fall and Joe Cheshire called me. And I should know better than to take Joe's calls. And he called me and said I have a case for you -- he had already tried to get me in the case once, by the way. And he told me you will never have a more innocent client than this young man. You have got to take this case.

And, of course, I was in the middle of a trial, I was tired, and I said look, let me get through this trial, I'll go up and talk to the family. And I spent two days with Kathy and Reade and Phil -- sat in their kitchen, talked to them, got to know them. And I cannot tell you the amount of pain that family was in.

The only comparison I can make was to a family who, god forbid, that had a child with a potentially fatal disease. And they woke up every morning not knowing whether their child was going to live and go on with a normal life or be taken from them favor.

Because make no mistake about that, if Mike Nifong had had his way, Reade Seligmann would have spent 30 years in jail and he never would have seen his parents alive again outside of a prison waiting room.

And, after spending that time with them, I decided that Joe was right, as he usually is, and I needed to be in this case.

And what I would like to do is take a couple of minutes and talk about heroes and cowards.

There are a number of heroes in this case that haven't been recognized, the magnificent professor Jim Coleman at Duke University, one of the few...

(APPLAUSE)

COONEY: ... one of the few professors who was willing to stay up -- stand up and say, this is not right. We have procedures for a reason. We have presumptions for a reason. What is going on is wrong.

And, as equally brave is a cab driver who is an immigrant to this country, Moez Elmostafa. Moez Elmostafa gave Reade Seligmann and Rob Wellington a ride one night. He didn't know it was a big deal. He got called at 12:14. He picked them up at 12:19. He dropped them off at Duke at 12:46.

And the one thing he really remembered is, they went to Cook Outs [fast food] and they smelled up his cab for a couple of days. And it turned out that that cab ride was the linchpin for Reade alibi, because, during that cab ride, this false accuser said my client was raping her.

And Moez Elmostafa gave an affidavit. He told the truth. He put it under oath, exactly the way we expect a citizen of this country to do. And what did that get him from Mike Nifong? They served a two-year-old warrant on him with no basis, and tried him for a bogus shoplifting charge to see if they could intimidate him. And Moez Elmostafa is still driving a cab in Durham. I don't know if he's listening to this. But he's one of the great heroes of this case.

(APPLAUSE)

COONEY: And, of course, [parents of Reade Seligmann].

I mean, imagine facing a district attorney who wants to put your child in jail for 30 years. And they kept saying, why can't you get it dismissed? Why can't you go here or why can't you go there? And I kept explaining, in North Carolina, no one has a check on a district attorney. There is no procedure for that.

What you have to do is trust me. And we will work together and we have got a plan. . . And it took a lot of courage and bravery for them to hang on and do what they did and not fall apart. Lesser people would have fallen part. They didn't. And they are truly part of the heroes of this case.

The final hero I want to talk about is Reade. Those of you who know me know I have got daughters. And I love them greatly. I always regretted we didn't have a son, because sons and mothers have a special relationship, and I was fine with my daughters.

But let me tell you something. If I had a son, if I had had a son, I would want him to be like Reade Seligmann. Reade Seligmann, in four semesters at Duke, was on the honor roll twice. In this semester, with Mike Nifong trying to put him in jail and mobs threatening his life in the streets, that young man still had a 3.5 grade-point average. Everything you need to know about that, you just heard.

And those are some of the heroes.

I want to talk a little bit about the cowards because, as Joe said, this is a bittersweet day. We're all delighted the justice system worked. But the reason it's bittersweet is because it never should have misfired to begin with. And the reason it misfired is because people were afraid to speak truth to power.

And I want to call out first the newspaper in Durham, North Carolina, "The Durham Herald-Sun," who, to this day...

has not written a single editorial critical of the way in which Mike Nifong proceeded. If "The Durham-Herald Sun" had bothered to stand up and demand proper processes, the presumption of innocence, and doing things the way our Constitution provides, do you think Mike Nifong would have rolled forward?

Instead, they published editorials talking about how bad all the lacrosse players were, and that the lacrosse players should have to prove their innocence, and that, in addition to the crimes that night, there was a crime of a cover-up. And you will not see a word of apology from them.

In fact, as recently as two weeks ago, they were still publishing what they knew were lies, and repeating them.

Now, we will never sue them. They have got way too much money. And, as a general proposition in the law, you don't sue people who buy newsprint by the gallon, because they always win.

But, if they had done what journalists are supposed to do and spoken truth to power, they could have slowed this train down. And there are a number of other people in Durham, some of whom teach for a living, who should have stood up and said, wait a second. Civil rights means something. We have spent careers studying civil rights. We're not going to throw them down the drain simply because a district attorney tells us to.

One wonders what would have happened if the newspaper had stood up for proper processes and if the teachers had stood up for proper processes, whether that would have slowed the last coward of the case down. And you know who I'm talking about.

Now, I'm not going to say anything else about him, because he's got a bar hearing coming up. And I want to give him what he tried to deny Reade, a fair hearing, where he can put on his evidence. And I have got confidence in the state bar. And I have got confidence in their ability to decide that case fairly.

And, quite frankly, we wouldn't be here if the state bar hadn't taken the unprecedented action of filing an ethics complaint against Mr. Nifong in the middle of an ongoing prosecution.

But I will leave him with this one thought. I want him to read Proverbs, Chapter 11, beginning at Verse 29. And I know everyone in here knows that, but I will tell it anyway. "He that troubleth his own house shall inherit the wind. And the fool shall be a servant to the brave-hearted."

Thank you.

(APPLAUSE)

The lacrosse case could never have happened in most of the states of the union, which have laws in place to protect defendants' rights. Some observers would suggest a hypothetical template for how an innocent defendant might be convicted in North Carolina:

Select the judge who will preside over the case. The District Attorney gets to select the judge under the Case Mangement system in use in Durham (and hence, can select a judge who will give him favorable rulings). And many of these rulings, being discretionary, may be very hard to overturn later. (In any event, such overrulings may well be post-conviction.)

Charge a defendant before a Grand Jury, using whatever distortions and false information is necessary. Since no transcript is kept of Grand Jury proceedings, there will be no record of what was said.

A defendant charged by a Grand Jury has no right to a Probable Cause hearing, in which he can challenge the prosecution's case. Hence, do not arrest the defendant until after he is indicted by the Grand Jury.

Inflame the media (make up stories); use innuendo, lies and a smear campaign. The media love a good story and can be spoon fed details by a prosecutor.

Make the public hate the defendant and one is halfway to a conviction. Give the jury a reason--any reason--to compromise and find the defendant guilty of something.

Intimidate through arrest or threat of arrest witnesses who might corroborate the defendant's story.

Coerce the defendant through threats of physical violence after conviction by prison gangs who will have been inflamed against him. Have these same gangs threaten witnesses, family members of the accused, of potential jurors. The prosecutor can disclaim responsibility for this, and lament that he has not sufficient resources to protect everyone at all times.

Delay the trial. A criminal trial in North Carolina can be postponed for a couple of years; in some instances, even longer. Pressure a defendant who is unable to afford the financial and emotional cost of defending himself for years before trial.

Dangle the prospect of a plea baragin before the defendant. His troubles can end, immediately, with the stroke of a pen by the District Attorney. All he has to do is be cooperative. Because it is the intention of the District Attorney to force a plea, nothing he does to get to that point matters, regardless of how much he has to violate the law and the defendant's rights. In these circumstances, the case will never see the inside of a courtroom and the defendant, by confessing to lesser charges, will have vindicated the prosecutor's original decision to charge him in the first place.

Thus, a defedant can be convicted not only of a crime which he did not commit, but which never even happened. That this is not a remote possibility is shown by the lacrosse case, in which three defendants--defendants who could afford the best of legal assistance--still came within a hair's breadth of being tried (and possibly convicted) of a crime which never occurred.

> I have said this from the beginning. This isn't so much about Reade [Seligmann], Collin [Finnerty] , or Dave [Evans]. And it isn't about Nifong or the DPD or even Duke University.
>
> It's about the next poor SOB that gets framed, no matter the color or social standing.
>
> --blogger

AGENDA FOR REFORM

1) Enact a Speedy Trial law

> Sixth Amendment to the Constitution of the United States
>
> In all criminal prosecutions, the accused shall enjoy the right to a speedy and public trial, by an impartial jury of the State and district wherein the crime shall have been committed, which district shall have been previously ascertained by law, and to be informed of the nature and cause of the accusation; to be confronted with the witnesses against him; to have compulsory process for obtaining witnesses in his favor, and to have the Assistance of Counsel for his defense.

Yet in North Carolina, courts had held that jailing a suspect and holding him without trial for up to four and a half years is not a denial of his Constitutional right to speedy justice.

NORTH CAROLINA COURT OF APPEALS

Filed: 7 May 2002

STATE OF NORTH CAROLINA v . HENRY BERNARD SPIVEY, JR.

This Court held in Hammonds that the delay of over four and one-half years between defendant's arrest and trial did not constitute denial of his constitutional right to a speedy trial.

In the present case, defendant was arrested on 10 October 1994 and charged with first-degree murder; he pled guilty on 3 May 1999. Defendant argues the State was not diligent in bringing him to trial in a speedy and prompt manner since his arrest. [i.e., he was held in jail four and a half years before being tried.]

———

The State in this case made a showing as it did in Hammonds, that the dockets were clogged with murder cases and this caused an unavoidable backlog of cases. We are bound by Hammonds holding of "no indication that court resources were either negligently or purposefully underutilized." [Ergo, the defendant's right to a Speedy Trial was not violated because North Carolina retained him in custody for four and a half years before bringing him to trial.]

> Depending on what type of crime has been committed, [in most states, but not including North Carolina] there is a set number of days involved in which to reach the limit of the speedy trial. For a violation, it's 30 days. In a B misdemeanor, it's 60 days. An A misdemeanor, it's 90 days. A felony, it's 180 days.
>
> --D.A., Prosecutors in Their Own Words,
> edited by Mark Baker

2) North Carolina also lacks an absolute Right to a Probable Cause hearing.

> The district court judge will determine if the defendant has or wishes to have an attorney, and will normally schedule a probable cause hearing. If a prosecutor obtains an indictment [from a grand jury] before the scheduled probable cause hearing, no hearing is held.
>
> --Report of Chief Chalmers to City Manager Patrick Baker
> on the Duke lacrosse investigation, May 11, 2007

3) Require transcripts to be kept of Grand Jury proceedings.

The lacrosse defendants' cases were presented to a grand jury which heard more than 80 other cases that day, with an average allotment for each case of only a few minutes. Once the true bill of indictment was voted, the defendants were not able to demand that the State produce any evidence for its prosecution. Nor were they entitled to learn what was presented against them as evidence. Had they been granted a Probable Cause hearing, they could have challenged the confused and contradictory statements made by the accuser. They could have presented the actual SANE medical report (showing the accuser had no injuries). They could have presented the DNA test results proving no lacrosse player had any contact with the accuser. Nifong's prosecution could have been exposed as a sham and stopped before it began.

> ZAHN: When you say it's impossible that that rape might have happened, are you suggesting that the DA is making up something here?
>
> CHESHIRE [defense attorney for indicted lacrosse player] : . . There's no record of what goes on in a grand jury. There's -- there's no tape recording, no court reporter. There are no rules of evidence. . . And grand jurors indict 99.9 percent of the time. So, the fact that they have a grand -- a grand jury indictment means absolutely nothing in the process here.
>
> --CNN, April 17, 2006

> "Eighty-one indictments were returned by the secret jury but none of the cases presented were rejected by the court [on the day the lacrosse defendants were indicted, averaging only a few minutes for each case].
>
> --Fox News, April 2006

> The grand jury returned 190 true bills of indictment Monday, an unusually high number because the March 2 grand jury was snowed out. One bill was found not to be true [no indictment was returned], and 63 were returned to the prosecutor because the jury did not have time to take them up.
>
> --Herald Sun, March 18, 2009

4) There is no effective right to a Bill of Particulars in North Carolina

Nifong did not provide specific details of his charges against the players, and Mangum did not give clear answers and kept changing her stories. Who assaulted her first? Who was second? How many took part? In what room of the house did she dance? In which bathroom of the house was she held against her will? When did this take place, and how long did it take? The accused were never interrogated by Nifong and only Evans ever spoke with police, on the night after the house on Buchanan St. was searched. Nifong claimed that he never talked with Mangum about the case until more than ten months after it began.

Without knowing the specifics of the charges, it would not have been possible to prepare a defense (by, for example, demonstrating that a defendant was not present in the house at the time of the alleged attack). To the end of the case, the charged players were never informed of specifically what each one of them was individually charged with doing.

> Nifong: Defense Attorneys 'Don't Know What My Timeline Is'
>
> --WRAL TV, May 3, 2006, after Seligmann's alibi evidence had been made public

5) There is no effective punishment for making false accusations.

> If rape is one of the most horrible experiences imaginable, isn't being falsely accused of it close behind?
>
> Ellis Henican, Newsday, September 18, 2009

At the time of the lacrosse case, making a false statement to the police could bring a maximum penalty of only a fine of a few hundred dollars and community service. (The penalty for making a false 911 emergency call was more severe.) To this day, persons making false accusations of rape rarely face severe penalties, and never anything near the sentence which would have been imposed on those they accused if found guilty. There is, in practice, no effective deterrent for lying to the police about someone else--even though the lives of the accused may be overturned as a result.

Rape shield laws protect only the accuser. Even if an accuser's previous history may be relevant to challenge her current accusation, it is often inadmissible in court. The accused in a rape case receive no protection, and their identities may be broadcast even before conviction, merely on the strength of an accusation. An innocent accused must bear thereafter the stigma of that accusation--as Dennis Prager says, "The rape of a name is also a rape."

"The lesson in all of this is there is nothing inevitable about justice. Justice is something you have to fight for every day... every hour, and every second."

--James Cooney, lacrosse defense attorney

REPORT OF THE KAUFMAN COMMISSION ON PROCEEDINGS INVOLVING GUY PAUL MORIN: THE HONORABLE FRED KAUFMAN CM QC 31 MARCH 1998

Guy Paul Morin was accused of murdering a young girl in Ontario, Canada. Many years after his conviction he was proven innocent by DNA testing. The Kaufman Commission was an investigation into his case to see how such wrongful convictions could be avoided in the future.

Recommendations:

———

89. Police Culture and Management
Style Police forces across the province must endeavor to foster within their ranks a culture of policing which values honest and fair investigation of crime, and protection of the rights of all suspects and accused. Management must recognize that it is their responsibility to foster this culture. This must involve, in the least, ethical training for all police officers.

———

94. Investigation of an Alibi
Where the defence discloses the existence of an alibi in a serious case, police should be encouraged to have the alibi investigated by officers other than those most directly involved in investigating the accused. Often, the investigation of an alibi need not draw extensively upon the knowledge of the investigating officers themselves. This recommendation permits a more objective, less predisposed approach to the potential alibi.

95. Accountability for Unsatisfactory Police Testimony
If police give testimony found to be false or which Crown counsel reasonably considers to be unreliable, Crown counsel should report these matters to the Chief of Police for investigation. The Ministries of the Attorney General and Solicitor General must implement measures to ensure that these situations are reported to the Chief of Police for investigation, that such investigation occurs, and that the results of the investigation are communication to Crown counsel or to the Court.

96. Police Videotaping of Suspects
1. The Durham [Canada] Regional Police Service should amend its operational manual to provide that all

interviews conducted with suspects within a police station be videotaped or audiotaped, absent truly exigent circumstances. Any practice of interviewing a suspect off-camera before a formal videotaped interview undermines this policy. Similarly, a practice of encouraging suspects to speak off the record or off-camera during an interview undermines this policy. Videotaping or audiotaping ultimately narrows trial issues, shortens trials, protects both the interviewer and the interviewee from unfounded allegations and encourages compliance with the law; such a policy also enables the parties and the triers of fact to evaluate the extent to which the interviewing process enhanced or undermined the reliability of the statement.

2. The Durham [Canada] Regional Police Service should investigate the feasibility of adopting the practice of the Australian Federal Police of carrying tape recorders on duty for use when interviewing on other locations, or indeed for use when executing search warrants or in analogous situations.

3. Where oral statements, which are not videotaped or audiotaped, are allegedly made by a suspect outside of the police station, the alleged statements should then be re-read to the suspect at the police station on videotape and his or her comments recorded. Alternatively, the alleged statement should be contemporaneously recorded in writing and the suspect ultimately permitted to read the statement as recorded and sign it, if it is regarded as accurate.

4. Where the policy is not complied with, the police should reflect in writing why the policy was not complied with.

5. The Ministry of the Solicitor General should work to implement this policy (in the very least) for al major Ontario police forces.

———

98. Police Videotaping of Designated Witnesses
The Durham Regional Police Service should implement a similar policy for interviews conducted of significant witnesses in serious cases where it is reasonably foreseeable that their testimony may be challenged at trial. This policy extends, but is not limited to, unsavory, highly suggestible or impressionable witnesses whose anticipated evidence may be shaped, advertently or inadvertently, by the interview process. The Ministry of the Solicitor General should assist in implementing this policy (in the very least) for all major Ontario police forces.

99. Crown Videotaping of Interviews
Crown counsel should not be mandated to videotape or audiotape their interviews with witnesses. However, the Ministry of the Attorney General should study, in consultation with the Ontario Crown Attorneys' Association or representative Crown counsel, the feasibility of limited videotaping or audiotaping of selected interviews, where the tenor of the anticipated interview or the nature of the person being interviewed would make such a contemporary record desirable to protect Crown counsel or would be in the interests of the administration of justice.

———

106. Crown Education Respecting Interviewing Practices
The Ministry of the Attorney General should establish educational programing to better train Crown counsel about interviewing techniques on their part which enhance, rather than detract, from reliability. The Ministry may also reflect some of the desirable and undesirable practices in its Crown policy manual.

107. Conduct of Crown Interviews

1. Counsel should generally not discuss evidence with witnesses collectively.
2. A witness' memory should be exhausted through questioning and through, for example, the use of the witness' own statements or notes before any reference is made (if at all) to conflicting evidence.
3. The witness' recollection should be recorded by counsel in writing. It is sometimes advisable that the interview be conducted in the presence of an officer or other person, depending on the circumstances.
4. Questioning of the witness should be non-suggestive.
5. Counsel may then choose to alert the witness to conflicting evidence and invite comment.
6. In doing so, counsel should be mindful of the dangers associated with this practice.
7. It is wise to advise the witness that it is his or her own evidence that is desired, that the witness is not simply to adopt the conflicting evidence in preference to the witness' own honest and independent recollection and that he or she is, of course, free to reject the other evidence. This is no less true if several other witnesses have given conflicting evidence.
8. Under no circumstances should counsel tell the witness that he or she is wrong.
9. Where the witness changes his or her anticipated evidence, the new evidence should be recorded in writing.
10. Where a witness is patently impressionable or highly suggestible, counsel may be well advised not to put conflicting evidence to the witness, in the exercise of discretion.

11. Facts which are obviously uncontested or uncontestable may be approached in another way. This accords with common sense.

---

117. Creation of a Criminal Case Review Board
The Government of Canada should study the advisability of the creation, by statute, of a criminal case review board to replace or supplement those powers currently exercised by the federal Minister of Justice pursuant to section 690 of the Criminal Code.

THE NEW ZEALAND INTEGRITY COMMISSION

The Police Integrity Commission is a completely independent agency and was established by the New South Wales [Australia] Parliament on the recommendation of the Royal Commission into the New south Wales Police Service.

Its principal functions are to detect, investigate and prevent police misconduct, and as far as practicable, it is required by law to turn its attention to serious police misconduct by NSW police officers.

What Does the Police Integrity Commission Do?

The Police Integrity Commission (the Commission) was established in 1996 upon the recommendation of the Royal Commission in to the New South Wales Police Service (the Royal Commission).

The Police Integrity Commission Act 1996 (the Act) sets out the principal functions of the Commission. These functions can be summarised briefly as: preventing, detecting or investigating serious police misconduct; and, managing or overseeing other agencies in the detection and investigation of serious police misconduct and other police misconduct. The Commission is also to manage those matters not completed by the Royal Commission. The Commission is, as far as practicable, required to turn its attention particularly to serious police misconduct.

Other functions of the Commission described in the Act relate to: police activities and education programs (s.14); the qualitative and strategic audit of the reform process (s.14A); and the collection of evidence and information (s.15).

Who Are the Commission Officers?

The Commission is not part of the NSW Police Service. It is an independent body. The Commission employs experienced and senior investigative staff made up of lawyers, accountants, current and former police investigators and analysts. The Commission is prevented from having serving or former members of the NSW Police Service on its staff and its police investigators are all drawn from other Australian and overseas police services.

Who Does the Commission Report to? How Does the Commission Report?

The Commission is situated within the portfolio of the Minister for Police.

The Parliamentary Joint Committee on the Office of the Ombudsman and the Police Integrity Commission monitors and reviews the Commission in the exercise of its functions.

The Commission may report on any matter that has been the subject of an investigation. The Commission must report on any matter as to which the Commission has conducted a public hearing. These reports are furnished to the Parliament of NSW as they are completed.

Guidelines of the New York Fair Trial Free Press Conference

Although they are commonplace, photographs of accused individuals in handcuffs or shackles are particularly likely to contribute to the views of readers and viewers that individuals are guilty, despite the fact that those individuals are legally entitled to a presumption of innocence before and during their trials.

Although the press normally argues for more, rather than less, access to news and news subjects, one major newspaper in the state published an editorial condemning the practice of the police of "walking the perp"—creating opportunities for photographers to get shots of accused individuals—because of the dangers of prejudice. Such pictures have become commonplace in newspaper crime coverage and on newscasts.

The Duke case was quite possibly the most irresponsible and indefensible prosecution in modern American history. The defendants were charged and indicted only after they had already been proven innocent by DNA testing.

How could the Duke case happen? It is probably safe to say that the Scottsboro case could not have taken place in New York or Minnesota or California, because the prejudices there, though they existed, were not sufficiently strong to warp the sense and system of justice. It is probably also safe to say that the Duke lacrosse case could not have taken place in those places, and for the same reasons.

Sam Liebowitz' profound belief was that if he proved the stories of Victoria Price and Ruby Bates to be lies, there would not be *"a red-blooded, upstanding citizen below the Mason-Dixon line who will not pray with their heart and soul"* for the acquittal of his clients, the Scottsboro boys. He was wrong about human nature. That same nature, albeit dressed in different clothes, was alive in Durham and bayed with all its might once again for the conviction of those it disliked.

Scottsboro saw the spectacle of a city accepting the testimony of two women--women who had reason to lie in order to avoid trouble with the law--over physical evidence which disproved their charges. Victoria Price and Ruby Bates feared being charged with riding a train illegally, and perhaps with prostitution. Confronted by police, they eagerly grasped at the suggestion that they might have been assaulted by other riders on the train. This set in motion the Scottsboro trials. Many observers believe that this scenario likely repeated itself in Durham, when Crystal Mangum feared she might be committed to a medical facility for observation, and that her custody of her children might be lost. Given the opportunity to say instead that she had been raped--which meant an immediate transfer to a hospital, with no commitment--she presumably leapt at the chance.

Dan T. Carter wrote in "Scottsboro, A Tragedy of the American South", that it was impossible to single out the chief prosecutor of the Scottsboro boys as the sole perpetrator of the travesty, "For his cynical tactics were made possible by the silent acquiescence of dozens of other business, religious, and political leaders. Nor was he the only individual--North or South--who exploited the case for personal and ideological reasons, however lofty." (p. 462)

Perhaps the same words could be applied to Nifong and Durham.

However reprehensible District Attorney Michael Nifong's words and actions have been throughout this case, it would be a serious mistake to see in this tawdry episode just the vileness of one man.

The larger tragedy is what this case revealed about the degeneration of our times and the hollowness of so many people in "responsible" positions . . .

--Thomas Sowell, Feb. 1, 2007

Going back to when we were children, I think most of us in this courtroom thought justice came automatically. That virtue was its own reward. That good triumphs over evil. But as we get older, we know this just isn't true. **Individual human beings have to create justice**, and this is not easy, because the truth often poses a threat to power, and one often has to fight power at great risk to themselves.

--Brad Bannon, lacrosse defense attorney

What is there to prevent this kind of miscarriage of justice from happening in the future? Very little. In North Carolina the state has unlimited resources and still has the deck stacked in its favor. There are observers who feel that it is only a matter of time before the next Duke lacrosse case; the next accusations, the next rush to judgment, the next condemnation before trial (in such circumstances a trial is held not to determine guilt but only to ratify it); and the next innocents to be paraded before the press and have their mug shots displayed.

The Bill of Rights is no more than a scrap of paper unless real people defend what it stands for.

--Walter Abbot

Take the evidence, sift it out and find the truths and untruths and render your verdict. It will not be easy to keep your minds solely on the evidence. Much prejudice has crept into it. It has come not only from far away, but from here at home as well...

You are not trying whether or not the defendant is white or black-- you are not trying that question; you are trying whether or not this defendant forcibly ravished a woman.

You are not trying lawyers, you are not trying State lines. You are here at home as jurors--a jury of citizens under oath sitting in the jury box taking the evidence and considering it, leaving out any outside influences.

Things may vex you. I might say that the court may have been vexed about a great many things. It may have been evident to you that a great many telegrams came in here to me since I have been here. But, gentlemen, they do not affect me whatever or the great principle which the court desires to see done, and that is to see justice done in this case...

We are a white race and a Negro race here together--we are here to live together--our interests are together. The world at this time and in many lands is showing intolerance and hate. It seems sometimes that love has almost deserted the human bosom. It seems that only hate has taken its place. It is only for a time gentlemen, because it is the great things in life, God's great principles, matters of eternal right, that alone live. Wrong dies and truth forever lasts, and we should have faith in that.

--Judge Horton in his charge to the
jury in the Scottsboro case

SELECTED BIBLIOGRAPHY

Baydoun, Nader, *A Rush to Injustice: How Power, Prejudice, Racism, and Political Correctness Overshadowed Truth and Justice in the Duke Lacrosse Rape Case;* Thomas Neslon, 2007.

Carter, Dan T., *Scottsboro, A Tragedy of the American South,* Louisiana State University Press, 1969

Chalmers, Allan, *They Shall Be Free*; Doubleday and Co., 1951.

Curriden, Mark; and Phillips Jr., Leroy; *Contempt of Court: The Turn of the Century Lynching that Launched a Hundred Years of Federalism;* Faber & Faber, 1999.

Goodman, James, *Stories of Scottsboro,* Vintage Books, 1994

Hays, Arthur Garfield, *Trial by Prejudice*; Covici, Freide, 1933

Maher, Michael, "The Case of the Scottsboro Boys" ; included in *The Press on Trial, Crimes and Trials as Media Events,* edited by Lloyd Chiasson Jr.; Greenwood Press, 1997

McAdam, Doug, *Freedom Summer,* Oxford University Press, 1988

Patterson, Haywood, and Conrad, Earl, *Scottsboro Boy*; Doubleday and Co., 1950

Reynolds, Quentin, Courtroom, *The Story of Sameul S. Liebowitz*; Farrar, Straus and Co., 1950

Taylor, Stuart, and Johnson, K.C., *Until Proven Innocent, Political Correctness and the Shameful Injustices of the Duke Lacrosse Rape Case*; Thomas Dunne Books, 2007

Yeager, Don, and Pressler, Mike, *It's Not About the Truth, the Untold Story of the Duke Lacrosse Case and the Lives it Shattered*; Threshold Editions, 2007

Selected Websites

Durham-in-Wonderland
http://durhamwonderland.blogspot.com/

Friends of Duke University
http://friendsofdukeuniversity.blogspot.com/

Liestoppers
http://www.liestoppers.blogspot.com/

Famous American Trials : Scottsboro
http://www.law.umkc.edu/faculty/projects/Ftrials/scottsboro/scottsb.htm

www.ingramcontent.com/pod-product-compliance
Lightning Source LLC
Chambersburg PA
CBHW071356170526
45165CB00001B/66

9781439235904